CHELSEA HOUSE PUBLISHERS

Modern Critical Views

Further titles in preparation.

Modern Critical Views

GERTRUDE STEIN

Modern Critical Views

GERTRUDE STEIN

Edited with an introduction by

Harold Bloom

Sterling Professor of the Humanities
Yale University

1986
CHELSEA HOUSE PUBLISHERS
New York
New Haven   Philadelphia

PROJECT EDITORS: Emily Bestler, James Uebbing
ASSOCIATE EDITOR: Maria Behan
EDITORIAL COORDINATOR: Karyn Gullen Browne
EDITORIAL STAFF: Laura Ludwig, Linda Grossman, Perry King
DESIGN: Susan Lusk

Cover illustration by Kye Carbone

Printed and bound in the United States of America

Library of Congress Cataloging in Publication Data

Gertrude Stein.
    (Modern critical views)
    Bibliography: p.
    Includes index.
    1. Stein, Gertrude, 1874–1946—Criticism and
interpretation—Addresses, essays, lectures.
I. Bloom, Harold.   II. Series.
PS3537.T323Z613 1986   818'.5209   85–25515
ISBN 0–87754–668–1

Chelsea House Publishers
Harold Steinberg, Chairman and Publisher
Susan Lusk, Vice President
A Division of Chelsea House Educational Communications, Inc.
133 Christopher Street, New York, NY 10014

Contents

Editor's Note

This volume gathers together a representative selection of the best criticism that has been devoted to the work of Gertrude Stein, reprinted here in the chronological order of its original publication. The editor wishes to thank Ms. Nancy Sales, whose erudition brought several of these articles to his attention. The editor's "Introduction" offers an appreciation of Stein's *The Geographical History of America*, in the belief that this book best represents what she called her "literary thinking," though by no means does it contain her very best writing.

The chronological sequence begins with five early portraits of Stein and her work by some of her distinguished literary contemporaries. Sherwood Anderson's "American Impression" is precisely that, a vignette movingly depicting a felt affinity. With Katherine Anne Porter's more complex tribute, and Edmund Wilson's judicious overview, we begin to enter the area of the problematical, where all of Stein's highly experimental writing chooses to dwell. Porter's comparison of Stein to Jakob Boehme, and Wilson's implication that Stein's influence may count for more than her actual work, both suggest that she is an anomaly among authors, a suggestion that is countered by the insistence of William Carlos Williams that Stein's books are what they must be—"the artist's articulation with existence." This early sequence ends lovingly with Thornton Wilder's whole-hearted paean to his mentor and friend, in his superb introduction to *Four in America*.

More detailed and precise criticism can be said to begin with Donald Sutherland's sympathetic reading of *Three Lives*, which studies Stein's assault upon nineteenth-century syntax and word order. Allegra Stewart's general account of Stein's creativity centers upon the meditative intensity of the work, its displacement of what traditionally had been religious concerns. A very different, indeed an overtly dissenting judgment of Stein is given by B. L. Reid, who rather harshly diminishes her stature to that of an enduring myth, to the memory of a great personality rather than of a great writer.

We return to more balanced views with Richard Bridgman's analysis of *Things As They Are* and *Three Lives*, both of which are seen as moving towards a wholly admirable inevitability of style in relation to idea. Norman Weinstein's description of *Four Saints in Three Acts* encompasses the work both as opera and as play, seeing it as a prophetic instance of audience involvement in a deliberately actionless performance, and as the forerunner of the theater of Ionesco and Beckett.

In the analysis of Stein's *Paris France* by Judith P. Saunders, we receive an effective guide to some of Stein's deeper relations to American literary tradition: to Thoreau, to Mark Twain, and I would think most certainly to Whitman. Stein's best critic, Catharine R. Stimpson, achieves an extraordinary series of insights in her essay upon the differences between masculine and feminine approaches to the mind/body problem, as these differences are articulated in Stein's thinking. A very different mode of criticism is exemplified, with characteristic verve and panache, in the stylistic analysis of *Tender Buttons* by William H. Gass. Marianne DeKoven's overview of Stein's poetry engagingly connects Stein's experimentalism to some contemporary critical modes. The volume ends with Jayne L. Walker's reading of history as a mode of repeating in *The Making of Americans*, perhaps returning us full circle to the editor's "Introduction," with its meditation upon Stein's repetitions.

Introduction

I

The greatest master of dissociative rhetoric in modern writing is Gertrude Stein. What makes that assertion surprising as well as true is that Stein was anything but a religious writer, and dissociative rhetoric usually is the mark of religious texts, even if the religion is as displaced as it is in Carlyle and Emerson. The function of dissociative rhetoric invariably is to break down preconceived patterns in our response, so as to prepare us for discourse that will touch upon the possibilities of transcendence. But Stein is a crucial episode in the history of the literature of American pragmatism, or as Richard Rorty grimly calls it, post-philosophy. She finds her patriarch in William James and, through James, her American intellectual ancestor in the pragmatic Emerson of the essay "Experience." Her affinity with Whitman is authentic, and the zany humor she turned against Bertrand Russell when she associated Emerson and the automobile as marking the American difference from England is finally a serious and valid insight into the American religion of self-reliance, the only religion her work espoused.

My own favorite among her books, though I grant it is far from her best, is the one audaciously titled *The Geographical History of America or the Relation of Human Nature to the Human Mind.* As Thornton Wilder observed, the book is about the psychology of the creative act, particularly in America, the vast land, so much of it flat, surrounded by the long straight lines of the sea. When Stein says that such an American context engenders an unusual power of abstraction, I think we must read "abstract" in both of its Emersonian senses, each much exploited by Wallace Stevens as well as Stein. The American writer fabricates by abstraction (to adopt Valèry's phrase, as Stevens does) because this is both the abstract or universal as opposed to the particular, and also the abstract as withdrawn from a stale reality for the sake of contriving a fresh reality. Stein's poems endlessly exemplify both these senses of abstract, but the theory of the abstract is reserved by her for the flawed but remarkable *Geographical History of America.* "What is a master-piece," Stein asks in a question without a question-mark, to which she magnificently replies: "Any one that is no one is deceived because although any one can quote it no one can make use of it," which leads her to a sublime meditation upon loss and achievement:

> It is not any loss to lose a master-piece.
>   Every once in a while one is lost.
>   I remember very well deciding not to worry even if a master-piece should get lost. Any master-piece ancient or modern because there is no such thing as ancient or modern in a master-piece how can there be when there is no time and no identity.
>   And if a master-piece is lost then there is just one less to know about and as there are so few after all does it make any difference.
>   Suppose you have them all or none at all.
>   But nevertheless master-pieces do have to have existence and they do each one they do although there are very few.
>   We know very well that master-pieces have nothing to tell how can they when after all anything that tells what every one tells tells what any one tells.
>   I tell you that any soldiers at all look as soldiers are.
>   Of course they do.
>   Anybody too.
>   And master-pieces do only master-pieces have to be what they tell well anybody can tell anything very well.

There is no time and no identity, no distinction between ancient and modern, in masterpieces because they are the product, according to Stein, of the human mind rather than of human nature, and Stein's rugged distinction assigns time and identity only to human nature, never to the mind. This is a ruthless strategy for subverting any author's sense of belatedness, of coming after Shakespeare, and it is therefore no surprise that Stein's refusal to mourn the loss of masterpieces is followed directly by a shrewd (if misplaced) attack on *Hamlet*:

> I said to Thornton Wilder but you do know that the psychology in Shakespeare is no psychology at all. A young man whose father was just murdered, would not act like Hamlet, Hamlet was not interested in his father, he was interested in himself, and he acted not like a young man who has lost a loved father but like a man who wants to talk about himself, that is psychology if you like but anybody in any village can do that.
>   Now in a master-piece what does anybody do they do what they do that is they say what they know and they only know what they are as they know what they are, there is no time and no identity, not at all never at all ever at all.

The village reference reminds us of Stein's devastating dismissal of Ezra Pound in *The Autobiography of Alice B. Toklas*:

Gertrude Stein liked him but did not find him amusing. She said he was a village explainer, excellent if you were a village, but if you were not, not.

Hamlet certainly is more interested in himself than in his dead father, and he splendidly acts like a man who wants to talk about himself. Stein knows but does not care to admit that anybody in any village can do that because the village schoolmaster, at least, has read Shakespeare. Denying time and identity is one thing, but denying that the human mind has learned its psychology from Shakespeare rather than from William James (or Gertrude Stein) is quite another. Outrageously original, Stein paid the cost of her confirmation as an American writer; she achieved originality by force of repetition, and repetition is an associative mode of rhetoric. *The Geographical History of America* begins to read like *The Geographical Biography of Gertrude Stein's Writing,* and we are compelled to peer closer to see Stein's own variety of belatedness at play.

II

Is there any difference between flat land and an ocean a big country and a little one.
Is there any difference between human nature and the human mind.
Poetry and prose is not interesting.
What is necessary now is not form but content.
That is why in this epoch a woman does the literary thinking.
Kindly learn everything please.

The Geographical History of America works hard at "literary thinking," which proves to be, inevitably, the tracing of the genealogy of the American literary imagination. "Repeating is a wonderful thing" always had been the Steinian motto, the wonder being that repetition induced resemblances that patterned into "an ordered system," such as the nation's literary tradition. This ordered repetition is the art of *Tender Buttons,* arguably Stein's best work, and of her more successful poems: *Stanzas In Meditation, Patriarchal Poetry,* and the erotic "Lifting Belly." The last of the *Stanzas In Meditation* is a singular triumph for her art:

> Why am I if I am uncertain reasons may inclose.
> Remain remain propose repose chose.
> I call carelessly that the door is open
> Which if they can refuse to open
> No one can rush to close.
> Let them be mine therefor.

Everybody knows that I chose.
Therefor if therefor before I close.
I will therefor offer therefor I offer this.
Which if I refuse to miss can be miss is mine.
I will be well welcome when I come.
Because I am coming.
Certainly I come having come.
                              These stanzas are done.

This may be read as *The Geographical History of America* in little, and yet is it not a coda, rather than a repetition, in its relation to Emersonian tradition? Retrospectively, Stein announces her own incarnation of the American Poetical Character, as Whitman had done before her, and she sublimely insists "that the door is open," a variant upon Whitman's trope of carelessly calling us to the open road. And the door to the geographical or imaginative freedom of America is a door "no one can rush to close" even if we go on refusing to open it. If, like the later Emerson of *The Conduct of Life*, we were to propose a darker realism or historicism to Stein, she would reply with scarcely less lyricism in *The Geographical History of America*:

If it were then the writing that has been written would not be writing that any human mind can read, it has really no memory nor any forgetting.
    Think of the Bible and Homer think of Shakespeare and think of me.
    There is no remembering and there is no forgetting because memory has to do with human nature and not with the human mind.
    Everybody says no when I say so but when I say so finally they do not say no.

But does this affirmative drive—early Emersonian and Whitmanian—not lose much of its force when it confronts its own belatedness? Is not the mode of Steinian repetition sadly related to that reiteration that drove Whitman's poetry into staleness and uneasiness after 1865? Stein's cunning answer plays variations upon any sense of maturation or development in history as being an imaginative defeat:

The human mind fails to be a human mind when it thinks because it cannot think that what is the use of being a little boy if you are going to grow up to be a man.

As a late master of the American Sublime, Stein formidably refuses this despair of human nature, and chooses what she calls human mind instead. The choice, Emersonian and William Jamesian, returns her to the Emersonian trope for American freedom, which is wildness:

By their used to be wild ones it is meant that no one was interested then in their being there except as they were there that is when they were wild ones as if they were wild ones. Now they see to it that they are still wild but continue to be there. That is what makes it be America over there that no one knows the difference between human nature and the wild animals there because there is more not being wild but being ones there there is more now there that they live as easily as anything since no one intends any things should happen to any one of them. In other words there in America wild ones are as if they were there with nothing to happen to them as if they lived there which they do so that nobody thinks they die there which they do.

    That is what peace is but always there is some one who has not felt that this could be done that any wild animal living where it is living could naturally go on being living until it became dead. Dead is not uninteresting and yet it is not any more uninteresting than that to any animal or human nature.

To know, with the Whitman of the first edition of *Leaves of Grass* (1855) that you are one of the American "wild ones" returns you to the peace of imaginative possibility. Though an apparent apostle of "writing," Stein is very much in the logocentric American oral tradition, recently attacked by the French philosophical rhetorician Jacques Derrida as the phenomenon he calls "American cultural nationalism," and which he condemns in such contemporary figures as Richard Rorty and myself. Stein, like Stevens and Hart Crane, is indeed an American cultural nationalist, but only in the sense that she insists upon the Emersonian stance of self-reliance. Her book, as she says, is "a poem of how to begin again." Against fresh inception, as she well knows, is the sense that the American stance itself has become a tradition, and to this she replies engagingly at the start of Chapter IV:

Everybody who has a grandfather has had a great grandfather and that great grandfather has had a father. This actually is true of a grandmother who was a granddaughter and her grandfather had a father.

    He had brothers and they lived on where he had come from. They always wrote to one another. At anytime anybody who knows how to write can write to one another.

    But what do they write about.

    They tell about the weather and sometimes what they have sold never what they have given to one another because and never forget that, they always have they always did they always can sell anything that is something to somebody.

    This is what makes the human mind and not human nature although a great many one might say anybody can say something about this not being so. But it is so.

The truths of belatedness are seen as an undoing repetition, which undoes identity and time, and even repetition itself, but not the human mind or authorial self. What Stein relies upon, like Whitman, is the expressionistic strength of her exuberant stance, her trope of freedom as wildness. Exuberance indeed both characterizes and constitutes what she calls "literary thinking." That is the strength of a wild book that ends:

> When he is young a dog has more identity than when he is older. I am
> not sure that is not the end.

Since identity belongs to mere human nature and not the creative human mind, Stein's final sentence is a delicious irony, identity and time constituting no end at all. We return therefore to the wonderful beginning of *The Geographical History of America* with its Whitmanian blend of wit and pride:

> In the month of February were born Washington Lincoln and I. These
> are ordinary ideas. If you please these are ordinary ideas.

We are pleased, because we recognize again, as we did with *Leaves of Grass*, that here is an American writer who has made ghostlier the demarcations between the ordinary and the extraordinary.

SHERWOOD ANDERSON

An American Impression

One who thinks a great deal about people and what they are up to in the world comes inevitably in time to relate them to experiences connected with his own life. The round hard apples in this old orchard are the breasts of my beloved. The curved round hill in the distance is the body of my beloved, lying asleep. I cannot avoid practicing this trick of lifting people out of the spots on which in actual life they stand and transferring them to what seems at the moment some more fitting spot in the fanciful world.

And I get also a kind of aroma from people. They are green healthy growing things or they have begun to decay. There is something in this man, to whom I have just talked, that has sent me away from him smiling and in an odd way pleased with myself. Why has this other man, although his words were kindly and his deeds apparently good, spread a cloud over my sky?

In my own boyhood in an Ohio town I went about delivering news-papers at kitchen doors, and there were certain houses to which I went—old brick houses with immense old-fashioned kitchens—in which I loved to linger. On Saturday mornings I sometimes managed to collect a fragrant cooky at such a place but there was something else that held me. Something got into my mind connected with the great light kitchens and the women working in them that came sharply back when, last year, I went to visit an American woman, Miss Gertrude Stein, in her own large room in the house at 27 rue de Fleurus in Paris. In the great kitchen of my fanciful world in which, ever since that morning, I have seen Miss Stein standing there is a most sweet and gracious aroma. Along the walls are many shining pots and pans, and there are innumerable jars of fruits, jellies and preserves. Something is going on in the great room, for Miss Stein is a worker in words with the same loving touch in her strong fingers that was characteristic of the women of the kitchens of the brick houses in the town of my boyhood. She is an American woman of the old sort, one who cares for the handmade goodies and who scorns the factory-made foods, and in her own great kitchen she is making something with her materials, something sweet to the tongue and fragrant to the nostrils.

That her materials are the words of our English speech and that we do not, most of us, know or care too much what she is up to does not greatly matter to me. The impression I wish now to give you of her is of one very intent and earnest in a matter most of us have forgotten. She is laying word against word, relating sound to sound, feeling for the taste, the smell, the rhythm of the individual word. She is attempting to do something for the writers of our English speech that may be better understood after a time, and she is not in a hurry.

And I have always that picture of the woman in the great kitchen of words, standing there by a table, clean, strong, with red cheeks and sturdy legs, always quietly and smilingly at work. If her smile has in it something of the mystery, to the male at least, of the Mona Lisa, I remember that the women in the kitchens on the wintry mornings wore often that same smile.

She is making new, strange and to my ears sweet combinations of words. As an American writer I admire her because she, in her person, represents something sweet and healthy in our American life, and because I have a kind of undying faith that what she is up to in her word kitchen in Paris is of more importance to writers of English than the work of many of our more easily understood and more widely accepted word artists.

KATHERINE ANNE PORTER

"*Everybody Is a Real One*"

All I know about Gertrude Stein is
what I find in her first two books, *Three Lives* and *The Making of Americans*.
Many persons know her, they tell amusing stories about her and festoon
her with legends. Next to James Joyce she is the great influence on the
younger literary generation, who see in her the combination of tribal wise
woman and arch-priestess of aesthetic.

This is all very well; but I can go only by what I find in [her work].
They form not so much a history of Americans as a full description and
analysis of many human beings, including Gertrude Stein and the reader
and all the reader's friends; they make a psychological source book and the
diary of an aesthetic problem worked out momently under your eyes.

One of the many interesting things about *The Making of Americans*
is its date. It was written twenty years ago (1906–1908), when Gertrude
Stein was young. It precedes the war and cubism; it precedes *Ulysses* and
Remembrance of Things Past. I doubt if all the people who should read it
will read it for a great while yet, for it is in such a limited edition, and
reading it is anyhow a sort of permanent occupation. Yet to shorten it
would be to mutilate its vitals, and it is a very necessary book. In spite of
all there is in it Gertrude Stein promises all the way through it to write
another even longer and put in it all the things she left unfinished in this.
She has not done it yet; at least it has not been published.

Twenty years ago, when she had been living in Paris only a few
years, Gertrude Stein's memory of her American life was fresh, and I think
both painful and happy in her. "The old people in a new world, the new

people made out of the old, that is the story that I mean to tell, for that is what really is and what I really know." This is a deeply American book, and without "movies" or automobiles or radio or prohibition or any of the mechanical properties for making local color, it is a very up-to-date book. We feel in it the vitality and hope of the first generation, the hearty materialism of the second, the vagueness of the third. It is all realized and projected in these hundreds of portraits, the death-like monotony in action, the blind diffusion of effort, "the spare American emotion," "the feeling of rich American living"—rich meaning money, of course—the billion times repeated effort of being born and breathing and eating and sleeping and working and feeling and dying to no particular end that makes American middle-class life. We have almost no other class as yet. "I say vital singularity is as yet an unknown product with us." So she observes the lack of it and concerns herself with the endless repetition of pattern in us only a little changed each time, but changed enough to make an endless mystery of each individual man and woman.

In beginning this book you walk into what seems to be a great spiral, a slow, ever-widening, unmeasured spiral unrolling itself horizontally. The people in this world appear to be motionless at every stage of their progress, each one is simultaneously being born, arriving at all ages and dying. You perceive that it is a word without mobility, everything takes place, has taken place, will take place; therefore nothing takes place, all at once. Yet the illusion of movement persists, the spiral unrolls, you follow; a closed spinning circle is even more hopeless than a universe that will not move. Then you discover it is not a circle, not machine-like repetition, the spiral does open and widen, it is repetition only in the sense that one wave follows upon another. The emotion progresses with the effort of a giant parturition. Gertrude Stein describes her function in terms of digestion, of childbirth: all these people, these fragments of digested knowledge, are in her, they must come out.

The progress of her family, then, this making of Americans, she has labored to record in a catalogue of human attributes, acts and emotions. Episodes are nothing, narrative is by the way, her interest lies in what she calls the bottom natures of men and women, all men, all women. "It is important to me, very important indeed to me, that I sometimes understand every one." . . . "I am hoping some time to be right about every one, about everything."

In this intensity of preoccupation there is the microscopic observation of the near-sighted who must get so close to their object they depend not alone on vision but on touch and smell and the very warmth of bodies to give them the knowledge they seek. This nearness, this immediacy, she communicates also, there is no escaping into the future nor into the past. All time is in the present, these people are "being living," she makes you no gift of comfortable ripened events past and gone. "I am writing every-thing as I am learning everything," and so we have lists of qualities and defects, portraits of persons in scraps, with bits and pieces added again and again in every round of the spiral: they repeat and repeat themselves to you endlessly as living persons do, and always you feel you know them, and always they present a new bit of themselves.

Gertrude Stein reminds me of Jacob Boehme in the way she sees essentials in human beings. He knew them as salt, as mercury; as moist, as dry, as burning; as bitter, sweet or sour. She perceives them as attacking, as resisting, as dependent independent, as having a core of wood, of mud, as murky, engulfing; Boehme's chemical formulas are too abstract, she knows the substances of man are mixed with clay. Materials interest her, the moral content of man can often be nicely compared to homely workable stuff. Sometimes her examination is almost housewifely, she rolls a fabric under her fingers, tests it. It is thus and so. I find this very good, very interesting. "It will repay good using."

"In writing a word must be for me really an existing thing." Her efforts to get at the roots of existing life, to create fresh life from them, give her words a dark liquid flowingness, like the murmur of the blood. She does not strain words or invent them. Many words have retained their original meaning for her, she uses them simply. Good means good and bad means bad—next to the Jews the Americans are the most moralistic people, and Gertrude Stein is American Jew, a combination which by no means lessens the like quality in both. Good and bad are attributes to her, strength and weakness are real things that live inside people, she looks for these things, notes them in their likenesses and differences. She loves the difficult virtues, she is tender toward good people, she has faith in them.

An odd thing happens somewhere in the middle of this book. You will come upon it suddenly and it will surprise you. All along you have had a feeling of submergence in the hidden lives of a great many people, and unaccountably you will find yourself rolling up to the surface, on the outer edge of the curve. A disconcerting break into narrative full of phrases that might have come out of any careless sentimental novel, alternates with scraps of the natural style. It is astounding, you read on out of chagrin. Again without warning you submerge, and later Miss Stein explains she was copying an old piece of writing of which she is now ashamed, the words mean nothing: "I commence again with words that have meaning," she says, and we leave this limp, dead spot in the middle of the book.

Gertrude Stein wrote once of Juan Gris that he was, somehow, saved. She is saved, too; she is free of pride and humility, she confesses to superhuman aspirations simply, she was badly frightened once and has recovered, she is honest in her uncertainties. There are only a few bits of absolute knowledge in the world, people can learn only one or two fundamental facts about each other, the rest is decoration and prejudice. She is very free from decoration and prejudice.

EDMUND WILSON

Gertrude Stein

Gertrude Stein, born in Allegheny, Pennsylvania, a student of psychology and medicine who is said to have been considered by William James the most brilliant woman pupil he had ever had, published in 1909 a book of fiction called "Three Lives." It was brought out by a small and obscure publisher and at that time attracted little attention, but, loaned from hand to hand, it acquired a certain reputation. "Three Lives," which bore on its title-page a quotation from Jules Laforgue, was a work of what would at that time have been called realism, but it was realism of rather a novel kind. The book consisted of three long short stories—the histories of three women, two of them German servant-girls, the other a mulatto girl. What is most remarkable in these stories—especially if we compare them with such a typically Naturalistic production as Flaubert's "Un Cœur Simple," in which we feel that the old family servant has been seen from a great distance and documented with effort—is the closeness with which the author has been able to identify herself with her characters. In a style which appears to owe nothing to that of any other novelist, she seems to have caught the very rhythms and accents of the minds of her heroines: we find ourselves sharing the lives of the Good Anna and Gentle Lena so intimately that we forget about their position and see the world limited to their range, just as in Melanctha's case—and this is what makes her story one of the best as well as one of the earliest attempts of a white American novelist to understand the mind of the modern Americanized negro—we become so immersed in Melanctha's world that we quite forget its inhabitants are black. And we discover that these histories have a significance different from that of ordinary realistic fiction: Miss Stein is interested in her subjects, not from the point of view of the social conditions of which they might be taken as representative, but as three fundamental types of women: the self-sacrificing Anna, who combines devotion with domination; the dreamy and passive Lena, for whom it is natural to allow herself to be used and effaced from life by other lives; and the passionate and complex Melanctha, who "was always losing what she had in wanting all the things she saw." Behind the limpid and slightly monotonous simplicity of Gertrude Stein's sentences, one becomes aware of her masterly grasp of the organisms, contradictory and indissoluble, which human personalities are.

"Three Lives," though not widely circulated, exercised a considerable influence. Carl Van Vechten wrote about it; Eugene O'Neill and Sherwood Anderson read it with admiration. It is interesting to note that all three of these writers were to occupy themselves later with negro life, in regard to which Miss Stein had given an example of an attitude not complicated by race-consciousness. And Sherwood Anderson seems to have learned from her, in his own even less Naturalistic, even more dreamlike, fiction, both his recurrent repetitions with their effect of ballad refrains and his method of telling a story in a series of simple declarative sentences of almost primer-like baldness.

Gertrude Stein's next book was a long novel, "The Making of Americans," written between 1906 and 1908, but not published till 1925. I confess that I have not read this book all through, and I do not know whether it is possible to do so. "The Making of Americans" runs to almost a thousand large pages of small closely-printed type. The first chapters show the same remarkable qualities as "Three Lives," though in a somewhat diluted form. Miss Stein sets before us the men and women of her German-Jewish families with all the strong sense we have already admired for the various and irreducible entities of human character; and we are made, as we are in "Three Lives," to feel life as her people feel it, to take for granted just as they do the whole complex of conditions of which they are part. But already some ruminative self-hypnosis, some progressive slowing-up of the mind, has begun to show itself in Miss Stein's work as a sort of fatty degeneration of her imagination and style. In "Three Lives," the rhythmic repetitions were successful in conveying the recurrences, the gradual unwinding of life, and in the dialogue they produced the effect of the speech of slow-minded people: "I never did use to think I was so much on being real modest, Melanctha, but now I know really I am, when I hear you talking. I see all the time there are many people living just as good as I am, though they are a little different to me. Now with you, Melanctha, if I understand you right what you are talking, you don't think that way of no other one that you are ever knowing." But, though in "The Making of Americans" this sort of thing is appropriate to the patient and brooding repetitiousness of the German-Jewish Americans of the first and second generations, it is here carried to such immoderate lengths as finally to suggest some technique of mesmerism. With sentences so regularly rhythmical, so needlessly prolix, so many times repeated and ending so often in present participles, the reader is all too soon in a state, not to follow the slow becoming of life, but simply to fall asleep. And the further we get, the more difficult we find it to keep our mind on what we are reading: Miss Stein abandons altogether for long stretches any attempt to tell her story by reporting what her characters do and say, and resorts to a curious abstract vein of generalization: "Some are needing themselves being a young one, an older one, a middle aged one, an older one, an old one to be ones realizing what any one telling about different ways of feeling anything, of thinking about anything, of doing anything is meaning by what that one is telling. Some are needing themselves being a young one, an older one, a middle aged one, an older one, an old one to be one being certain that it is a different thing inside in one being a young one, from being an older one, from being a middle aged one, from being an older one, from being an old one," etc., etc. The psychological truth is still there, no doubt, but it is in a solution of about one percent to the total volume of the dose, and the volume of the dose is enormous.

This repetitive and abstract vein of the last pages of "The Making of Americans" persists still in the psychological portraits of Picasso and Matisse published in 1912: "One was quite certain that for a long part of his being one being living he had been trying to be certain that he was wrong in doing what he was doing and then when he could not come to be certain that he had been wrong in doing what he had been doing, when he had completely convinced himself that he would not come to be certain that he had been wrong in doing what he had been doing he was really certain then that he was a great one and he certainly was a great one. Certainly every one could be certain of this thing that this one is a great one."

This is queer and very boring, like a good deal of "The Making of Americans," but it is still intelligible. A little later, however, Miss Stein published privately another "portrait" which represented something of a new departure. In the "Portrait of Mabel Dodge," she seems to be groping for the instinctive movements of the mind which underlie the factitious conventional logic of ordinary intercourse, and to be trying to convey their rhythms and reflexes through a language divested of its ordinary meaning.

"Tender Buttons," which appeared in 1914 and was the first of Miss Stein's books to attract attention, went even further than the "Portrait of Mabel Dodge" in the direction of dislocating words from their meanings. The pieces in "Tender Buttons" are in a different vein from anything she had published before: she has here given up her long rhythms and writes pungently, impressionistically, concisely. Miss Stein had by this time gone to live in Paris (where she has remained ever since) and had become interested in the modern French painting of the generation of Picasso and Matisse, which she was one of the first to appreciate and collect; and the pieces in "Tender Buttons"—the title was supposed to describe the contents—are said to have been intended as prose still-lifes to correspond to those of such painters as Picasso and Braque. A pattern of assorted words, though they might make nonsense from the traditional point of view, would be analogous to a Cubist canvas composed of unidentifiable fragments.

Red Roses. A cool red rose and a pink cut pink, a collapse and a sold hole, a little less hot.

A Sound. Elephant beaten with candy and little pops and chews all bolts and reckless rats, this is this.

Custard. Custard is this. It has aches, aches when. Not to be. Not to be narrowly. This makes a whole little hill.

It is better than a little thing that has mellow real mellow. It is better than lakes whole lakes, it is better than seeing.

Chicken. Alas a dirty word, alas a dirty third, alas a dirty bird.

Gertrude Stein is said, at this period, to have made a practice of shutting herself up at night and trying utterly to banish from her mind all the words ordinarily associated with the ideas she had fixed upon. She had come to believe that words had other values than those inherent in their actual meanings, and she was attempting to produce a kind of literature which should work with these values exclusively.

In "Have They Attacked Mary He Giggled—A Political Satire" (1917), she developed, however, still another genre, which at least partially left to language its common meanings—a sort of splintered stenographic commentary made up of scraps of conversation as they reverberate in the mind and awaken unspoken responses. The volumes of miscellaneous pieces which have followed—"Geography and Plays" (1922) and "Useful Knowledge" (1928)—contain examples of all her previous styles as well as several variations, including a curious kind of "play" which consists simply of long lists of phrases divided into acts. Among these, some of the satires are funny, some of the portraits rather interesting and bits of the "abstract" impressionism charming, and there are one or two really excellent short stories such as "Miss Furr and Miss Skeene," in which the repetitive rig-marole manner is admirably suited to render the monotony and insipidity of the feminine lives which are being narrated. But most of what Miss Stein publishes nowadays must apparently remain absolutely unintelligible even to a sympathetic reader. She has outdistanced any of the Symbolists in using words for pure purposes of suggestion—she has gone so far that she no longer even suggests. We see the ripples expanding in her consciousness, but we are no longer supplied with any clew as to what kind of object has sunk there.

Sometimes these writings of Gertrude Stein make us laugh: her humor is perhaps the one of her qualities which comes through in her recent books most clearly; and I should describe them as amusing nonsense, if "nonsense" were not a word which had so often been used in derogation both of the original Symbolists and of [various other] contemporary writers. . . . If I should say that Miss Stein wrote nonsense, I might be thought to be implying that she was not serious or that she was not artistically suc-cessful. As a matter of fact, one should not talk about "nonsense" until one has decided what "sense" consists of—and one cannot investigate this without becoming involved in questions which go to the bottom of the whole Symbolist theory and throw further light on the issues it raises.

The original Symbolists supposed themselves to be defending the value of suggestion in literature as against the documentation of Naturalism and the logic of rationalism—and both they and their opponents seemed to tend to take it for granted that the suggestion was all on one side and the sense all on the other. . . . Now, as a matter of fact, all literature, all writing, all speech, depends equally upon suggestion; the "meaning" of words is what they suggest. Speaking accurately, it is impossible to say that one kind of writing suggests, whereas another kind proves or states. Any literary work, if it accomplishes its purpose, must superinduce in the reader a whole complex of what we are accustomed to call thoughts, emotions and sensations—a state of consciousness, a state of mind; it depends for its effectiveness upon a web of associations as intricate and in the last analysis as mysterious as our minds and bodies themselves. Our words themselves are the prime symbols, and the only originality of the Symbolists consisted in reminding people of the true nature and function of words. It is of course possible to think of words abstractly so that they shall seem to have pure definite meanings, but the fact remains that as soon as we begin to use them, we cannot help pouring them full of suggestion by our inflections, our pauses, our tones or by their order and collocation on the page, and in any case by selecting them in such a way as to bring out certain previous associations.

. . . It is well to remember the mysteriousness of the states with which we respond to the stimulus of works of literature and the primarily suggestive character of the language in which these works are written, on any occasion when we may be tempted to characterize as "nonsense," "balderdash" or "gibberish" some new and outlandish-looking piece of writing to which we do not happen to respond. If other persons say they do respond, and derive from doing so pleasure or profit, we must take them at their word.

Gertrude Stein is a singular case in this respect. Widely ridiculed and seldom enjoyed, she has yet played an important rôle in connection with other writers who have become popular. I have spoken of her influence on Sherwood Anderson—and Ernest Hemingway, not only in such short stories as "Mr. and Mrs. Elliot" (who recall Miss Furr and Miss Skeene), but also in certain passages of "The Sun Also Rises" and "A Farewell to Arms," where he wants to catch the slow rhythm of time or the ominous banality of human behavior in situations of emotional strain, owes her a similar debt. Most of us balk at her soporific rigmaroles, her echolaliac incantations, her half-witted-sounding catalogues of numbers; most of us read her less and less. Yet, remembering especially her early work, we are still always aware of her presence in the background of contemporary literature—and we picture her as the great pyramidal Buddha of Jo Davidson's statue of her, eternally and placidly ruminating the gradual developments of the processes of being, registering the vibrations of a psychological country like some august human seismograph whose charts we haven't the training to read. And whenever we pick up her writings, however unintelligible we may find them, we are aware of a literary personality of unmistakable originality and distinction.

WILLIAM CARLOS WILLIAMS

The Work of Gertrude Stein

Let it be granted that whatever is new in literature the germ of it will be found somewhere in the writings of other times; only the modern emphasis gives work a present distinction.

The necessity for this modern focus and the meaning of the changes involved are, however, another matter, the everlasting stumbling block to criticism. Here is a theme worth development in the case of Gertrude Stein—yet signally neglected.

Why in fact have we not heard more generally from American scholars upon the writings of Miss Stein? Is it lack of heart or ability or just that theirs is an enthusiasm which fades rapidly of its own nature before the risks of today?

> The verbs auxiliary we are concerned in here, continued my father, are am; was; have; had; do; did; could; owe; make; made; suffer; shall; should; will; would; can; ought; used; or is wont . . . —or with these questions added to them;—Is it? Was it? Will it be? . . . Or affirmatively . . . — Or chronologically . . . —Or hypothetically . . . —If it was? If it was not? What would follow?—If the French beat the English? If the Sun should go out of the Zodiac?
>
> Now, by the right use and application of these, continued my father, in which a child's memory should be exercised, there is no one idea can enter the brain how barren soever, but a magazine of conceptions and conclusions may be drawn forth from it.—Didst thou ever see a white bear? cried my father, turning his head round to Trim, who stood at the back of his chair.—No, an' please your honour, replied the corporal.— But thou couldst discourse about one, Trim, said my father, in case of

need?—How is it possible, brother, quoth my Uncle Toby, if the corporal never saw one?—'Tis the fact I want, replied my father,—and the possibility of it as follows.

A white bear! Very well, Have I ever seen one? Might I ever have seen one? Am I ever to see one? Ought I ever to have seen one? Or can I ever see one?

Would I had seen a white bear! (for how can I imagine it?)

If I should see a white bear, what should I say? If I should never see a white bear, what then?

If I never have, can, must, or shall see a white bear alive; have I ever seen the skin of one? Did I ever see one painted?—described? Have I never dreamed of one?

Note how the words *alive, skin, painted, described, dreamed* come into the design of these sentences. The feeling is of words themselves, a curious immediate quality quite apart from their meaning, much as in music different notes are dropped, so to speak, into repeated chords one at a time, one after another—for themselves alone. Compare this with the same effects common in all that Stein does. See *Geography and Plays,* "They were both gay there." To continue——

Did my father, mother, uncle, aunt, brothers or sisters, ever see a white bear? What would they give? . . . How would they behave? How would the white bear have behaved? Is he wild? Tame? Terrible? Rough? Smooth?

Note the play upon *rough* and *smooth* (though it is not certain that this was intended), *rough* seeming to apply to the bear's deportment, *smooth* to surface, presumably the bear's coat. In any case the effect is that of a comparison relating primarily not to any qualities of the bear himself but to the words rough and smooth. And so to finish——

Is the white bear worth seeing?
Is there any sin in it?
Is it better than a black one?

In this manner ends Chapter 43 of *The Life and Opinions of Tristram Shandy.* The handling of the words and to some extent the imaginative quality of the sentence is a direct forerunner of that which Gertrude Stein has woven today into a synthesis of its own. It will be plain, in fact, on close attention, that Sterne exercises not only the play (or music) of sight, sense and sound contrast among the words themselves which Stein uses, but their grammatical play also—i.e. for, how, can I imagine it; did my . . . , what would, how would, compare Stein's "to have rivers; to halve rivers," etc. It would not be too much to say that Stein's development over a lifetime is anticipated completely with regard to subject matter, sense and grammar—in Sterne.

Starting from scratch we get, possibly, thatch; just as they have always done in poetry.

Then they would try to connect it up by something like—The mice scratch, beneath the thatch.

Miss Stein does away with all that. The free-versists on the contrary used nothing else. They saved—The mice, under the . . . ,

It is simply the skeleton, the "formal" parts of writing, those that make form, that she has to do with, apart from the "burden" which they carry. The skeleton, important to acknowledge where confusion of all knowledge of the "soft parts" reigns as at the present day in all intellectual fields.

Stein's theme is writing. But in such a way as to be writing envisioned as the first concern of the moment, dragging behind it a dead weight of logical burdens, among them a dead criticism which broken through might be a gap by which endless other enterprises of the understanding should issue—for refreshment.

It is a revolution of some proportions that is contemplated, the exact nature of which may be no more than sketched here but whose basis is humanity in a relationship with literature hitherto little contemplated.

And at the same time it is a general attack on the scholastic viewpoint, that medieval remnant with whose effects from generation to generation literature has been infested to its lasting detriment. It is a breakaway from that paralyzing vulgarity of logic for which the habits of science and philosophy coming over into literature (where they do not belong) are to blame.

It is this logicality as a basis for literary action which in Stein's case, for better or worse, has been wholly transcended.

She explains her own development in connection with *Tender Buttons* (1914). "It was my first conscious struggle with the problem of correlating sight, sound and sense, and eliminating rhythm;—now I am trying grammar and eliminating sight and sound" (*transition* No. 14, fall, 1928).

Having taken the words to her choice, to emphasize further what she has in mind she has completely unlinked them (in her most recent work) from their former relationships in the sentence. This was absolutely essential and unescapable. Each under the new arrangement has a quality of its own, but not conjoined to carry the burden science, philosophy and every higgledy-piggledy figment of law and order have been laying upon them in the past. They are like a crowd at Coney Island, let us say, seen from an airplane.

Whatever the value of Miss Stein's work may turn out finally to be, she has at least accomplished her purpose of getting down on paper this much that is decipherable. She has placed writing on a plane where it may deal unhampered with its own affairs, unburdened with scientific and philosophic lumber.

For after all, science and philosophy are today, in their effect upon the mind, little more than fetishes of unspeakable abhorrence. And it is through a subversion of the art of writing that their grip upon us has assumed its steel-like temper.

What are philosophers, scientists, religionists, they that have filled up literature with their pap? Writers, of a kind. Stein simply erases their stories, turns them off and does without them, their logic (founded merely on the limits of the perceptions) which is supposed to transcend the words, along with them. Stein denies it. The words, in writing, she discloses, transcend everything.

Movement (for which in a petty way logic is taken), the so-called search for truth and beauty, is for us the effect of a breakdown of the attention. But movement must not be confused with what we attach to it but, for the rescuing of the intelligence, must always be considered aimless, without progress.

This is the essence of all knowledge.

Bach might be an illustration of movement not suborned by a freight of purposed design, loaded upon it as in almost all later musical works; statement unmusical and unnecessary, Stein's "They lived very gay then" has much of the same quality of movement to be found in Bach—the composition of the words determining not the logic, not the "story," not the theme even, but the movement itself. As it happens, "They were both gay there" is as good as some of Bach's shorter figures.

Music could easily have a statement attached to each note in the manner of words, so that C natural might mean the sun, etc., and completely dull treatises be played—and even sciences finally expounded in tunes.

Either, we have been taught to think, the mind moves in a logical sequence to a definite end which is its goal, or it will embrace movement without goal other than movement itself for an end and hail "transition" only as supreme.

Take your choice, both resorts are an improper description of the mind in fullest play.

If the attention could envision the whole of writing, let us say, at one time, moving over it in swift and accurate pursuit of the modern imperative at the instant when it is most to the fore, something of what actually takes place under an optimum of intelligence could be observed. It is an alertness not to let go of a possibility of movement in our fearful bedazzlement with some concrete and fixed present. The goal is to keep a beleaguered line of understanding which has movement from breaking down and becoming a whole into which we sink decoratively to rest.

The goal has nothing to do with the silly function which logic, natural or otherwise, enforces. Yet it is a goal. It moves as the sense wearies, remains fresh, living. One is concerned with it as with anything pursued and not with the rush of air or the guts of the horse one is riding—save to a very minor degree.

Writing, like everything else, is much a question of refreshed interest. It is directed, not idly, but as most often happens (though not necessarily so) toward that point not to be predetermined where movement is blocked (by the end of logic perhaps). It is about these parts, if I am not mistaken, that Gertrude Stein will be found.

There remains to be explained the bewildering volume of what Miss Stein has written, the quantity of her work, its very apparent repetitiousness, its iteration, what I prefer to call its extension, the final clue to her meaning.

It is, of course, a progression (not a progress) beginning, conveniently, with "Melanctha" from *Three Lives,* and coming up today.

How in a democracy, such as the United States, can writing which has to compete with excellence elsewhere and in other times remain in the field and be at once objective (true to fact) intellectually searching, subtle and instinct with powerful additions to our lives? It is impossible, without invention of some sort, for the very good reason that observation about us engenders the very opposite of what we seek: triviality, crassness and intellectual bankruptcy. And yet what we do see can in no way be excluded. Satire and flight are two possibilities but Miss Stein has chosen otherwise.

But if one remain in a place and reject satire, what then? To be democratic, local (in the sense of being attached with integrity to actual experience) Stein, or any other artist, must for subtlety ascend to a plane of almost abstract design to keep alive. To writing, then, as an art in itself. Yet what actually impinges on the senses must be rendered as it appears, by use of which, only, and under which, untouched, the significance has to be disclosed. It is one of the major problems of the artist.

"Melanctha" is a thrilling clinical record of the life of a colored woman in the present-day United States, told with directness and truth.

It is without question one of the best bits of characterization produced in America. It is universally admired. This is where Stein began. But for Stein to tell a story of that sort, even with the utmost genius, was not enough under the conditions in which we live, since by the very nature of its composition such a story does violence to the larger scene which would be portrayed.

True, a certain way of delineating the scene is to take an individual like Melanctha and draw her carefully. But this is what happens. The more carefully the drawing is made, the greater the genius involved and the greater the interest that attaches, therefore, to the character as an individual, the more exceptional that character becomes in the mind of the reader and the less typical of the scene.

It was no use for Stein to go on with *Three Lives.* There that phase of the work had to end. See *Useful Knowledge,* the parts on the U.S.A.

Stein's pages have become like the United States viewed from an airplane—the same senseless repetitions, the endless multiplications of toneless words, with these she had to work.

No use for Stein to fly to Paris and forget it. The thing, the United States, the unmitigated stupidity, the drab tediousness of the democracy, the overwhelming number of the offensively ignorant, the dull nerve—is there in the artist's mind and cannot be escaped by taking a ship. She must resolve it if she can, if she is to be.

That must be the artist's articulation with existence.

Truly, the world is full of emotion—more or less—but it is caught in bewilderment to a far more important degree. And the purpose of art, so far as it has any, is not at least to copy that, but lies in the resolution of difficulties to its own comprehensive organization of materials. And by so doing, in this case, rather than by copying, it takes its place as most human.

To deal with Melanctha, with characters of whomever it may be, the modern Dickens, is not therefore human. To write like that is not in the artist, to be human at all, since nothing is resolved, nothing is done to resolve the bewilderment which makes of emotion an inanity: That, is to overlook the gross instigation and with all subtlety to examine the object minutely for "the truth"—which if there is anything more commonly practiced or more stupid, I have yet to come upon it.

To be most useful to humanity, or to anything else for that matter, an art, writing, must stay art, not seeking to be science, philosophy, history, the humanities, or anything else it has been made to carry in the past. It is this enforcement which underlies Gertrude Stein's extension and progression to date.

THORNTON WILDER

"Four in America"

Miss Gertrude Stein, answering a question about her line

A rose is a rose is a rose is a rose,

once said with characteristic vehemence:

"Now listen! I'm no fool. I know that in daily life we don't say 'is a . . . is a . . . is a . . .' "

She knew that she was a difficult and an idiosyncratic author. She pursued her aims, however, with such conviction and intensity that occasionally she forgot that the results could be difficult to others. At such times the achievements she had made in writing, in "telling what she knew" (her most frequent formulization of the aim of writing) had to her the character of self-evident beauty and clarity. A friend, to whom she showed recently completed examples of her poetry, was frequently driven to reply sadly: "But you forget that I don't understand examples of your extremer styles." To this she would reply with a mixture of bewilderment, distress, and exasperation:

"But what's the difficulty? Just read the words on the paper. They're in English. Just read them. Be simple and you'll understand these things."

Now let me quote the whole speech from which the opening remark in this introduction has been extracted. A student in her seminar at the University of Chicago had asked her for an "explanation" of the famous line. She leaned forward giving all of herself to the questioner in that unforgettable way which has endeared her to hundreds of students and to hundreds of soldiers in two wars; trenchant, humorous, but above all urgently concerned over the enlightenment of even the most obtuse questioner:

"Now listen! Can't you see that when the language was new—as it was with Chaucer and Homer—the poet could use the name of a thing and the thing was really there? He could say 'O moon,' 'O sea,' 'O love' and the moon and the sea and love were really there. And can't you see that after hundreds of years had gone by and thousands of poems had been written, he could call on those words and find that they were just worn out literary words? The excitingness of pure being had withdrawn from them; they were just rather stale literary words. Now the poet has to work in the excitingness of pure being; he has to get back that intensity into the language. We all know that it's hard to write poetry in a late age; and we know that you have to put some strangeness, something unexpected, into the structure of the sentence in order to bring back vitality to the noun. Now it's not enough to be bizarre; the strangeness in the sentence structure has to come from the poetic gift, too. That's why it's doubly hard to be a poet in a late age. Now you all have seen hundreds of poems about roses and you know in your bones that the rose is not there. All those songs that sopranos sing as encores about 'I have a garden; oh, what a garden!' Now I don't want to put too much emphasis on that line, because it's just one line in a longer poem. But I notice that you all know it; you make fun of it, but you know it. Now listen! I'm no fool. I know that in daily life we don't go around saying 'is a . . . is a . . . is a . . .' Yes, I'm no fool; but I think that in that line the rose is red for the first time in English poetry for a hundred years."

[*Four in America*] is full of that "strangeness which must come from the poetic gift" in order to restore intensity to images dusted over with accustomedness and routine. It is not required in poetry alone; for Miss Stein all intellectual activities—philosophical speculation, literary criticism, narration—had to be refreshed at the source.

There are certain of her idiosyncrasies which by this time should not require discussion—for example, her punctuation and her recourse to repetition. Readers who still baulk at these should not attempt to read this volume, for it contains idiosyncrasies far more taxing to conventional taste. The majority of readers ask of literature the kind of pleasure they have always received; they want "more of the same"; they accept idiosyncrasy in author and period only when it has been consecrated by a long-accumulated prestige, as in the cases of the earliest and the latest of Shakespeare's styles, and in the poetry of Donne, Gerard Manley Hopkins, or Emily Dickinson. They arrogate to themselves a superiority in condemning the novels of Kafka or of the later Joyce or the later Henry James, forgetting that they allow a no less astonishing individuality to Laurence Sterne and to Rabelais.

This work is for those who not only largely accord to others "another's way," but who rejoice in the diversity of minds and the tension of difference.

Miss Stein once said:

"Every masterpiece came into the world with a measure of ugliness in it. That ugliness is the sign of the creator's struggle to say a new thing in a new way, for an artist can never repeat yesterday's success. And after every great creator there follows a second man who shows how it can be done easily. Picasso struggled and made his new thing and then Braque came along and showed how it could be done without pain. The Sistine Madonna of Raphael is all over the world, on grocers' calendars and on Christmas cards; everybody thinks it's an easy picture. It's our business as critics to stand in front of it and recover its ugliness."

[Four in America] is full of that kind of ugliness. It is perhaps not enough to say: "Be simple and you will understand these things"; but it is necessary to say: "Relax your predilection for the accustomed, the received, and be ready to accept an extreme example of idiosyncratic writing."

Distributed throughout Miss Stein's books and in the Lectures in America can be found an account of her successive discoveries and aims as a writer. She did not admit that the word "experiments" be applied to them. "Artists do not experiment. Experiment is what scientists do; they initiate an operation of unknown factors in order to be instructed by its results. An artist puts down what he knows and at every moment it is what he knows at that moment. If he is trying things out to see how they go he is a bad artist." A brief recapitulation of the history of her aims will help us to understand her work.

She left Radcliffe College, with William James's warm endorsement, to study psychology at Johns Hopkins University. There, as a research problem, her professor gave her a study of automatic writing. For this work she called upon her fellow students—the number ran into the hundreds—to serve as experimental subjects. Her interest, however, took an unexpected turn; she became more absorbed in the subjects' varying approach to the experiments than in the experiments themselves. They entered the room with alarm, with docility, with bravado, with gravity, with scorn, or with indifference. This striking variation reawoke within her an interest which had obsessed her even in very early childhood—the conviction that a description could be made of all the types of human character and that these types could be related to two basic types (she called them independent-dependents and dependent-independents). She left the university and settling in Paris, applied herself to the problem. The result was the novel of one thousand pages, *The Making of Americans*, which is at once an account of a large family from the time of the grandparents' coming to this country from Europe and a description of "everyone who is, or has been, or will be." She then went on to give in *A Long Gay Book* an account of all possible relations of two persons. This book, however, broke down soon after it began. Miss Stein had been invaded by another compelling problem: how, in our time, do you describe anything? In the previous centuries writers had managed pretty well by assembling a number of adjectives and adjectival clauses side by side; the reader "obeyed" by furnishing images and concepts in his mind and the resultant "thing" in the reader's mind corresponded fairly well with that in the writer's. Miss Stein felt that that process did not work any more. Her painter friends were showing clearly that the corresponding method of "description" had broken down in painting and she was sure that it had broken down in writing.

In the first place, words were no longer precise; they were full of extraneous matter. They were full of "remembering"—and describing a thing in front of us, an "objective thing," is no time for remembering. Even vision (a particularly overcharged word), even sight, had been dulled by remembering. The painters of the preceding generation, the Impressionists, had shown that. Hitherto people had known that, close to, a whitewashed wall had no purple in it; at a distance it may have a great deal of purple, but many painters had not allowed themselves to see purple in a distant whitewashed wall because they remembered that close to it was uniformly white. The Impressionists had shown us the red in green trees; the Post-impressionists showed us that our entire sense of form, our very view of things, was all distorted and distorting and "educated" and adjusted by memory. Miss Stein felt that writing must accomplish a revolution whereby it could report things as they were in themselves before our minds had appropriated them and robbed them of their objectivity "in pure existing." To this end she went about her house describing the objects she found there in the series of short "poems" which makes up the volume called *Tender Buttons*.

Here is one of these:

Red Roses

A cool red rose and a pink cut pink, a collapse and a sold hole, a little less hot.

Miss Stein had now entered upon a period of excited discovery, intense concentration, and enormous productivity. She went on to writing portraits of her friends and of places. She revived an old interest in drama and wrote scores of plays, many of which are themselves portraits of friends and of places. Two of her lectures in *Lectures in America* describe her aims in these kinds of work. She meditated long on the nature of narration and wrote the novel *Lucy Church Amiably*. This novel is a description of a landscape near Bilignin, her summer home in the south of France. Its subtitle and epigraph are: "A Novel of Romantic Beauty and Nature and which Looks Like an Engraving . . . *'and with a nod she turned her head toward the falling water. Amiably.'* "

Those who had the opportunity of seeing Miss Stein in the daily life of her home will never forget an impressive realization of her practice of meditating. She set aside a certain part of every day for it. In Bilignin she would sit in her rocking chair facing the valley she has described so often, holding one or the other of her dogs on her lap. Following the practice of a lifetime she would rigorously pursue some some subject in thought, taking it up where she had left it on the previous day. Her conversation would reveal the current preoccupation: it would be the nature of "money," or "masterpieces," or "superstition," or "the Republican party." She had always been an omnivorous reader. As a small girl she had sat for days at a time in a window seat in the Marine Institute Library in San Francisco, an endowed institution with few visitors, reading all Elizabethan literature, including its prose, reading all Swift, Burke, and Defoe. Later in life her reading remained as wide but was strangely nonselective. She read whatever books came her way. ("I have a great deal of inertia. I need things from outside to start me off.") The Church of England at Aix-les-Baines sold its Sunday School library, the accumulation of seventy years, at a few francs for every ten volumes. They included some thirty minor English novels of the 'seventies, the stately lives of colonial governors, the lives of missionaries. She read them all. Any written thing had become sheer phenomenon; for the purposes of her reflections absence of quality was as instructive as quality. Quality was sufficiently supplied by Shakespeare whose works lay often at her hand. If there was any subject which drew her from her inertia and led her actually to seek out works it was American history and particularly books about the Civil War.

And always with her great relish for human beings she was listening to people. She was listening with genial obsorption to the matters in which they were involved. "Everybody's life is full of stories; your life is full of stories; my life is full of stories. They are very occupying, but they are not really interesting. What is interesting is the way everyone tells their stories"; and at the same time she was listening to the tellers' revelation of their "basic nature." "If you listen, really listen, you will hear people repeating themselves. You will hear their pleading nature or their attacking nature or their asserting nature. People who say that I repeat too much do not really listen; they cannot hear that every moment of life is full of repeating. There is only one repeating that is really dead and that is when a thing is taught." She even listened intently to dog nature. The often-ridiculed statement is literally true that it was from listening to her French poodle Basket lapping water that she discovered the distinction between prose and poetry.

It can easily be understood that the questions she was asking concerning personality and the nature of language and concerning "how you tell a thing" would inevitably lead to the formulization of a metaphysics. In fact, I think it can be said that the fundamental occupation of Miss Stein's life was not the work of art but the shaping of a theory of knowledge, a theory of time, and a theory of the passions. These theories finally converged on the master-question: what are the various ways in which creativity works in everyone? That is the subject of [Four in America]. It is a subject which she was to develop more specifically in a book which of all her works is most closely related to this one: The Geographical History of America or the Relation of Human Nature to the Human Mind. It led also to a reconsideration of all literature, reflected in the beautiful lecture, "What are Masterpieces and Why are There So Few of Them?"

Miss Stein held a doctrine which permeates [Four in America], which informs her theory of creativity, which plays a large part in her demonstration of what an American is, and which helps to explain some of the great difficulty which we feel in reading her work. It is the Doctrine of Audience; its literary aspect is considered in the Theory of the Moment of Recognition. In The Geographical History of America it is made to illustrate a Theory of Identity.

Let me enter into the subject by again quoting from her words in a conversation:

"Why is it that no preachers, no teachers, no orators, no parliamentary debaters ever have any ideas after the age of thirty-five? It is because when they talk they only hear what the audience is hearing. They get mixed up in their head and think that it is possible for one person to agree totally with another person; and when you think that you are lost and never have any ideas any more. Now what we know is formed in our head by thousands of small occasions in the daily life. By 'what we know' I do not mean, of course, what we learn from books, because that is of no importance at all. I mean what we really know, like our assurance about how we know anything, and what we know about the validity of the sentiments, and things like that. All the thousands of occasions in the daily life go into our head to form our ideas about these things. Now if we write, we write; and these things we know flow down our arm and come out on the page. The moment before we wrote them we did not really know we knew them; if they are in our head in the shape of words then that is all wrong and they will come out dead; but if we did not know we knew them until the moment of writing, then they come to us with a shock of surprise. That is the Moment of Recognition. Like God on the Seventh Day we look at it and say it is good. That is the moment that some people call inspiration, but I do not like the word inspiration, because it suggests that someone else is blowing that knowledge into you. It is not being blown into you; it is very much your own and was acquired by you in thousands of tiny occasions in your daily life. Now, of course, there is no audience at that moment. There is no one whom you are instructing, or fighting, or im-proving, or pleasing, or provoking. To others it may appear that you are doing all those things to them, but of course you are not. At that moment you are totally alone at this recognition of what you know. And of that thing which you have written you are the first and last audience. This thing which you have written is bought by other people and read by them. It goes through their eyes into their heads and they say they agree with it. But, of course, they cannot agree with it. The things they know have been built up by thousands of small occasions which are different from yours. They *say* they agree with you; what they mean is that they are aware that your pages have the vitality of a thing which sounds to them like someone else's knowing; it is consistent to its own world of what one person has really known. That is a great pleasure and the highest compliment they can pay it is to say that they agree with it.

"Now these preachers and orators may have had such moments of recognition when they were young; they may even have had them when they are addressing an audience—though that is very rare. After they have faced a great many audiences they begin to think that the audiences are literally understanding, literally agreeing with them, instead of merely being present at the vitality of these moments of recognition, at their surprising themselves with their own discovery of what they know. Then they grad-ually slip in more of the kind of ideas that people can agree with, ideas which are not really ideas at all, which are soothing but not exciting—oh,

yes, they may be exciting as oratory, but they are not exciting as creation—
and after a while they dry up and then they do not have any real ideas any
more."

A portion of the ideas expressed above is found in the "Henry James"
section of [*Four in America*]:

> Mr. Owen Young made a mistake, he said the only thing he wished his
> son to have was the power of clearly expressing his ideas. Not at all. It
> is not clarity that is desirable but force.
>
> Clarity is of no importance because nobody listens and nobody
> knows what you mean, nor how clearly you mean what you mean. But if
> you have vitality enough of knowing enough of what you mean, somebody
> and sometime and sometimes a great many will have to realise that you
> know what you mean and so they will agree that you mean what you
> know, what you know you mean, which is as near as anybody can come
> to understanding any one.

Miss Stein never claimed that these doctrines were new. She delighted in finding them in the great works of the past. She was never tired
of saying that all real knowledge is common knowledge; it lies sleeping
within us; it is awakened in us when we hear it expressed by a person who
is speaking or writing in a state of recognition.

From consciousness of audience, then, come all the evils of thinking,
writing, and creating. In *The Geographical History of America* she illustrates
the idea by distinguishing between our human nature and our human mind.
Our human nature is a serpents' nest, all directed to audience; from it
proceed self-justification, jealousy, propaganda, individualism, moralizing,
and edification. How comforting it is, and how ignobly pleased we are when
we see it expressed in literature. The human mind, however, gazes at
experience and without deflection by the insidious pressures from human
nature tells what it sees and knows. Its subject matter is indeed human
nature; to cite two of Miss Stein's favorites, *Hamlet* and *Pride and Prejudice*
are about human nature, but not of it. The survival of masterpieces, and
there are very few of them, is due to our astonishment that certain minds
can occasionally report life without adulterating the report with the grat-
ifying movements of their own self-assertion, their private quarrel with
what it has been to be a human being.

Miss Stein pushed to its furthest extreme this position that at the
moment of writing one rigorously excludes from the mind all thought of
praise and blame, of persuasion or conciliation. In the early days she used
to say: "I write for myself and strangers." Then she eliminated the strangers;
then she had a great deal of trouble with the idea that one is an audience

to oneself, which she solves in this book with the far-reaching concept: "I am not I when I see."

It has often seemed to me that Miss Stein was engaged in a series of spiritual exercises whose aim was to eliminate during the hours of writing all those whispers into the ear from the outside and inside world where audience dwells. She knew that she was the object of derision to many and to some extent the knowledge fortified her. Yet it is very moving to learn that on one occasion when a friend asked her what a writer most wanted, she replied, throwing up her hands and laughing, "Oh, praise, praise, praise!" Some of the devices that most exasperate readers—such as the capricious headings of subdivisions in her work, such sequences as Book IV, Book VII, Book VIII, Volume I—though in part they are there to make fun of pompous heads who pretend to an organic development and have no development, are at bottom merely attempts to nip in the bud by a drastic intrusion of apparent incoherence any ambition she may have felt within herself to woo for acceptance as a "respectable" philosopher. It should be noted that another philosopher who wrestled with the problem of restating the mind of man in the terms of our times and who has emerged as perhaps the most disturbing and stimulating voice of the nineteenth century—Søren Kierkegaard—delayed his recognition and "put off" his readers by many a mystification and by an occasional resort to almost Aristophanic buffoonery.

There is another evidence of Miss Stein's struggle to keep her audience out of her mind. *Four in America* is not a book which is the end and summary of her thoughts about the subjects she has chosen; it is the record of her thoughts, from the beginning, as she "closes in" on them. It is *being written* before our eyes; she does not, as other writers do, suppress and erase the hesitations, the recapitulations, the connectives, in order to give us the completed fine result of her meditations. She gives us the process. From time to time we hear her groping toward the next idea; we hear her cry of joy when she has found it; sometimes, it seems to me that we hear her reiterating the already achieved idea and, as it were, pumping it in order to force out the next development that lies hidden within it. We hear her talking to herself about the book that is growing and glowing (to borrow her often irritating habit of rhyming) within her. Many readers will not like this, but at least it is evidence that she is ensuring the purity of her indifference as to whether her readers will like it or not. It is as though she were afraid that if she went back and weeded out all these signs of groping and shaping and reassembling, if she gave us only the completed thoughts in their last best order, the truth would have slipped away like water through a sieve because such a final marshaling of her thoughts would have been directed toward audience. Her description of existence would be, like so many hundreds of thousands of descriptions of existence, like most literature—dead.

Another spiritual exercise she practices is no less disconcerting. She introduces what I like to call "the irruption of the daily life." If her two dogs are playing at her feet while she is writing she puts them into the text. She may suddenly introduce some phrases she has just heard over the garden wall. This resembles a practice that her friends the Post-impressionist painters occasionally resorted to. They pasted a subway ticket to the surface of their painting. The reality of a work of art is one reality; the reality of a "thing" is another reality; the juxtaposition of the two kinds of reality gives a bracing shock. It also insults the reader; but the reader is not present, nor even imagined. It refreshes in the writer the sense that the writer is all alone, alone with his thoughts and his struggle and even with his relation to the outside world that lies about him.

The fourth section of this book, by far the most difficult, seems to me to be full of these voices and irruptions. She is sitting on the terrace of her villa at Bilignin toward the end of day. The subject of George Washington comes toward her from a distance:

Autumn scenery is warm if the fog has lifted.
    And the moon has set in the day-time in what may be drifting clouds. . . .
    George Washington was and is the father of his country. . .
    It should not be a disturbance if they can mistake a bird for a bat and a bat for a bird and find it friendly.

At first view the plan of this book appears to furnish little more than a witty diversion, a parlor game—what kind of novels would George Washington have written? What kind of military strategy would Henry James have devised? One soon discovers, however, that it is a very earnest game indeed. It asks about "how creativity works in any one," about the relations between personality and gifts, personality and genius. No less searchingly, it asks another question: what is an American and what makes him different from a citizen of any other country?

Soon after Miss Stein settled in France for an almost unbroken residence of over forty years a very unusual thing happened to her: she was really taken into a number of French homes. She was told their secrets, told their finances, and told their politics. That must seldom have happened to any American who was at once so loved, so tirelessly ready to listen to details, and who had so consuming a passion to reduce the multitudinous occasions of the daily life to psychological and philosophical laws.

In addition, she spent some time in England during the earlier part of the War of 1914–18. She spent a number of summers in Spain and related what she saw to the characters of her three close friends the Spanish painters, Picasso, Juan Gris, and Picabia. All the time, however, she was meeting and "listening" to Americans and the contacts with Europeans continued to sharpen her perception of specific American nature. When after thirty-five years' absence she returned to America and traveled it from coast to coast her delight was not only in the experience itself; it was also the delight of seeing her conclusions confirmed and extended.

The section on Ulysses S. Grant begins with a lively discussion of the relations between people and the Christian names they bear. She relates it to superstition and to religion, as later she will relate it to the spell cast by novelists, the novelist Henry James and the hypothetical novelist George Washington.

She is tracking down certain irrational ways we have of knowing things, of believing things, and of being governed by these ways of believing. Even the strongest minds have been nonplussed and rendered angry by the extent to which they can be caught up into belief by imaginative narration. One remembers St. Augustine's anguished repudiation of the hold which theatrical performances had taken of him in Carthage. "Novels are true," says Miss Stein. Similarly, great minds have tried to revolt from the sway that superstition can exert over them—involuntarily downcast by omens, predictions, recurrences of certain numbers—just as lesser minds can be given courage by a palm reading and can be crossed with fear by a broken mirror. There is no "truth" in these things, people say; but perhaps man knows nothing and will never know anything; the important thing is that he behaves as though he knew something and the irrational ways of knowing which are found in religion and superstition and in submission to a novel are among the more powerful driving forces toward how he behaves.

Miss Stein is talking about religion throughout this section and she is furnishing analogies to the kind of "knowing" that goes to make up religious belief. One of them is the haunting sense that your name is the right name for you.

Religion, as Miss Stein uses the term, has very little to do with cults and dogma, particularly in America. She makes a score of attempts to define it, but the attempts result in fragmentary analogies, straining the syntax of the English language to express flashes of insight. Religion is what a person knows—knows beyond knowing, knows beyond anyone's power to teach him—about his relation to the existence in which he finds himself. It is the tacit assumption that governs his "doing anything that he does do," his creativity. "Religion is what is alright if they have to have their ups and downs." "Religion is not a surprise but it is exciting." "There is no advice in American religion." "American religion is what they could not compare with themselves." "Nobody in America need be careful to be alone, not in American religion . . ."

To illustrate what American religion is she first chooses the figure of a camp meeting. There is no leader, or to put it more exactly, there is a leader but the people are not led. Here is the first striking difference from European religion. It is in the open; there is even some deliberation as to whether the trees have to be there. Just as we hear that Americans have no home, just because their whole country is their home, so their church really has no house. The fact is Americans do not localize anything, not even themselves, as the whole book constantly reiterates. Here again we are a long way from European religion. Moreover, American religion is thanking, not supplication. Americans do not even wish. We shall see the extent to which they do not "wait"; they are not "ready," except in limited contingencies, they do not "prepare"—so little does an American believe that one forces circumstances to one's will. It is at the very heart of American religion that the majority of Americans "like what they have," and readers of *The Geographical History of America* will see how this relative absence of resenting the universe, despising the universe, trying to subjugate or reshape a "destiny" derives from the physical constitution of our country and the problems our pioneers met. Now in a camp meeting some walk up and down, some stand, some sing, some kneel, some wail; there is a leader but they are not led; and a congregation of four hundred is not four hundred, but it is one and one and one and one . . . up to four hundred.

The foregoing does not mean that Americans are passive. The true passivity, that is the true slavery and the true ineffectiveness, is to wish and to wait and to yearn and to conspire. Nor does the group that is one and one and one, and so on, mean that the American is an uncurbed individualist, for "they all go forward together." "They act as if they all go together one by one and so any one is not leading." "Go forward" has no moralizing sense; in Gertrude Stein it is hard to find a moralizing sense. Moralizing comes from that realm of belief which is acquired, learned, arrogated to oneself and promulgated; but which is not truly believed or lived by.

The passage to the effect that Americans cannot earn a living or be a success is likely to cause the bewildered astonishment that it first aroused in Miss Stein. ("Now, Lizzie, do you understand?") It is conceded that some Americans can make money, and that they can do what they have to do and that they can become "names which everyone knows," but that is not the same thing. Again Miss Stein is seeing Americans against her immense knowledge of French domestic life, compared to which the American relation to money is frivolous and the American relation to the whole practical side of life is without perseverance, foresight, or thorough application. The French would put it overwhelmingly that we are not *"serieux."* In conversation, Miss Stein went even further; she said that "Americans are really only happy when they are failures," and laughing deeply she would furnish a wealth of illustration. Again the reader should be warned against interpreting this passage in moralizing terms; this is not the sentimental commonplace that life's failures are the true successes nor does it mean that Americans are unworldly knight errants. An American's inability to make a living is not a consequence of his "values" but of the way his mind works in him.

The portrait of an American is then beginning to assemble about the image of General Grant and his hypothetical alter ego, Hiram Grant, retired from the army and become very busily a failure in the harness store at Galena, Illinois. He did not wait for the great position that would someday fall to him, because Americans do not wait, that is they do not live in the expectation that circumstance is coming toward them bearing gifts. There is no animism in American religion. The skies do not pity nor punish nor bring gifts. Nor does her American yearn, strain, or intrigue for the situations he may profit by; he is what he is, and what he *is*, not what he *wills*, is his expression. Some of the most exasperating of Miss Stein's phrases are employed to express this aspect of her subject. She seems to have a low opinion of the verb "sit" which to her expresses both the passivity and the expectancy which are not present in her American. Apparently, the word "there" and the verbs "come" and "go" all imply a degree of intention that is not in her Americans. So we get such upsetting combinations of these usages as: "Ulysses Simpson Grant was there as often as he came but he never came."

All this prepares us for the statement that Americans never die; they are killed or they go away, but they are not dead. This is in great contrast, of course, to the Europeans who "wait for" their death, prepare, resist, foresee, bewail, or accept their death. This she puts down to the American sky, which is not really a sky but is just air; but it is obviously related to the other elements of the American religion, that all you have is in every moment of your consciousness (and that you like all that you have) and so self-contained is every moment of consciousness that there is nothing left over for expectation or memory. The American, then, who has lost that moment of consciousness is not that European thing called "dead"—so fraught with immemorial connotations—he has gone away. For this Miss Stein finds the striking image that every American is an only child—is *one*, has everything, and is the center of everything—is then naturally very solemn and cannot die.

This is followed by an apparently difficult passage which, however, yields us some light on a number of Miss Stein's most characteristic locutions. General Grant was not "one of two" or "one of three"; for relief or guidance or comfort or support he did not ally himself with anyone else and even when he came to fill that high station for which he had not been waiting he was "not differently surrounded by himself"—surrounded, of course, he was, as we all are, but "surround does not mean surrender" (and surrender is here not the act of war but the loss of one's own knowing: "This is what I mean and this will I do").

So we begin to see what kind of a saint General Grant would have been if he had been a leader in religion. And now we see another reason why I went to some length to discuss Miss Stein's theory of Audience and her theory of the distinction between human nature and the human mind. It looks as though General Ulysses S. Grant and the saint he might have been had it in common that they did not listen to those seductive appeals from the Audience which keep crowding up from human nature. Neither Grant waited nor was anxious; neither came nor sat; both "knew what they knew at the moment of knowing it," a knowledge unsullied by expectation or memory. They did not let will or determination order them about; they did what they did, but they did not set about to do what they were to do.

One word hovers over the entire book and is never spoken. It is the word "abstract." American religion is presented as very abstract, and so are the mentalities of the Americans described here who are certainly prototypes of the generalized American. In *The Geographical History of America* she goes on to explain that such minds are so formed by the physical character of the environment in which they live. "Everyone is as their land and water and sky are," and in America there is no sky—there is just air; there is just "up"; the majority of Americans, in addition, either know the straight line of the sea or the lake, or they know a land so devoid of natural features that "when they made the boundary of a State they have to make it with a straight line." In European geography there are no boundaries which are straight lines.

The section on Wilbur Wright begins with another teasing play with Christian names. The reader can now share Miss Stein's delighted consternation on receiving a letter from a man named Ulysses Lee. "And there is nothing more to be said is there. Names call to names as birds call to birds." We have learned what a "Ulysses" nature is; a nature of that degree of abstraction could conceivably be born into a situation in which he would find himself called Ulysses Lee.

In driving through Le Mans Miss Stein once came upon the monument which the French had raised to Wilbur Wright. She tells us that she was struck with the "funny feeling" that Wilbur Wright was not there. France contains many monuments to its eminent dead and in a way she felt that their eminent dead were there. As she has told us, Americans do not die, they go away; but it was very clear that they do not go away to their monuments. This set her brooding again about American religion and American death and about Wilbur Wright and how he made what he made. Presently she found a relationshp between aviation and painting and between painting and acting.

Now a writer is not confronted by his past books. They are not even there in his mind, staring at him. His past work is not an audience to him. He is not his work and he is not connected to his work, save at the moment of creation. All painters, however, and particularly European painters, are surrounded by their paintings, even if their paintings are distributed all over the world. They are "extended" to their paintings. They are not alone. And the paintings are not "left"—are not relegated to a place outside consciousness. We are repeatedly told that no painting can be "left."

This has something to do with seeing, and leads to a similar situation in actors and in Wilbur Wright. Actors in a profound sense see rather than hear what they say. (The words are but a small part of the creativity in their art and the words having been created in the "recognition" of the dramatist are resumed by the actor into his total creation which is preponderantly visual. He "paints" a role employing the words of the dramatist as the raw material of his painting, just as his face, body, voice, and dress are raw material. It is in this sense that he "sees what he says.")

These creators who see their past work are eternally surrounded by it and are not alone. This is not urged as a reproach upon them; it is the character of their creativity; nor is their past work an audience to them in a bad sense, for they are their creativity, past and present. In the vocabulary of Miss Stein seeing always stands high. She enjoyed repeating that "seeing is believing." Readers will remark that among these thousands of references to creativity there is no reference to music. "Music is for adolescents" she used to say. The eye is closer to the human mind, the ear to human nature. She had passed through a phase of her life as an impassioned and informed music-lover and had put it behind her. Only once have I heard her concede that music—it was after a hearing of Beethoven's "Archduke" Trio—can occasionally issue from the human mind.

A reader having reached the middle point in the Wilbur Wright section is presumably becoming accustomed to Miss Stein's disregard for the first or generally received meanings of words and to her powerful compressions. (They have a relationship by contrast with her repetitions: a repetition is a small degree of progression by alteration and emphasis; a compression is a sweeping summary or a violent leap into new matter.) A reader is ready for such a passage as the following (the punctuation is impertinently mine): "A painting is something seen after it has been done and—in this way—left alone; nobody can say: 'he—or I—left it alone.' No painting is left alone."

The airplane was that kind of creation and the man whose work it was to make the flying machine and to fly it saw himself moving; he was in his creation as a painter is in and of his painting.

There are many difficulties in this section for which I am not competent to furnish a gloss. The day will come when devoted readers of Miss Stein will furnish a lexicon of her locutions. There are hundreds of them which may strike a first reader as incoherent expressions thrown off at random; but they are found recurringly distributed throughout her work. The task of her future commentators will consist in tracing them to their earliest appearances embedded in a context which furnishes the meaning they held for her. Thereafter they became bricks in her building, implements in her meditation. To her their meaning is "self-evident"; she forgets that we have not participated in the systematic meditation which was her life.

I leave to the reader's contemplation also the spectacle of the extraordinary emotion which accumulates toward the end of each of these sections. Miss Stein loves, overwhelmingly loves, each of the heroes of this volume. "Who knows what Grant did. I do." "It is Ulysses S. Grant that is interesting, very interesting." "I cannot think of Ulysses Simpson Grant without tears." "Wilbur Wright is fine." "East and West. George Washington is best."

The Henry James section begins with Miss Stein's account of how she came to make an important discovery concerning writing. It is a curious thing to me that in each of her retellings of this story she has omitted a fact that throws further light on it. This fact is that when she wrote the poems called *Before the Flowers of Friendship Faded Friendship Faded* she began writing them as translations of a group of poems in French by her friend Georges Hugnet. They are far from being literal translations, even in the beginning, but they take their point of departure from his poems, and they remained, as her discussion shows, "the poems he would have written if he had written them."

Hence, she was not writing "what she wrote, but what she intended to write." A sort of ventriloquism had introduced itself into the process of writing, and she became aware that the words had a sort of smoothness which they did not have in the poems which she wrote "from herself alone." Suddenly this smoothness reminded her of a smoothness she had long noticed in Shakespeare's Sonnets. She says (in the fourth lecture on *Narration*):

> I concluded then that Shakespeare's sonnets were not written to express his own emotion. I concluded he put down what some one told him to do as their feeling which they definitely had for each sonnet as their feeling and that is the reason that the words in the sonnets come out with a smooth feeling with no vibration in them such as the words in all his plays have as they come out from them.

Many scholars have reached a similar conclusion as to Shakespeare's Sonnets, and not only in regard to the series written on the preposterous theme "Go, young man, and get married in order that you may leave a copy of your excellences to the afterworld."

Miss Stein was perhaps a little nettled to find also that the poems of *Before the Flowers of Friendship Faded* gave more pleasure to her friends than her earlier poems had given. This discovery led her straight to the problem of audience. There are two kinds of writing: the kind in which the words mean what they say and the kind in which the "meaning has to be meant as something [that] has been learned"—it has been written to satisfy a preconceived notion as to what it will be like when it is finished, or to satisfy someone else's expectation of it. It is surprising that at this stage of drawing up this distinction she expresses so little disapproval of the second type of writing. She appears to be reconciled to it, it is the way in which the majority of all books have been written.

Henry James, it appears, wrote in a combination of the two ways of writing. In this he resembled a general whose activity consists in doing what he has to do in a situation that has already been prepared. In a general's work for a while "nothing happens together and then all of a sudden it all happens together." For a general and for Henry James "everything that could happen or not happen would have had a preparation."

This treatment of Henry James does indeed awaken a feeling which one had had about his work. It does not mean that other novelists like Fielding, Jane Austen, and Anthony Trollope—to name three for whom she had the highest admiration—did not likewise follow a design and know well in advance the pattern their book was to take. Henry James went further; he finished the book before he wrote it; he wrote the book to resemble a book which he had completely envisaged. Like a general he arrived on a scene which had already been prepared or as we are repeatedly told had "been begun." He was to an unprecedented degree an audience to his own composition. We could wish that Miss Stein had helped us through these subtle distinctions by an occasional specific illustration. One is indebted to her, however, for two exquisite characterizations of Henry James's quality. She is speaking of a woman who lived in a chateau near Belley: "She lived alone and in the country and so did Henry James. She was heavy set and seductive and so was Henry James. She was slow in movement and light in speech and could change her speech without changing her words so that at one time her speech was delicate and witty and at another time slow and troubling and so was that of Henry James." And again: "He had no fortune and misfortune and nevertheless he had no distress and no relief from any pang . . . He had no failure and no success and he had no relief from any failure and he had no relief from any distress."

There is an extended portion of this section in which Miss Stein gradually changes into a different style. It is the style of the "Portraits." In fact, when she alludes to this book in one of her *Narration* lectures, she calls it a book of portraits. In her lecture "Portraits and Repetition" she says:

> And so I am trying to tell you what doing portraits meant to me. I had to find out what it was inside any one, and by any one I mean every one. I had to find out inside every one what was in them that was intrinsically exciting and I had to find out not by what they said not by what they did not by how much or how little they resembled any other one but I had to find out by the intensity of movement that there was inside in any one of them.

In another place in the lecture she calls this work catching "the rhythm of personality." Opinions on this extreme style vary even among Miss Stein's greatest admirers. Some assure us that from the first reading they obtain a clear image of the personality so described; others acknowledge occasional flashes of insight but hold that Miss Stein was mistaken in thinking that she had been able to convey the "movement" of her sitters' personalities to anyone but herself. Readers who are indebted to her other writings for so wide a variety of pleasures—for the narrative brilliance of *The Autobiography of Alice B. Toklas*, the massive grasp of *The Making of Americans*, the critical insight and aphoristic skill of her lectures, the il-

lumination and the trenchant thinking about fundamentals contained in
the present book—such readers will return again and again to the most
difficult pages not willingly conceding that these are forever closed to them.

The fourth section, "Scenery and George Washington," has the
subtitle "A Novel or a Play." Its characters are "Scenery" and "George
Washington." The section opens, as I have said, with an evocation of the
valley below her villa at Bilignin toward which comes, as from a distance,
the figure of Washington and the inquiry as to what kind of novels he
would have written.

Now Miss Stein felt that the novel was threatened with extinction
and she was much concerned with whether it could be saved. Her fears
concerning it were not based, as those of many critics have been, on the
fact that the assumption of omniscience on the part of the storyteller is
untenable in our time. Her objection was that what happens "from outside"
is no longer important to us, that we are aware of so much happening that
the event is no longer exciting; and that we no longer feel that the sequence
of events, the succession in time, is of much significance. As she says in
the fourth *Narration* lecture:

> . . . and this has come to be a natural thing in a perfectly natural way
> that the narrative of today is not a narrative of succession as all the writing
> for a good many hundreds of years has been. . . . There is at present not
> a sense of anything being successively happening, moving is in every
> direction beginning and ending is not really exciting, anything is anything,
> anything is happening . . .

And in the lecture "Portraits and Repetition" she says:

> A thing you all know is that in the three novels written in this generation
> that are the important things written in this generation, there is, in none
> of them a story. There is none in Proust in The Making of Americans or
> in Ulysses.

Miss Stein interrupts her discussion to give samples of the event-
novel, the succession-novel, and she assures us that is not the kind of novel
George Washington wrote. What he wrote was "the great American novel,"
an entirely new kind of novel and a thing which, if we can know it, will
throw invaluable light on the American nature. With what she calls "Volume VI" begins a flood of definitions, that is, analogical definitions of what
this novel is, just as the Grant section furnished a flood of descriptions of
what "American religion" is.

In the first place, it has to do with the American time-sense. In
the lecture "What is English Literature" she shows how the English, living

for centuries their "daily island life," made their literature out of it. "They relied on it so completely that they did not describe it they just had it and told it . . . In America . . . the daily everything was not the daily living and generally speaking there is not a daily everything. They do not live every day . . . and so they do not have this as something they are telling." We are back at the abstractedness of the American mind. It does not draw its assurance of knowing anything from an intense localization in time and place. The endless procession of phenomena separate themselves from their specific contingency and reform themselves as a generalized knowing.

> And so . . . Henry James just went on doing what American literature had always done, the form was always the form of the contemporary English one, but the disembodied way of disconnecting something from anything and anything from something was the American one . . . Some say that it is repression, but no it is not repression it is a lack of connection, of there being no connection with living and daily living because there is none, that makes American writing what it always has been and what it will continue to become."

It should be unnecessary to say that this George Washington was not a novelist because he aesthetically composed his life or because he stood off at a distance and viewed his life. A novelist is sovereign over the elements of his imagined world; but they have also an objective life (derived from the "knowing" that he has acquired); he may not force or wrench them, nor make them report a fairer world than he has experienced. We seem to be told by Miss Stein that George Washington moved among events like a novelist among his characters at the moment of their creation. ("I am fond of talking about Napoleon but that has nothing to do with novel writing. Napoleon could not write a novel, not he. Washington could. And did.") And because he was an American novelist, George Washington was disattached from the concrete and the specific. He could and did love concrete things. ("He was charmed with the dresses of the little baby"—how astonishing are Miss Stein's ways of enclosing the general in the specific! That is an example of the writing which she exalts in the Henry James section, where the "writing and the writer are alike," of a "sound heard by the eyes," and that "does not mean what it says because it just is"—that is, lands squarely on its truth and is only watered down by "preparation" and explanation, as I have watered it down here.) George Washington's love of the concrete in our human life and his pleasure in baby-dresses was of the American order; it tended to transmute its experiences from things of human nature to things of the human mind. The human mind cannot be consoled by things nor rendered proud; it does not preach nor despise; it merely sees and tells what it sees. Such a novel George Washington was writing every day.

The pages begin to bristle with Miss Stein's most idiosyncratic expressions and we are again in the "portrait" style. This [essay] is already too long to permit of an attempt to wrestle with them. The solution of many of them, however, can be found elsewhere in Miss Stein's work. For example, the long passage on Washington's youth beginning with the disconcerting phrases: "He could just smile if he was born already . . . And he was not born. Oh indeed no he was not born," has a history in her work. As early as *A Long Gay Book* Miss Stein was observing that many people are rendered uneasy, are even crippled, by the thought that they were once helpless babies, passed about and tended by others. The dignity of their human mind (which, of course, knows no age) is undermined by thoughts of themselves in infancy. It is this idea which grows into fuller statement in *The Geographical History of America* in the development of the astonishing question: "What is the use of being a little boy if you are going to grow up to be a man?"

The word "tears" occurs frequently in this book. What things in our human lot seem to have moved Miss Stein to tears? It was not the misfortunes of our human nature, though she was a greatly sympathetic resource to her friends when their griefs were real. What moved her deeply was the struggle of the human mind in its work which is to know. It was of Henry James's mind (and the phrase applies as beautifully to those great heroines of his last novels who live not to assert themselves but to understand) that she says "he had no relief from any pang."

She said to me once: "Everyone when they are young has a little bit of genius, that is they really do listen. They can listen and talk at the same time. Then they grow a little older and many of them get tired and they listen less and less. But some, a very few continue to listen. And finally they get very old and they do not listen any more. That is very sad; let us not talk about that." This book is by an impassioned listener to life. Even up to her last years she listened to all comers, to "how their knowing came out of them." Hundreds of our soldiers, scoffing and incredulous but urged on by their companions, came up to Paris "to see the Eiffel Tower and Gertrude Stein." They called and found bent upon them those gay and challenging eyes and that attention that asked nothing less of them than their genius. Neither her company nor her books were for those who have grown tired of listening. It was an irony that she did her work in a world in which for many reasons and for many appalling reasons people have so tired.

DONALD SUTHERLAND

"Three Lives"

At all events the early work of Gertrude Stein accepts and loves the middle class as being the vital class in America. Very much later she had wicked things to say about our lower middle class, but as late as *The Making of Americans* she said passionately, against other claims, that anything worth while had always come from the middle class. Even if that is not entirely so, the attitude is far from foolish.

In *Three Lives* she deals with the poor, whom she had known as servants and patients in Baltimore, but there is very little if any political meaning to it. They are primarily human and not social types. She had what was then not a sentimental or programmatic but a natural democratic feeling that any human being was important just as that, as a human being. This feeling was no doubt reinforced and made confident by her philosophical and medical training, but it was, to start with, a native and direct curiosity about everybody. Later, as I will show, this basic democratic feeling in her developed not into political theory but into a sort of secular saintliness.

So "the good Anna" is first of all a human type, living and dying as that type does. She is presented first not as a child or a young girl but in her full development, in a situation which gives full expression to her typical kind of force, which is incessant managing will. The first chapter gives her as the type of that, the second chapter gives her life, and the third chapter her death. It is a curious kind of construction, which derives from "Un Coeur Simple." Flaubert begins: "Pendant un demi-siècle, les bourgeois de Pont-L'Evêque envièrent à Mme Aubain sa servante Félicité.

Pour cent francs par an, elle faisait la cuisine et le mènage, cousait, lavait, repassait, savait brider un cheval, engraisser les volailles, battre le beurre, et resta fidèle à sa maitresse,—qui cependant n'était pas une personne agréable." After this summary presentation Flaubert goes on to recount assorted episodes demonstrating Félicité's courage, loyalty, generosity, affection, etc. "Elle avait eu, comme une autre, son histoire d'amour." "The Good Anna" begins: "The tradesmen of Bridgepoint learned to dread the sound of 'Miss Mathilda,' for with that name the good Anna always conquered." And later: "The widow Mrs. Lehntman was the romance in Anna's life."

Now while the situations and episodes in "The Good Anna" are chosen and arranged to show the character of the subject in various relationships, the qualities of the character are not primarily moral. The word "good," which is repeated as constantly as a Homeric epithet before the name Anna, does not indicate an evaluation of the character or a conclusion about it but the constantly present essence of the character which is there as a fact and not as a value. Like the word "poor" which is used of Anna, Melanctha, and Lena, it gives a rather perfunctory general shape to the character, like the terribly simple shape of a Cézanne head or apple. Both the epithet and the shape of the apple look awkward and crude from the point of view of more graceful and less serious art, say that of Whistler or Pater, but these raw simplicities are necessary to hold down or stabilize an extreme complexity of interrelationship. It is like the melodrama of Henry James. Not to press these parallels too far, but as the Cézanne apple has weight and existence not by its shape or by perspective but by an equilibrium of relationships within the space of the picture, so the good Anna gets weight and existence, almost as a physical consistency, from her relationships within the account.

> Anna found her place with large, abundant women, for such were always lazy, careless or all helpless, and so the burden of their lives could fall on Anna, and give her just content. Anna's superiors must be always these large helpless women, or be men, for none others could give themselves to be made so comfortable and free.
>
> Anna had no strong natural feeling to love children, as she had to love cats and dogs, and a large mistress. She never became deeply fond of Edgar and Jane Wadsmith. She naturally preferred the boy, for boys love always better to be done for and made comfortable and full of eating, while in the little girl she had to meet the feminine, the subtle opposition, showing so early always in a young girl's nature.
>
> Miss Mary was sitting in a large armchair by the fire. All the nooks and crannies of the chair were filled full of her soft and spreading body. She was dressed in a black satin morning gown, the sleeves, great monster

things, were heavy with the mass of her soft flesh. She sat there always, large, helpless, gentle. She had a fair, soft, regular, good-looking face, with pleasant, empty, grey-blue eyes, and heavy sleepy lids.

Behind Miss Mary was the little Jane, nervous and jerky with excitement as she saw Anna come into the room.

"Miss Mary," Anna began. She had stopped just within the door, her body and her face stiff with repression, her teeth closed hard and the white lights flashing sharply in the pale, clean blue of her eyes. Her bearing was full of the strange coquetry of anger and of fear, the stiffness, the bridling, the suggestive movement underneath the rigidity of forced control, all the queer ways the passions have to show themselves all one.

"Miss Mary," the words came slowly with thick utterance and with jerks, but always firm and strong. "Miss Mary, I can't stand it any more like this. When you tell me anything to do, I do it. I do everything I can and you know I work myself sick for you. The blue dressings in your room makes too much work to have for summer. Miss Jane don't know what work is. If you want to do things like that I go away."

Anna stopped still. Her words had not the strength of meaning they were meant to have, but the power in the mood of Anna's soul frightened and awed Miss Mary through and through.

Like in all large and helpless women, Miss Mary's heart beat weakly in the soft and helpless mass it had to govern. Little Jane's excitements had already tried her strength. Now she grew pale and fainted quite away.

This last scene is as an event no more than a slapstick episode. It comes from a gift Gertrude Stein had and never lost, for extremely broad and reckless farce. In this same story she distinguishes two varieties or gradations of it.

Her freakish humor now first showed itself, her sense of fun in the queer ways that people had, that made her later find delight in brutish servile Katy, in Sally's silly ways and in the badness of Peter and of Rags.

Anna always had a humorous sense from this old Katy's twisted peasant english, from the roughness on her tongue of buzzing s's and from the queer ways of her servile brutish humor.

As the passions are all one the humor is all one through its gradations, and very much continuous with Gertrude Stein. She had an extraordinary mimetic faculty that allowed her not only to take on the full nature of her subject—in this case to the point of composing her episode in the manner of her characters—but to follow the gradations of a theme or feeling into its farthest and faintest developments. For example the character of dogs becomes quite comparable to the character of people, and this not sentimentally or metaphorically but as the brain of a dog can be studied with the human brain and is not very different.

> And then Peter never strayed away, and he looked out of his nice eyes and he liked it when you rubbed him down, and he forgot you when you went away, and he barked whenever there was any noise.
>
> When he was a little pup he had one night been put into the yard and that was all of his origin she knew. The good Anna loved him well and spoiled him as a good german mother always does her son.
>
> Little Rags was very different in his nature. He was a lively creature made out of ends of things, all fluffy and dust color, and he was always bounding up into the air and darting all about over and then under silly Peter and often straight into solemn fat, blind, sleepy Baby, and then in a wild rush after some stray cat.
>
> Rags was a pleasant, jolly little fellow. The good Anna liked him very well, but never with her strength as she loved her good looking coward, foolish young man, Peter.
>
> Baby was the dog of her past life and she held Anna with old ties of past affection. Peter was the spoiled, good looking young man, of her middle age, and Rags was always something of a toy. She liked him but he never struck in very deep.

Gertrude Stein is here dealing with broad classifications or types of character and relationship, minutely distinguished and identified. The scientific accuracy or the accuracy of intuition very consciously overrides the inaccuracies of common sense which would say one's feeling about a dog have little or no relation to one's feelings about a person. The humor of this kind of paradox, a rather broad sympathetic irony, is, as I suggested, the pervading tone of this work. The same irony carries the scene with Miss Mary, where the event is broad to the point of vulgarity, but where the feelings involved are distinguished and identified with great finesse. This intricate and accurate elaboration of the broad, the normal, the commonplace, is a method she used all her life. . . .

She was trained to a very sharp scalpel and there is a medical neatness about how Miss Mary fills her chair and Anna's being just inside the door. It is a somewhat forced neatness of contour as one finds it in Cézanne and in Flaubert, in Juan Gris. With Gertrude Stein it is, among other things, a sort of feminine daintiness that can become a fussiness now and then, and that can work either as an irritation or a personal charm on the reader. But here it makes very clear the constant definition of Anna's character by the description of its functions in a variety of relationships. For closer and closer definition and distinction the terms naturally have to be very simple, if it is all going to be clear. The terms of the definition or expression are used in as absolute a sense as may be. In the sentence "The tradesmen of Bridgepoint learned to dread the sound of 'Miss Mathilda,' for with that name the good Anna always conquered" the word "conquered" is used absolutely. It is *le mot juste* with a vengeance. It does not depend, for the expression of the present subject, on connotations of Alexander the Great or Cortez. It is used in its essential or axiomatic meaning of succeeding and dominating in an enterprise against resistance. It is used without historical resonance and suggestion, without, so to speak, the conventional perspective of literary language. To some extent, in this early work, it may play *against* conventional perspective, as the relational depth in Cézanne seems to play paradoxically against traditional perspective, but that paradox is a secondary interest. As with Cézanne, the new usage stands by itself as solid and accurate, without reference to what it contradicts. The verbal irony here, such as it may be, is only a minor distraction, at most an incidental reflection of the larger and more serious irony at the heart of the work. At any rate, she relied less and less on the rather cosmetic interest of verbal irony, and made no apologies for absolute and categorical meaning. This was directly against another contemporary movement, of composition by the multiplication of resonances and ambiguities.

If the character then is defined by its relationships and its consistency of force, there is the question of presentation. The narrative becomes episodic, as I have explained, and there are plenty of flat statements, generalities, and discourses. That is, the *presentation* does still rely on demonstration and even on explanation. But the really extraordinary thing about the good Anna is that the character is thought of also as a musical continuity. Already in Radcliffe Gertrude Stein had described the conflict between the conscious and the automatic parts of her subjects in experiments as being like two themes going on together in music, one and the other dominating alternately. This and the opera may have been the beginning of the idea. Solomons noted that her attention was mainly auditory, and she herself speaks of doing a great deal of listening then, not to what was being said so much as to the way it was being said, the rise and fall, and the characteristic variety of emphasis. She used to call this "the rhythm of a personality." The phrase sounds now like a rather fancy affectation, but it had an exact and responsible meaning within what was being thought about human psychology at the time. It was not rhythm for pleasure in rhythm but a thing existing in the living personality that could be accurately registered and described. The means for registering this was inevitably the language as spoken or as written. In *Three Lives* this is conveyed clearly enough in the dialogue parts. There is a handsome example of this projection by rhythm in dialogue in a scene between the good Anna and Mrs. Lehntman.

"I know you was careless, Mrs. Lehntman, but I didn't think that you could do this so. No, Mrs. Lehntman, it ain't your duty to take up with no others, when you got two children of your own, that got to get along just any way they can, and you know you ain't got any too much money all the time, and you are all so careless here and spend it all the time, and Julia and Willie growin' big. It ain't right, Mrs. Lehntman, to do so."

This was as bad as it could be. Anna had never spoken her mind so to her friend before. . . . And then too Mrs. Lehntman could not really take in harsh ideas. She was too well diffused to catch the feel of any sharp firm edge.

Now she managed to understand all this in a way that made it easy for her to say, "Why, Anna, I think you feel too bad about seeing what the children are doing every minute in the day. Julia and Willie are real good, and they play with all the nicest children in the square. . . . No indeed Anna, it's easy enough to say I should send this poor, cute little boy to a 'sylum when I could keep him here so nice, but you know Anna, you wouldn't like to do it yourself, now you really know you wouldn't, Anna, though you talk to me so hard.—My, it's hot to-day, what you doin' with that ice tea in there Julia, when Miss Annie is waiting all this time for her drink?"

Julia brought in the ice tea. . . .

"Here Miss Annie," Julia said, "Here, Miss Annie, is your glass of tea, I know you like it good and strong."

"No, Julia, I don't want no ice tea here. Your mamma ain't able to afford now using her money upon ice tea for her friends. It ain't right she should now any more. . . ."

"My, Miss Annie is real mad now," Julia said, as the house shook, as the good Anna shut the outside door with a concentrated shattering slam.

In this passage the hard rage of Anna, the bland diffusion of Mrs. Lehntman, and the nasty silliness of Julia are conveyed by the rhythm of the talk I think very well. But in prose, since there can be no explicit indication of staccato or legato or speed or *dolce,* the exact phrasing can easily be lost by the reader. Gertrude Stein supplies some direction, not only from the natural assumptions of the scene but by such words as sharp, firm, hard, and then for Mrs. Lehntman, diffused, easy. With these directions one can so to speak interpret the piece fairly accurately. But the rhythm involves much more than the matters of beat and phrasing and metrics. The physical verbal rhythm is in itself relatively simple and heavy, like the vocabulary. It would correspond to say a simple ¾ time in comparison to the elaborate syncopations and runs and glides and suspensions of late 19th century prose, or poetry—or to the palette of Cézanne as against an infinitely graduated impressionist palette, say that of Monet. But as with the vocabulary, the simplification of the rhythm is there to carry and clarify something complicated. . . . The functioning of the attention of the characters in speech (which would be according to Gertrude Stein's early definition a reflex of their total character) goes on against a simplified verbal rhythm. It has to be simple to disengage the special personal emphasis and to carry a rhythm of ideas. By a rhythm of ideas I mean only that as anyone goes on talking, or as we say expressing himself, there is in the sequence and force of the things said a very definite rate of change and a pattern of recurrence. The rate of change is largely a matter of the duration of interest, or as we would say the attention span, or as they said at Radcliffe a pulse beat of consciousness, quickened or sluggish. This is much more natural than it sounds. In the 19th century novel the thing said expresses the character insofar as it shows an attitude or, in Aristotle's word, a predilection. What a man has to say about his mother, about foreigners, about the new wing to the rectory expresses his character. We get not the essence of the character in process so much as little incidents or lights about the character. After an accumulation of them one can feel the character is all there and alive, that one knows what to expect of him in any little action. The pattern passages of Jane Austen, Trollope, and Dickens do go beyond this, to presenting the mind of the character in process directly, but it all tends to be crippled by the conventions of current grammar and literary style or dialect, or obstructed by material furthering the plot or the atmosphere or the philosophy.

In the passage quoted above and in the scene with Miss Mary quoted earlier, the ideas expressed have hardly any personal idiosyncrasy, they are in themselves the bleakest commonplaces, and this neutrality serves as a foil to make clear the extremely delicate sequence and emphasis of the ideas as they come out of the character in accordance with the vital intensity and frequency of that character. The ideas of the enraged Anna come with a steady insistence as well as abrupt change. Consider how the pressure that has to be put not only on the metric but on the meaning of the phrase "to do so" expresses the violence in Anna more directly than external description or greater eloquence of vocabulary and idea. The petition of the name Mrs. Lehntman is Anna's way of making the woman stay there and hold still under the pounding reproaches. The use of the word "here" in the phrase "and you are all so careless here and spend it all the the time" is again a way of arresting the household for the attack. The repetition of the phrase "all the time" is again a way of enveloping their behavior for total condemnation. In contrast the charming "easy" maundering expostulation of Mrs. Lehntman dwells softly on irrelevances until the final incoherence of calling for the ice tea. Gertrude Stein says earlier, "It was wonderful how Mrs. Lehntman could listen and not hear, could answer and yet not decide, could say and do what she was asked and yet leave things as they were before."

This differs from the method of Proust. With him the peculiarities of speech, the curious idiom of vocabulary, both verbal and ideal, all project the precise social or historical coloring of the character. Not that drama and an expressive rhythm are not in it, but they are not disengaged from an extremely complex harmonics in every phrase uttered by Françoise or Charlus, for example. Gertrude Stein reduces the tonality, the pedal, and disengages the pure melody and rhythm. We are out of Wagner say into Satie. This is one part of what she called the destruction of associational emotion.

In "The Good Anna" she tries numerous other methods for presenting the characters alive, besides direct dialogue. One attempt is to run Anna's abrupt rhythm across the dialogue into the narrative: " 'Peter!,'— her voice rose higher,—'Peter!,'—Peter was the youngest and the favorite dog,—'Peter if you don't leave Baby alone,'—Baby was an old, blind terrier that Anna had loved for many years,—'Peter if you don't leave Baby alone, I take a rawhide to you, you bad dog.' " The consistency corresponding to the rhythm is given in physical descriptions: "At this time Anna, about twenty-seven years of age, was not yet all thin and worn. The sharp bony edges and corners of her head and face were still rounded out with flesh, but already the temper and the humor showed sharply in her clean blue eyes, and the thinning was begun about the lower jaw, that was so often strained with the upward pressure of resolve." The quality of incessant strain and pressure, Anna's particular quality, pervades nearly everything in the story, from the structure and transitions to the least matters of style. It is, like the work of Flaubert, exhaustively coordinated. It seems all to be written on the signature as it were of one of the earliest sentences: "Anna led an arduous and troubled life."

Whatever this analysis may make it look like, "The Good Anna" is not merely an exercise in technique, though certainly very brilliant as an exercise. The story comes really from a simple animal necessity to express something living. It is more a matter of feeling than philosophy that decides that remarks about people or the story of what happened to them does not adequately or directly express them living. It takes a very vivid, even rank sense of life and a great intellectual vitality not to sacrifice the intuition of the living to the inadequate but accepted form, and then to use all available means and inventions to express that living as truly as one can. "The Good Anna" is an effort to do so.

But the impact and influence of *Three Lives* were mainly by its verbal novelty. It destroyed the extenuated rhetoric of the late 19th century. Wordsworth and the romantics had broken up the late classical rhetoric and regulated the written language on the natural idiom or on personal impulse. Language, like people, put off the perruque and wore an open collar. But the complex and ineffable longings of the natural life became standardized into attitudes, Byronic and others, and the language settled into as perfunctory a rhetoric as the classical. It wound up as art for art. And people did their hair correspondingly, making necessary the anti-macassar. Then Gertrude Stein inevitably came to the crew cut.

Three Lives, more radically than any other work of the time in English, brought the language back to life. Not the life of the peasantry or the emotions or the proletariat but life as it was lived by anybody living in the century, the average or normal life as the naturalists had seen it. Gertrude Stein in this work tried to coordinate the composition of the language with the process of consciousness, which, we have seen, was to her a close reflex of the total living personality. If this was to be done at least two serious things had to happen to the language:

First the word had to have not its romantic or literary meaning but the immediate meaning it had to the contemporary using it, a literal axiomatic meaning confined to the simple situations of the average life. The heroines of *Three Lives,* two German women and a Negress, have no connection whatever with the literary past of the language. The words are not used either as the authentic dialect of Baltimore Germans or Negroes; rather the perfunctory dialect convention serves as a pretext for liberating the language from literary convention.

The second necessity was to destroy 19th century syntax and word order, which could not follow the movement of a consciousness moving naturally, this movement being, in the early 20th century, of the utmost importance. Gertrude Stein had read a great deal of Elizabethan prose and poetry, in particular the prose of Robert Greene, and to that extent had a precedent and model for an extremely loose syntax which could follow the immediate interest and impulse of the consciousness, whether lively and extravagant or simply ruminant. The prose of Greene is normally full of the rather swaggering rapid movement and brutal emphasis of his person. The prose and construction of "The Good Anna" are based on something of the same quality in the character of the heroine.

As Whitman for example had destroyed 19th century metrics and verse forms, Gertrude Stein destroyed 19th century syntax and word order. Her work at this is comparable to what G. M. Hopkins was doing with syntax in his poetry, but there is a very great difference between them. Hopkins had as a Jesuit a casuist training in very fine distinctions of idea, a training corresponding considerably to the medical and philosophical training of Gertrude Stein. But, and I believe this is important, Hopkins was a straight baroque poet. The baroque style is equivalent to the Jesuit style, none too roughly, and they are both creations of the Counter Reformation, motivated by a desire to keep an escaping thing under. Under authority or under a formula or under the intellect or under the eye, it does not much matter. The baroque means, as a conquest, to bring everything under a closed system and within reach of the authorities. ("Glory be to God for dappled things.") The tension of the baroque is simply that struggle, heroic or sometimes just frantic. In the time of Hopkins the religious motive happened to coincide with a similar motive on the part of 19th century science and also the British Empire. All in all it leads to a closed and finished art, the stuffing of something inside something else, even if it wrenches the container considerably. Joyce, in the 20th century, went on with this, cramming everything into the scheme of the *Odyssey* or cyclic time, so that one may say that he was the last hypertrophy of the 19th century and destroyed it by overdoing it.

The early work of Gertrude Stein is still rather haunted by the pretention to universal inclusion, not of Catholicism of course but of naturalistic or evolutionary science. *The Making of Americans* is a universal history of human types and *Three Lives* has the paradigmatic force of naturalist writing. But the form and method and intent differ greatly from the insular Catholic product. The virtue of that product is to re-create the corporeal presence of everything within its little room, but the art of Gertrude Stein, being not insular but continental, is, even so early, generalized and disembodied, representing rather than including the totality of cases by single simple axioms. The form itself makes an enclosure, but this, as a reflection of a theory of consciousness, does not stand as a receptacle but as a field of activity, "a space of time that is filled always filled with moving." Otherwise her work, like that of Whitman, is all wide open spaces. It is absolutely not institutional or sectarian, it cannot be cathartic or tragic or salvationist, it is not out to justify or condemn or set things right. She had, to a startling degree, no sense of alienation from the universe but took it as a miraculously given thing. She speaks somewhere of the daily miracle that happens to the artist. The religious parallel to this very secular art would be not doctrine or ritual or institution but arbitrarily the state of grace. She teased everyone by calling this her being a genius. She was, I have no doubt, but the importance of that for the reader is not in the value but in the orientation it gives her work.

"The Good Anna," as pioneer work, does have its uncertainties and imperfections. I do not see how, for example, it is not a mistake to use the word "nay," or to mention the Struldbrugs, or to speak of "the dust which settles with the ages." But if these are errors they are errors with a meaning. They take up the prophetic tone of voice used loudly enough by Whitman, Melville, and later Hart Crane and Wolfe, to carry over the wide open spaces. In the case of Gertrude Stein it is the first appearance of the sibylline manner that is found in a great deal of her later work, where it perfectly belongs.

The third story of *Three Lives*, "The Gentle Lena," contains no great novelty beyond "The Good Anna." It is in a way a pendant to the first story in that Lena is a study of a soft and fluid and even absent consciousness and character as against the emphatic and hard presence of Anna. "Lena was patient, gentle, sweet and german." It is a delicious little story and prettily turned. It at least shows that Gertrude Stein was even this early capable of grace and easy elegance in the midst of her revolution. Further, it has a simple tenderness within complete clarity which so far as I know is unique in our literature. The nearest thing to it would be Sherwood Anderson.

But according to the general agreement the big thing in *Three Lives* is the middle story, "Melanctha." It is a tragic love story ending in death from consumption, so that it is available to the traditional literary taste and the educated emotions. Furthermore it is, as Carl Van Vechten says, "perhaps the first American story in which the Negro is regarded as a human being and not as an object for condescending compassion or derision." It is a good deal to have attained that clarity and equilibrium of feeling in a difficult question, but "Melanctha" as a piece of literature does much more.

Where "The Good Anna" and "The Gentle Lena" are composed as the presentation of a single type in illustrative incidents, "Melanctha" is composed on the dramatic trajectory of a passion. If "The Good Anna" roughly corresponds to "Un Coeur Simple," "Melanctha" corresponds roughly to *Madame Bovary*. Very roughly, and there is most likely no direct influence, but it makes an illuminating comparison.

Madame Bovary and the course of her passion are presented in an elaborate series of incidents, situations, landscapes, interiors, extraneous issues; in short they are measured and realized against a thick objective context as the things in the context are measured against her desire. Strangely enough this desire is never directly presented. It is measured somewhat by its casual source in her romantic reading—as Don Quixote is casually accounted for by his reading of the romances of chivalry—and it is known later by its various objects such as travel in far lands, luxuries, poetry written to her, and so on. As a blind desire, and probably as a death wish, it is symbolized by the awful blind beggar who is as it were Emma's *Doppelgänger* and who is finally put out of the way by Homais, the type of cheap rationalism. Emma's power is measured again by her being too much for Charles, for Léon, and even for Rodolphe, and by the pathetic infatuation of the boy Justin. She has certainly a variety of states of mind, wild desire, remorse, boredom, religiosity, fear, and so on, but they are a succession of distinct states, presented as complete and not as in process. In brief, Flaubert's art was spatial and intensely pictorial, not temporal and musical. Expressing directly and exactly the immediate movement, pulse, and process of a thing simply was not his business. But it was in this early period Gertrude Stein's business, and in "Melanctha" she did express at length the process of a passion.

She did not yet disengage the essential vitality entirely from its natural context. There are some few descriptions of railroad yards, docks, country scenes, houses, yards, rooms, windows, but these are reduced to a telling minimum. There is also some accounting for the complex forces in the heroine's character by the brutality of her father and the sweet indifference of her mother. She is described at the beginning of the story by contrast and association with Rose Johnson, her hard-headed decent friend, and again by the same contrast enlarged at the end of the story, when Rose casts her off. But the real demonstration of the story is the dialogue between Melanctha and her lover Jeff Campbell. In this long dialogue, which is like a duel or duet, the traditional incoherence between the inner and the outer life has been replaced by an incoherence between two subjectivities. It is conceived of as a difference in tempo, the slow Jeff against the quick Melanctha. Also there is already very much present in this story the difference, the radical and final difference in people, defined in *The Making of Americans* as the attacking and the resisting kinds or types. It is not quite the difference between active and passive, as both kinds are based on a persistence in being or in living, and they are further complicated by a deviousness and modulation in function. For example, how does a naturally attacking kind resist and how does a naturally resisting kind get provoked to attack? All this is elaborately and dramatically worked out in the long dialogue. "It was a struggle, sure to be going on always between them. It was a struggle that was as sure always to be going on between them, as their minds and hearts always were to have different ways of working." Their differences, shade by shade, and their gradual reconciliations are presented through the whole course of the affair from indifference to gradual fascination to the struggle for domination by a variety of means, to the decline into brotherly and sisterly affection, and finally to the final break.

Gertrude Stein had already, in a story written in 1903 and called *Quod Erat Demonstrandum* but not published until 1950 and under the title *Things as They Are*, worked out a very similar dialectic of a passion. It is very interesting as a preliminary exercise for "Melanctha." As its first title suggests, it is an intensive and exhaustive study of relations in a triangle. In its way it is a Jamesian study or demonstration, and its heroine mentions and quotes the heroine and/or villainess of James' novel *The Wings of the Dove*, Kate Croy. But *Things as They Are* bears a more striking resemblance to the *Adolphe* of Benjamin Constant, it has the same merciless directness and concentration, and though Gertrude Stein had probably not read *Adolphe* in 1903 this earliest work belongs to the tradition of *Adolphe* and of *La Princesse de Clèves*. It has the same unwavering intellectual clarity applied to the perpetually shifting relationships of a passion throughout its course. That much is already mastered in this first work, but the handling tends more to commentary than to presentation and has not the sure grasp of the personal cadences of a character's thought and feeling that makes the analyses in "Melanctha" a direct expression of character in movement. This is partly the fault of the characters themselves in *Things as They Are*. They are white American college women, whose speech and thought are bound to be at odds with their feeling. Gertrude Stein treats this difficulty handsomely enough as subject matter, but the expressive power of the prose is limited by its very propriety to the subject matter. It is very pure, immensely intelligent, and astonishing for a first work in 1903, but it is polite, cultivated, educated, literary. Compare with the passage from "Melanctha," quoted above, the following from *Things as They Are*:

> Time passed and they renewed their habit of desultory meetings at public places, but these were not the same as before. There was between them now a consciousness of strain, a sense of new adjustments, of uncertain standards and of changing values.

"Melanctha," in which the characters are Negroes, has thereby the advantage of "uneducated" speech, and of a direct relationship between feeling and word, more fundamental or universal drama. It is a measure of her strength that in making the most of the advantage Gertrude Stein abandoned polite or cultivated writing completely and forever, so completely that the press where she had *Three Lives* printed sent to inquire if she really knew English.

At all events, "Melanctha" is, as I said the work of Henry James was, a time continuum less of events than of considerations of their meaning. The events considered in "Melanctha" are mostly the movements of the passion, how Jeff and Melanctha feel differently toward each other from moment to moment.

Like the characters of James, Melanctha and Jeff are preternaturally articulate about their feelings, but where James keeps the plausibilities by using highly cultivated characters to express the complicated meaning in an endless delicacy of phrasing, Gertrude Stein uses the simplest possible words, the common words used by everybody, and a version of the most popular phrasing, to express the very complicated thing. It is true and exciting that James often used the simplest possible word for his complicated meaning, but he had a tendency to isolate it to the attention, to force it to carry its full weight by printing it in italics or putting it in quotes, or dislocating it from its more usual place in the word order, or repeating it. Gertrude Stein uses repetition and dislocation to make the word bear all the meaning it has, but actually one has to give her work word by word the deliberate attention one gives to something written in italics. It has been said that her work means more when one reads it in proof or very slowly, and that is certainly true, the work has to be read word by word, as a succession of single meanings accumulating into a larger meaning, as for example the words in the stanza of a song being sung. Unhappily all our training and most of our reasons for reading are against this. Very likely the desire for simplicity in style is most often a desire that the words and ideas along the way to the formulated conclusion, the point, be perfectly negligible and that we have no anxious feeling we are missing anything as we rush by. But as an example of how Gertrude Stein forces the simplest negligible words to stay there in a full meaning:

> "Can't you understand Melanctha, ever, how no man certainly ever really can hold your love for long times together. You certainly Melanctha, you ain't got down deep loyal feeling, true inside you, and when you ain't just that moment quick with feeling, then you certainly ain't ever got anything more there to keep you. You see Melanctha, it certainly is this way with you, it is, that you ain't ever got any way to remember right what you been doing, or anybody else that has been feeling with you. You certainly

Melanctha, never can remember right, when it comes what you have done and what you think happens to you." "It certainly is all easy for you Jeff Campbell to be talking. You remember right, because you don't remember nothing till you get home with your thinking everything all over, but I certainly don't think much ever of that kind of way of remembering right, Jeff Campbell. I certainly do call it remembering right Jeff Campbell, to remember right just when it happens to you, so you have a right kind of feeling not to act the way you always been doing to me, and then you go home Jeff Campbell, and you begin with your thinking, and then it certainly is very easy for you to be good and forgiving with it. No, that ain't to me, the way of remembering Jeff Campbell, not as I can see it not to make people always suffer, waiting for you certainly to get to do it. . . ."

The passage is, if one likes, about the synchronization of feeling upon the present activity. Anyone can see what is meant by the argument if the feeling discussed is understood to be sexual feeling. But the thing which makes this passage absolutely accurate and not euphemistic is that the subject is literally feeling, all feeling, inasmuch as all the passions are one. In brief, making abstraction of objects and situations, sexual feeling behaves no differently from other feelings. The readiness, slowness, concentration or absentmindedness, domination or dependence in sexual feeling are about the same as in all the other activities of a character. So that we have here a perfect propriety and fullness of diction.

The relatively simple dislocations of "you ain't got down deep loyal feeling, true inside you," from the more commonplace order "you have no true feeling of loyalty deep down inside you," not only jar the words awake into their full meaning but follow with much greater exactitude the slow, passionate, clumsy emphasis of Jeff Campbell's feeling.

The phrase "remembering right" could be replaced by a more familiar cliché, "profiting aptly by past experience," or by scientific gabble like "the coordination of habitual reflexes upon the present object," but the advantage of the simpler new phrase is that it expresses the matter in terms of the fundamental and final activities and categories of the mind. It is part of the "impulse to elemental abstraction," the description in terms of the final and generic as against description by context and association. It is like the generically round and sitting apple of Cézanne as against a delicately compromised and contextuated and reverberating apple of the impressionists. The propriety of the simple popular abstraction used in "Melanctha" is in this, that the two subjectivities at odds are seen, and so to be described, directly—directly from common knowledge, and not, as with *Madame Bovary*, seen refracted and described indirectly through an exterior context embodying considerable special knowledge. The immediate terms of *Madame Bovary* are saturated with French history, the immediate terms of "Melanctha" are the final categories of mental process—to know, to see, to hear, to wish, to remember, to suffer, and the like.

However, "Melanctha" is more than an exact chart of the passions. The conjugation or play of the abstractions proceeds according to the vital rhythm or tempo of the characters. In this way the essential quality of the characters is not only described but presented immediately. As Emma Bovary is *seen* against the rake Rodolphe and then against the pusillanimous Léon, and is thereby defined, so Melanctha is, in her quick tempo, *played* against the slow Jeff Campbell and then against the very fast "dashing" Jem Richards.

Gertrude Stein later made some remarks about *Three Lives* in the light of her later problems of expression. In *Composition as Explanation* she said:

> In beginning writing I wrote a book called *Three Lives* this was written in 1905. I wrote a negro story called *Melanctha*. In that there was a constant recurring and beginning there was a marked direction in the direction of being in the present although naturally I had been accustomed to past present and future, and why, because the composition forming around me was a prolonged present. A composition of a prolonged present is a natural composition in the world as it has been these thirty years [1926] it was more and more a prolonged present. I created then a prolonged present naturally I knew nothing of a continuous present but it came naturally to me to make one, it was simple it was clear to me and nobody knew why it was done like that, I did not myself although naturally to me it was natural. . . .
>
> In the first book [*Three Lives*] there was a groping for a continuous present and for using everything by beginning again and again.

The difference between a prolonged and a continuous present may be defined as this, that a prolonged present assumes a situation or a theme and dwells on it and develops it or keeps it recurring, as in much opera, and Bach, for example. The continuous present would take each successive moment or passage as a completely new thing essentially, as with Mozart or Scarlatti or, later, Satie. This Gertrude Stein calls beginning again. But the problem is really one of the dimensions of the present as much as of the artist's way with it. The "specious" present which occupied William James is an arbitrary distinction between past and future as they flow together in time. But for purposes of action and art it has to be assumed as an operable space of time. For the composer this space of time can be the measure, or whatever unit can be made to express something without dependence on succession as the condition of its interest. For the writer it can be the sentence or the paragraph or the chapter or the scene or the page or the stanza or whatever. Gertrude Stein experimented with all these units in the course of her work, but in the early work the struggle was mainly with the sentence and the paragraph.

ALLEGRA STEWART

The Quality of
Gertrude Stein's Creativity

O n the basis of her first short stories
in *Three Lives* and her long novel, *The Making of Americans*, Gertrude Stein
has often been classified as a writer of fiction, perhaps because the great
body of her work is so difficult to classify in any way at all. Since 1914,
however, when she published *Tender Buttons*, most of her writing defies
classification under the familiar categories of literature, although she made
a few sallies into autobiography, fiction, and the essay. Her publications,
to be sure, can be discriminated as poetry and prose, but she herself discarded
the distinction as irrelevant. She called her psychological word-paintings
of personalities and objects "portraits," and her descriptions of things moving in space (landscapes and scenes) she called "plays" and "operas." But
her compositions in these literary genera are the very reverse of what one
would expect, because she was always "in" her own consciousness, attempting to put into words, regardless of their associational meanings, the
union of two inner realities (those of subject and object) or the marriage
of outer and inner realities as it took place in presentational immediacy:

> When I see a thing it is not a play to me because the minute I see it it
> ceases to be a play for me, but when I write something that somebody
> else can see then it is a play for me. When I write other things not plays
> it is something that I can see and seeing it is inside of me but when I
> write a play then it is something that is inside of me but if I could see it
> then it would not be.

From *American Literature*, vol. 28 (January 1957). Copyright © 1957 by Duke University
Press.

Thus her "portraits" really leave out what everyone else can see, and her "plays" make visible what nobody else can see. The portraits objectify the personality or essential nature of people and things as distilled in the alembic of Gertrude Stein's consciousness, while the plays objectify her imaginative ideas and constructions excited by the motion and arrangement of objects in space. The portraits are impressionistic, the plays, expressionistic. Or, to put it another way, the portraits reflect her receptivity to the substantial, whereas her plays reflect the "play" of her mind with the purely phenomenal. She subjectifies the world in portraits and objectifies the contents of her consciousness in plays.

This *bouleversement* of the portrait and the play is all of a piece with her deliberate efforts to destroy the associational meanings of words in order to express pure quality apart from the forms which carry it. Her first portraits, written in 1909, represent an abrupt break with all forms of discursive writing, and with all the conventional symbolisms of language. From the point of view of contemporary literature, her compositions were part of a general revolt against surface realism and the constricting effects upon the imagination of scientific and historical data; and her rejection of conventional plot and chronological narrative was part of the general effort to restore to reality that inwardness which had been lost to life and literature in the general materialism of thought and life in our time.

In the twentieth century, organization and mechanization have supplanted both the rationalism of the enlightenment and the extreme individualism of the romantic period, with the result that society tends to be collectivized and depersonalized and the individual lost in the statistical table of averages. To all these forces Gertrude Stein's work (like that of many of her contemporaries) paradoxically opposed an irrationalism and an impersonalism of an entirely different kind. Inevitably her writing appeared to be part of a cult of unintelligibility, or a manifestation of a new barbarism. For in a period when there seemed to be nothing that had not been explained or that could not be understood, and among sophisticates who "knew" everything and believed nothing, she was seeking to recover mystery, and to reawaken wonder.

After 1909, this affirmative effort of hers consisted chiefly of recording the motions of her own mind. Writing became for her an exercise (or ritual) in concentration, for the act of concentrating one's attention liberates consciousness from every necessity except its own autonomous activity. But the struggle for such freedom imposed upon her a stern *ascesis*, requiring as it did the perception and then the verbal expression of her own inner motions, stripped of everything but presentational immediacy.

Such introversion differs radically, of course, from the introspection asso-ciated with anxiety or other neurotic maladjustments.

In seeking such interior freedom, Gertrude Stein suppressed all sub-ject matter as such in behalf of this on-going inner movement, which she tried to express without interposing any conscious purpose between her mind and its object, excluding both memory and conceptual forms. Unlike the chronological time of history and nature, the interior time of con-sciousness—duration, as Bergson called it—is always present time. It is in the present moment that the mind is free to act creatively and to "make" out of the "given" subject matter new objects that have no causal con-nections with the course of events in the external world. Gertrude Stein attempted in many different ways to record the time of duration in herself and in others as always the same, yet always different—the same because it is always present, different because it is filled with the fleeting stream of its own contents and the flux of things in chronological time. "Content without form," she was fond of saying, meaning that structures and forms should not be permitted to tyrannize over direct experience—that they are less important than the quality of life by which the forms themselves are actually distinguished.

As the activity of the individual soul alone with its "object," writing affirms the freedom and autonomy of man amid the flux of things and the determinations of space and time. Writing is "sacred," and Gertrude Stein often warned writers against trying to serve two masters, "god and mam-mon":

> When I say god and mammon concerning the writer writing, I mean that any one can use words to say something. And in using these words to say what he has to say he may use words directly or indirectly. If he uses these words indirectly he says what he intends to have heard by somebody who is to hear and in so doing inevitably he has to serve mammon. Mam-mon may be a success, mammon may be an effort he is to produce, mammon may be a pleasure he has from hearing what he himself has done, mammon may be his way of explaining, mammon may be a laziness that needs nothing but going on, in short mammon may be anything done indirectly. Now serving god for a writer who is writing is writing anything directly, it makes no difference what it is but it must be direct, the relation between the thing done and the doer must be direct.

In her own struggle for directness, Gertrude Stein strained words and exerted pressure upon them, and renounced "names" (nouns), and dissected grammar. Whatever she concentrated her attention upon became isolated from all the relations in which it stood to other things. A thing-in-itself with its own existence, *sui generis,* the object entered into a process of reciprocal excitement with a knowing consciousness and became open on all sides to the understanding in contact with it. The intellectual perception of sheer existence is an act of ingatheredness, or recollection, in which the knower feels outside of time and freed from the demands of the ego. He becomes a spiritual entity whose only action is the incarnation of what it knows in the word. This, Gertrude Stein believed, is the final creative act, the mystery in which knower and known are joined in unity.

To eternize in this way a fleeting moment of life is to create a new value from what would otherwise have been carried along in the temporal flux to oblivion. Such a value need never have been realized even fleetingly, of course, because there is no necessary relation between knower and known. The conjunction between them is accidental and contingent, but the act of realization is an exchange between two finalities of experience, and no matter how trivial the object may seem to be in terms of the world's work the value of the interchange is infinite. The product of exchange serves no purpose beyond itself; its measure is devotion rather than use. In Gertrude Stein's vocabulary it is variously called a "hymn," a "prayer," a "song," a "meditation," a "master-piece" of human experience—given an immortality beyond the life of both the knowing subject and the known object, in an object totally new.

Thus Gertrude Stein could write with words "together" and "apart," dedicated to the task of resurrecting them from the smooth, dead phrases of descriptive science, surface realism, factual narrative, and philosophical abstraction: "I have of course always been struggling with this thing, to say what you nor I nor nobody knows, but what is really what you and I and everybody knows." To restore to the imagination the living word, to bring back an interest in man as man, to revive an interest in the normal and the ordinary—in what everybody knows and nobody knows—such was the task she undertook. It required drastic renunciations and ascetic intellectual discipline, and it involved not being understood as well as being misunderstood.

If writing is a sacred activity, a hymn or a prayer, then the traditional classifications of literature are irrelevant. It does not matter very much what Gertrude Stein called her compositions, not only because she was not concerned with forms, but because, no matter what she wrote, it was a "piece" of an integrated consciousness, a work of the human mind absorbed in knowing. As Hegel said, the "well-known," the familiar, is never intelligibly known, since acquired knowledge is formal and not contentual. Gertrude Stein had set herself the goal of discovering what knowing is, and therefore she directed her knowing against this "being-familiar" and "being well-known." In *The Geographical History of America* she maintained that hers were ordinary ideas: "That is what I mean to be I mean to be the one who can and does have as ordinary ideas as these."

Whitehead once remarked that "it requires an unusual mind to undertake the analysis of the obvious. Familiar things happen, and mankind does not bother about them." Gertrude Stein's analysis of the obvious, however, confronts the given in ordinary human experience with full awareness of its mystery. She raises questions as to the nature of perception, the meaning of being, the boundlessness of space and the roundness of the world, the passage of time and the nature of personality and identity, and the activities of genius. To contemplate the obvious is to confront the polarities in the universe and the contradictions in man. It is to become aware of the dualism which runs through all things.

Meditation upon these subjects has been the exercise of reflective minds in all ages, but it has been considered the work of philosophers and religious thinkers rather than of creative writers. There is a vast body of writing, however, which, while differing radically in form and content, is unclassifiable except as "meditation." Of this class are Cicero's *De Officiis*, Erasmus's *Moriae Encomium*, Pascal's *Pensées*, Traherne's *Century of Meditations*, and—to mention a sensitive modern thinker—Gabriel Marcel's *Mystery of Being.* One might say, too, that the quality of the best poetry of Wordsworth, of Yeats, and of T. S. Eliot is meditative, and that the novels of Kafka, Mann, Joyce, Hesse, and Proust are fictionalized meditations. The emergence of the meditative element in modern poetry and fiction is correlative with the secular movement in the western world, but the lyrical element itself is reflective, and one need only recall such elegiac pieces as "Night Thoughts" or *The Anatomy of Melancholy* to recognize the diverse forms in which meditation upon "first and last things" has been the "object" of the writing. Hegel's *Phenomenology* and Emerson's essay on *Nature* are brought together under this mode of classification. In fact, all distinctions of form are dissolved in the masterpieces of literature, if the "object" is viewed in terms of content and not in terms of form. The actual subject matter and the personality of the mind that reflects upon it survive in the written word, stripped of all that is accidental and changing, and the written word itself becomes a "moving" power, a dynamic and living entity.

The meditative element became dominant in the writings of Gertrude Stein when she began to write portraits—in other words, at the time when she ceased to worry about communication and emphasized communion. During the writing of *The Geographical History of America,* she was concerned primarily with being, not with time and change. From *Tender Buttons* on, however, all her work is a kind of communion. She detached herself from "mechanical civilizations and the world being round," convinced that the dialectical process in time leads only from one pole to another—from communism to individualism and back again in a never-ending cycle, in which the individual is always lost in the collective or the solipsistic. The union of opposites is a creative act, but that action itself can never become the object of knowledge. To perform the act is to assert man's freedom from every necessity except that of existence itself. "The only interesting thing is that no one knows the limits of the universe," she said. "You live on this earth and you cannot get away from it and yet there is a space where the stars are which is unlimited and that contradiction is there in every man and every women and so nothing is ever settled."

Like space, knowledge is infinite, but actual knowing is an individuated process within a finite world where all things change. In view of the contradiction between finite and infinite and in view of the fact that all living creatures die, the important thing is to affirm this life by living it in full consciousness—that is, by living in the present. But it is very difficult to live in the present consciously. "Somebody has to have an individual feeling"; "any time is the time to make a poem. The snow and the sun below"; but the weight of the past and the hope for, or fear of, the future prevent most people from really living in the present. "Being men is a very difficult thing to be," for the primary fact is that time passes. "After all that is what life is and that is the reason there is no Utopia." Human institutions are not static and will never become so. All forms of action upon the world must consume themselves in the process except the immediate knowing of the present, but it is just as well that most people are so engaged in the struggle for existence, so occupied by the mere business of living, that they do not have time to dwell upon the mystery of existence. For they do not have the vitality to concentrate upon the present: "you have to be a genius to live in it and to exist in it and express it to accept it and deny it by creating it. . . ."

Life is mysterious and can never be understood. "The only thing that anybody can understand is mechanics," but machines are neither interesting nor essential: "you cannot exist without living and living is something that nobody is able to understand while you can exist without machines it has been done but machines cannot exist without you. . . ."

The modern world, overmechanized and overorganized, is an empty world, a world in which few have an individual feeling, because it has lost the sense of strangeness and mystery. To restore to it the feeling of life, writers must achieve a direct vision of the world. The novel, for example, is a dead form, because people have lost their belief in the reality of fictional characters. "I tell all the young ones now to write essays, after all since characters are of no importance why not just write meditations, meditations are always interesting, neither character nor identity are necessary to him who meditates."

For Gertrude Stein, meditation is more than reflection: it is communion, participation—an act of presence. Direct, immediate—it is the only way to master the contradictions and oppositions of discursive thinking and experience and to give a content to the "now." Only through participation will the word have life, and only through the written word can life be immortalized. The written word is the one medium in which all mediation disappears. Words on the written page bear no resemblance to the things they signify, and they are therefore entirely closed to sense perception and open immediately to the inward eye. Through written words one can commune in silence across space and time by signs which in themselves need make no appeal to the senses. All other forms of expression create an object with extension in space or time that is a necessary part of them; they are bound by one or the other and therefore appeal to eye or ear. Thus, paradoxically, the written word is the most immediate of all the modes of expression. In it the writer is disembodied but enduring. "Mention me if you can," Gertrude Stein said, "because I am here." She also said, "How can a language alter. It does not it is an altar."

In contrast to the written word, the spoken word is mediated both by the voice and by the physical presence of the speaker. Gertrude Stein found lecturing difficult because it brought her into contact with an audience, and so she sought to isolate herself in every way possible in order that communication should not interfere with communion. When a writer is writing, "that physical something by existing does not connect him with anything but concentrates him on recognition," whereas when he is addressing, or writing for, an audience, that physical something diverts his energies and deprives his words of authenticity. Only in so far as the consciousness is concentrated upon its object—is really present to it—can there be anything created. "By written I mean made. And by made I mean felt," she said, and over and over again she defined the genius as the one who talks and listens at the same time. "One may really indeed say that that is the essence of genius, of being most intensely alive, that is being one who is at the same time talking and listening. . . ." Talking and listening are not consecutive acts: they occur simultaneously in concentration, "The two in one and the one in two," "like the motor going inside the car and the car moving, they are part of the same thing."

In the act of presence, by which the dualism of experience is overcome here and now, an exchange occurs, in which the objects of contemplative perception and knowing become mental phenomena. Knower and known are joined in an object—the masterpiece—through which they become intelligible to our intuition and feeling, but not to our reason. The transaction occurs in time, but it is not a time-process, and the masterpiece itself has a life beyond life. It "does nothing." Though it can be destroyed, it cannot be used. Since creative writers are contemporaries in the "continuous now," the loss of a masterpiece does not really matter because it would remain the possession of those who had known it and no one else would miss it.

The number of masterpieces is of no importance, and no one of them has any necessity either to be or not to be. They are the gratuitous acts of "presence" itself, and the witnesses to man's freedom in this world. Through them the world-and-life-negation fostered by the thought of death is overcome and the contents of time rescued from the flux. Writing thus becomes ritual, in which the writer affirms himself as one who continues to exist after his death as long as he has readers—indeed, even if he has no readers.

Such a theory of creative writing equates the work of genius with the activity of saints, and the creativity itself with grace. Yet in the work of Gertrude Stein neither the prayers nor the grace seems to involve either a transcendent deity or an immanent world spirit. "It is the habit to say there must be a god but not all the human mind has neither time or identity therefore enough said." The human mind is a dynamism within the life force which moves in the individuated consciousness in a dimensionless inner space—a constructive agency, which is capable of individuating its own objects, free from causal necessity. To Gertrude Stein, the human mind was mysterious, but she was not mystical about it. She had "an intellectual passion for exactitude in the description of inner and outer reality," and neither had nor sought mystical experience. She defined mysticism as a kind of metamorphosis: "if you believe in anything deeply enough it turns into something else and so money turns into not money. That is what mysticism is. . . ."

Such transubstantiation is not the act of the human mind which knows and distinguishes. "A rose is a rose is a rose is a rose" to all eternity for Gertrude Stein, and the function of the human mind is not to dissolve itself in either the One or the All, nor to be turned into something else through transubstantiation, but to maintain itself courageously against all collectivisms and Nirvanas and to bound the infinite at every moment by its own autonomous acts of knowing. Thus she seems to deny nearly everything that we ordinarily call religion—mystical and nonmystical alike. And yet her view seems to me to be one legitimate view of man, and to merit the name of religion as defined by James, Bergson, and Whitehead.

William James denied that there is any such entity as religious emotion; nor is religion "conscience and morality." He defines religion as "the feelings, acts, and experiences of individual men in their solitude, so far as they apprehend themselves to stand in relation to whatever they may consider the divine," and points out that divine means "God-like, whether it be a concrete deity or not." In his chapters on saintliness, James ascribes saintliness to the susceptibility of the individual to "sovereign excitements" of a spiritual order: "the saintly character is the character for which spiritual emotions are the habitual centre of the personal energy," so that the claims of the non-ego are always met with "yes, yes" instead of "no, no."

According to James, among all the shiftings from self-centeredness to love, perhaps the most important is the one in which the individual passes from tenseness and self-responsibility to equanimity, receptivity, and peace, not by an act of will—"not by doing, but by simply relaxing and throwing the burden down." The difference between ordinary people and geniuses depends solely on "the amount of steam-pressure chronically driving the character in the ideal direction, or on the amount of ideal excitement transiently acquired." Thus the "genius with the inborn passion seems not to feel [the inhibitions to action] at all; he is free of all that inner friction and nervous waste." James praised the saintly life, but he felt that there were many ways of being saintly—of being true to one's mission and vocation. He was particularly ambivalent about "mere devotion, divorced from the intellectual conception which might guide it towards bearing useful fruit." For James, the universe was open; he was hospitable to mysticism, although himself not mystical. A moralist, he judged mystical experience by its fruits, not by its transports; a psychologist, he described the facts, without passing judgment upon their metaphysical meaning.

Bergson, on the other hand, was decidedly mystical, and saw the whole universe as "a machine for the making of Gods." In opposing static to dynamic religion, he associates the intellect in its myth-making faculty with static religion, and intuition and the vital impetus with dynamic religion. "Religion is to mysticism what popularization is to science," he said. In connection with the activity of intuition, he distinguished between writing intellectually and writing through "the imperative demand of creation," characterizing the latter as an "image of the creation of matter by form." It is important to point out here that Gertrude Stein attended Bergson's lectures in Paris in the winter of 1908, just before she began to write portraits, and it may well be that the impact of those lectures turned her attention from the problem of time in narrative to the problem of objectifying purely qualitative perceptions. Certainly her anti-intellectualism resembles Bergson's and was directed against the static and formal aspects of knowledge just as his was. It may be, too, that the Bergsonian mystical intuition and Gertrude Stein's "human mind" are so similar as to be almost indistinguishable. But Gertrude Stein herself was much less optimistic about the universe than Bergson was and believed much less in progressive evolution and the efficacy of action.

In my opinion, Whitehead's definition of religion comes closest to Gertrude Stein's attitude toward writing. Whitehead says that "religion is what the individual does with his own solitariness," and he related individual solitariness to universality, because "universality is a disconnection from immediate surroundings. It is an endeavour to find something permanent and intelligible by which to interpret the confusion of immediate detail." The great reflective books of the Old Testament, for example, seek neither to reform society nor to express religious emotion; instead, "there is a self-conscious endeavour to apprehend some general principles." In analyzing the aesthetic experience, Whitehead says that it is "feeling arising out of the realization of contrast under identity." "Expression is the one fundamental sacrament. It is the outward and visible sign of an inward and spiritual grace." A written piece, if it is really first-hand expression, is a masterpiece, and its creation is an act of loyalty to the universe. Geniuses display their originality in precisely that part of their expression which remains unformulated: "They deal with what all men know, and they make it new. They do not bring to the world a new formula nor do they discover new facts, but in expressing their apprehension of the world, they leave behind them an element of novelty—a new expression forever evoking its proper response."

It seems to me that Gertrude Stein's correlation of creative writing with the activity of saints is closest to James's idea of a religious vocation, that her view of the essential dynamism of the creative process is very close to Bergson's theory of intuition, and that her view of writing as "the fundamental sacrament" is very close to Whitehead's. But Gertrude Stein rejected all philosophical systems, believing that neither ontology nor epistemology could resolve the dualism of the universe. Like the existentialists, she began and ended with experience. And experience meant coming to grips with what Charles Sanders Peirce calls "firstness," or pure quality in all its immediacy, and with "secondness," or brute fact in all its starkness; and it meant rejecting utterly the realm of law—as either immanent or transcendent—which is what Peirce meant by "thirdness." For laws in Gertrude Stein's philosophy are constructs of the human mind, and the human mind is not subject to them.

Observation and construction, the activities of the imagination, have nothing to do with the will to live, either:

> If a master-piece is what it is how can then its not being one effect it.
> All that is silence because it makes longing and longing and feeling have nothing to do with what a master-piece is.

The human mind bridges the chasm between the fluctuating polarities of the universe, not by asserting the supremacy of either spirit or matter, but by maintaining always the distinction between them. In the act of knowing (either "in a glance or in looking"), man asserts his freedom to create this bridge; freedom is not asserted in the reconstructions of memory and habit. It is direct acquaintance that marries subject and object without destroying the separate existence of mind and the world, and Gertrude Stein declared that no one could know how this was done. It "happened" from time to time in the activity of genius. Such action is a force, an impulsion in individuals, but it is not Bergson's *élan vitale* rushing through matter. Nor is it the will to live of Schopenhauer, or James. It has nothing to do with progress or the struggle for existence. It is not something that arises out of the *negation* of the will to live, however, but rather an excess of vital energy, or abundance of life itself. It is an existential freedom, to which Gertrude Stein gives the name of the "human mind." Like the muse of Homer or of Milton, it is not a function of the ego, but the function of spirit.

For inspiration, psychology has no name but genius. Nordau treated it as a disease of personality, degenerate and aberrant. Others, notably Frederick W. H. Myers, have seen it as a subliminal self. Jung identified it with the collective unconscious, working through the intuition. James considered it an inexplicable form of selectivity which directed the attention towards a particular class of objects. Gertrude Stein compared it to lightning, which strikes in a particular time and place, occasioned by natural phenomena, but itself the cause of its own activity. The motions of genius are impulsive but unnecessitated, processes of attention rather than motives. For in genius, intention is freedom to know and to create.

The knower, according to this way of putting the case, is an individual, but to his feeling he is not existing in time; nor is he existing in eternity, though he may feel as if he were. Gertrude Stein's phrase for the condition of knowing is "being existing"—her way of expressing the permanence which endures through change. The "be" in become is a reminder that things persist—that there is a continuous present in which actual beings exist and sustain themselves as entities amid the flux. A masterpiece is such an entity. It carries within it its own measure of value and is therefore open to everyone who has a human mind in any conceivable here and now. It is thus universal in its content, not as a mere form.

In this connection, it is interesting to note what Charles Sanders Peirce has to say about abstraction and the present. According to him, the present is just what cannot be abstracted; it cannot be "aufgehoben," for the abstract is always "what the concrete makes it be." The concrete is always a "surprise," different from what we thought it would be, something that we had not expected, and for which we cannot prepare. To recognize it demands the independent existence of both the knower and the known, in an accidental relationship, independent of everything except the interplay of subject and object.

This interplay is really the activity of the human mind as it is present to the world at any moment. Peirce called it "musement,"

> an occupation of the mind which "involves no purpose save that of casting aside all serious purpose," and which consists in wonder either at some striking characteristic within one of the universes or at some purposeful connection between two of the universes, together with speculation about the cause of these features. The attitude of mind involved is closest to *pure play* because it is not fraught with serious purpose of any kind; on the contrary, it is actually an attempt to cut through the layers of conscious purpose and arrive at that state of mind which is close to the naïveté and freshness of children in the face of some awe-inspiring wonder. If, however, some ulterior purpose is allowed to enter, the proper attitude is destroyed.

Gertrude Stein's writing increasingly became "musement" of this order—play—particularly in *Tender Buttons* and *Geography and Plays*, in which she was seeking to express the successive moments of realizing the objects or the scene arbitrarily selected for attention, or to convey the essential nature of living creatures or of objects moving in space. "As I said if you like, it was like a cinema picture made up of succession and each moment having its own emphasis that is its own difference and so there was the moving and the existence of each moment as it was in me." Impersonal, objective, even mechancial, such writing is unconcerned with hopes and fears. Thus she could later say, "Finally a prayer has nothing to do with I care."

No matter what her subject matter was—and paradoxically, as she became more playful, she wrote more and more frequently about "saints and singing"—she was never solemn or conventionally religious. She had wit and a love of the comic, and since her object was only to be present both to her writing and to her reader, she gives the impression of childlike intentness, as though she were concentrating upon each movement in an absorbing game. Thus her work is dominated by the spirit of play, and is filled with a peculiarly pervasive feeling of delight and freedom from care, even when she is describing the wars she has seen. She wrote without tears, for there is something that sings in life—that is gratuitous and free. We do not know how to name it:

> Dogs and birds and a chorus and a flat land.
> How do you like what you are. The bird knows, the
> dogs know and the chorus well the chorus yes the chorus
> if the chorus which is the chorus.
> The flat land is not the chorus.
> Human nature is not the chorus.
> The human mind is not the chorus.
> Tears are not the chorus.
> Food is not the chorus.
> Money is not the chorus.
> What is the chorus.

For Gertrude Stein, there is a harmony between man and the universe, but it is not a heavenly harmony—not a music of the spheres. It is not a process in time nor a result of progress nor an event in history. It is perhaps "the choir invisible of those immortal dead who live again" in masterpieces, who were present to the world and to themselves, participating in experience, contemplating it, loving it, dreaming about it, and expressing it in words. But she rejected all mysticism, all theology, and all systematic philosophy which placed the oneness of things beyond experience; and the chorus as she conceived it is a harmony of separate and distinct voices, not a transcendent or an immanent paean in which the many are resolved into the One. Consequently there is little exalted rhetoric in her writing. But there is a great deal of joy—joy in the pleasures of perception, of imagination, of play. She sings a song that we all can sing in those moments when we really live consciously in the actual present and affirm life as an end in itself. In singing this song, one is "doing nothing" in exactly the way the saints are "doing nothing" when they pray or sing or perform their ritual tasks. The song is childlike and gay in its quality, solemn and serious only in the attention devoted to it. It asks for nothing, but finds everything. "They liked it as much as they ever liked it before because the wind blew and blew the birds about and they liked it they liked it as much when the wind did that."

This seizing of the present moment and savoring it is very characteristic of all forms of real participation. Contemplative participation is only another name for the process of knowing in which, according to Schopenhauer, the artist becomes the "pure will-less subject of knowledge." In *The Geographical History of America*, Gertrude Stein seems to be speaking of herself when she writes: "She says she wanted that she should be the only ideal one, but she is, what else is she but that, she is, and so the human mind rests with what is." Like Schopenhauer, she saw in the Idea the abiding and the essential, and in art, the embodiment of reality. Though her emphasis is different, it seems to me that she must have agreed with nearly everything that Schopenhauer says about the work of art.

> It repeats or reproduces the eternal Ideas grasped through pure contemplation, the essential and abiding in all the phenomena of the world; and according to what the material is in which it reproduces, it is sculpture or painting, poetry or music. Its one source is the knowledge of Ideas; its one aim the communication of this knowledge. While science, following the unresting and inconstant stream of the fourfold forms of reason and consequent, with each end attained sees further, and can never reach a final goal nor attain full satisfaction, any more than by running we can reach the place where the clouds touch the horizon; art, on the contrary, is everywhere at its goal. For it plucks the object of its contemplation out of the stream of the world's course, and has it isolated before it. And this particular thing, which in that stream was a small perishing part, becomes to art the representative of the whole, an equivalent of the endless multitude in space and time. It therefore pauses at this particular thing; the course of time stops; the relations vanish for it; only the essential, the Idea, is its object.

Ordinary people do not linger over the mere perception of an object or focus their attention sufficiently upon it to see it as a thing-in-itself. The man of genius lets us see the world through his eyes. It is his presence of mind which enables others to see. The value of vision does not arise from the subject matter; the insignificance of the matter may even intensify aesthetic experience as in still-life paintings or in the paintings of common country scenes by Ruisdael. It is for this reason that Gertrude Stein's writings give the appearance of triviality, and convey an impression of fragmentariness and inconsequentiality. But this is only on the surface. Like Henry James, she knew that it is the quality of life in the work of art that really counts.

The isolation of an object by the human mind was carried much farther by Gertrude Stein than it has been carried by other writers. Many of her portraits and plays, taken in isolation, seem fragmentary and unintelligible. The whole of her work, however, has unity and meaning. Her writings have the kind of unity which she ascribes to the continents on this planet. They are one as the land is one, separated into continents and islands by the waters of the world, but connected beneath by the vast floor of rivers and oceans, and so really one land, though to our eyes this one land appears as so many different "pieces" of various contours and sizes. The literal indivisible oneness of the ground beneath the waters is one of her recurrent ideograms for the oneness of the human mind under the flow of history and amid the diversity of peoples. "Do you see that there is the land which nobody can see because there is the sea, and yet there is the land in America, there is the land salt lake land where there is no sea."

To penetrate beneath the separating seas of literary forms to the substratum of consciousness requires one to ignore for the most part the separations in time and space which force upon us the isolated parts and fragments rather than the whole. The mind of man is still largely a *terra incognita;* it is revealed, if at all, primarily through the lives of saints and the creations of the artist, both often seeming to be occupied in doing nothing immediately useful. Masterpieces and the life of sanctity are "presences" across the centuries; they are always "here" to the mind that attends.

But this is a rather exalted way of describing Gertrude Stein's works. After all, her favorite illustration of the way one exists in eternity is Robinson Crusoe's discovery of Friday's footprints. "[It] is one of the most perfect examples of the non-existence of time and identity, which makes a master-piece," she said. For in any moment of absorbed wonder the self is recollected in an experience of heightened awareness. And the beautiful paradox is that the artist, the saint, or the philosopher—like Crusoe in this dramatic confrontation of the "otherness" in the world—becomes most truly himself, is most truly a Self, precisely in the moment of self-forgetfulness. It was to this paradox that Gertrude Stein pointed when she said that "the human mind is like not being in danger but being killed," and that "At any moment when you are you you are you without the memory of yourself because if you remember yourself while you are you you are not for purposes of creating you."

B. L. REID

An Evaluation: "Think of Shakespeare and Think of Me"

Ⅰt would be a great deal easier to measure Gertrude Stein if she would let us alone. It would be much easier if she would let us weigh her as a minor writer rather than a major one, or as a scientist-philosopher rather than a creative artist, or as a follower of a bypath rather than of the highroad of literature. I am suggesting, obviously, that these alternatives seem to be the essential truths about her, but she will have none of them. The critic has to cut his way through a jungle of Miss Stein's ponderous pronouncements on the subject of herself, backed by all the weight of her full assurance and supported in some degree by the evidences of her wholly real independence and intelligence and the acclamation of eloquent and respectable friends.

Gertrude Stein's ego is one of the great egos of all time. It is monumental; it is heroic. Flat assertion of her own genius is a leitmotiv in virtually all her books. "Think of the Bible and Homer think of Shakespeare and think of me," she says; "I am one of the masters of English prose"; "In this epoch the only real literary thinking has been done by a woman"; "in english literature in her time she is the only one"; "I know that I am the most important writer writing today"; "I have been the creative literary mind of the century." She makes Miss Toklas say: "The three geniuses of

From *Art by Subtraction: A Dissenting Opinion of Gertrude Stein.* Copyright © 1958 by University of Oklahoma Press.

whom I wish to speak are Gertrude Stein, Pablo Picasso and Alfred White-head. . . . I have known only three first class geniuses and in each case on sight within me something rang."

I am inclined to think she gave Miss Toklas only a two-thirds chance of being right. Of course, Gertrude Stein became accustomed to the kind of carping insensitivity I am according her here, and she took it as one of the unavoidable tribulations attendant on genius. "Naturally I have my detractors," she said to Wombley Bald. "What genius does not?" It may be true indeed that Miss Stein needs to be seen as a genius to be seen at all. That is, we evaluate her as a being essentially not measurable at all, as apart, unique. When we try to fit her into a context involving normality or moderate supranormality, she does not fit; there is no common yardstick; the scales refuse to function. Perhaps we must agree with Julian Sawyer's judgment of her "absolute perspicacity." If she has that, she is beyond us; we cannot know her—and the critic's job is simplified into one of awe.

If Gertrude Stein is a genius, she is one in the vulgar sense of the term: perversely elevated, isolated, inhuman. Hers is not the friendly, communicative genius of her masters, James and Whitehead, or even Picasso, pulling us gently or roughly up to the heights of their new insight. She is a genius with a tragic flaw, one curiously like the old flaw of Oedipus and Lear—the fatal combination of pride and power and blindness. We must say this with the full knowledge that Gertrude Stein seemed all her life to be trying to communicate to us, that she worked with sweat and occasional humility to make us know her mind. That, however, is her colossal blindness and her arrogance; convinced of the absolute rightness of her vision and of her literary record of that insight, she refused all moderation or compromise.

It seems to me that Miss Stein is a vulgar genius talking to herself, and if she is talking to herself, she is not an artist. It is because she does talk to herself that she offers insuperable difficulties to both reader and critic. I suggest, therefore, that she be defined out of existence as an artist. To be an artist, she must talk to us, not to the dullest or the most tradition bound or the most unsympathetic of us, but to those of us who are flexible, those willing to be fruitfully led. There is not world enough or time enough for Gertrude Stein's kind of writing; too much in literature is both excellent and knowable.

What I am trying to say is that most of the confusion about Gertrude Stein seems the result of trying to understand her in a mistaken context. The original mistake is Miss Stein's; it happened when she defined herself as an artist, thereby obscuring from herself and her readers the fact that both her ends and her means pointed toward philosophy by way of science. The whole cast and capability of her mind was scientific, reflective, rational, philosophic. Of the truly creative ability to fabricate and counterfeit, to excite and to move and to instruct by fact or fiction conceived as dramatic, narrative, or lyric, she had only a rudimentary portion, and this she studiously suppressed until it was very nearly dead. Her works are not, properly speaking, art at all. Her aim was to "describe reality," but description alone is not art but science. In her aesthetics she reflects on reality as well, and it becomes philosophy.

Her "art" is one of subtraction and narrowing throughout. In her art she does not reflect, for reflection entails consciousness of identity and audience, an awareness fatal to the creative vision. She rules out the imagination because it is the hunting ground of secondary talent. She rules out logical, cause-effect relations: "Question and answer make you know time is existing." She rules out distinctions of right and wrong: "Write and right. Of course they have nothing to do with one another." She will have no distinctions of true and false: "The human mind is not concerned with being or not being true." She abjures beauty, emotion, association, analogy, illustration, metaphor. Art by subtraction finally subtracts art itself. What remains as the manner and matter of the specifically "creative" works of Gertrude Stein is the artist and an object vis-à-vis. This is not art; this is science. Miss Stein would turn the artist into a recording mechanism, a camera that somehow utters words rather than pictures.

It is vastly ironic that in a century in which the arts have been in pell-mell flight from the camera, she, who thought herself always galloping in the van of "contemporaneousness," has fled toward the camera. That hers is an eccentric camera, a literal camera obscura, does not make it less a camera. That in her early writing she was interested in what was under the surface, in the "inside," does not make her less a photographer. There she may be operating an X ray, but even its function is to take the picture, not to comment upon it, clothe it, or give it life in beauty or ugliness. Hers is still the "intellectual passion for exactitude in description."

Gertrude Stein's mistake, one must think, lies in conceiving as a sufficient ideal the thing William James handed her as a tool, the tool of rigidly objective scientific observation. She was conscious of this orientation toward science to some degree at one point in her work, *The Making of Americans*; after that she thought she had lost it and embarked upon a purely creative tack. But it seems that she never truly lost the scientific point of view. Whatever her subject, her "art" remained, within its idiosyncrasy, photographic in intention and in method.

Miss Stein makes a passing observation about painting in *The Autobiography of Alice B. Toklas* that is highly significant for an insight into her own work:

> One of the things that always worries her about painting is the difficulty that the artist feels and which sends him to painting still lifes, that after all the human being essentially is not paintable . . . if you do not solve your painting problem in painting human beings you do not solve it at all.

Yet she "always made her chief study people." Thus her chief study is people, who essentially are not paintable, and she is committed by the terms of her creed to painting them. One of the critical verities about Gertrude Stein is that she would never be instructed by impossibility, and one suspects that this particular impossibility is the focal dilemma of her work. It is her commitment to this impossibility, more than any of her ostensible dilemmas—the realization of "the complete actual present" or "the sense of immediacy"—that makes her twist and turn, that "made me try so many ways to tell my story" as she puts it.

True, "abjectly true," as William James would say, the human being is not paintable. Nor is he photographable; no matter whether one snaps his exterior or X-rays his bones and his liver and lights, one still does not have a human being. All great artists have recognized this abject truth; it is the reason they have set about apprehending the "poor, bare, forked animal"—still imperfectly, of course—by a means other than painting or by a means in addition to painting, by all the proliferation of the resources of language and thought and imagination they could command.

Gertrude Stein never effectively admitted that she could not paint or photograph man. She continued to try as long as she lived. And she, like the painters, was driven, in a very curious and retributively just way, into the retreat of still life. There was the difference, however, that the retreat became for her not occasional but chronic, not therapy but the disease itself. She retreated into the outright still life of the unpopulated *Tender Buttons,* or she sterilized and transfixed man until he was virtually a still-life element, no more humanly alive than Cézanne's applies or Braque's guitars. Why else should a play resemble a landscape, as she insists it should? In a very real sense, all the later works of Gertrude Stein, with the exception of those that are in some way autobiographical, are still lifes. To become an artist in the true sense of the word, Miss Stein would have had to surrender to the impossibility of apprehending man by unaided science.

It is significant, surely, that the one work of Gertrude Stein's with real artistic stature is the one that is least exclusively painterly. *Three Lives* is written as one feels, vaguely, a work of art should be written. It is written, that is, by a process of imagination applied to life experienced and directed by an informing philosophical theme and purpose; it is long and thoughtful in gestation; it envisions a reader to be enlightened and moved, and therefore it proceeds with a consciousness of form applied to part and whole, of language to be shaped and disciplined to delight and clarify. In a word, it is art achieved by the addition or multiplication of the tools of the writer. *Three Lives* was written, too, before experience became "sheer phenomenon" to Gertrude Stein, while she yet retained the desire to select and evaluate and be herself moved by her experience, before the encroachment of science upon her art imposed the necessity of removing herself emotionally from her subject and enjoined her to see mechanically rather than qualitatively.

The peripatetic origin of *Three Lives* reminds one of the method of the early Joyce, and indeed this book marks the one point in her work where one is moved to suspect that she, too, had within her the equipment of a first-rate creative writer. The book formed itself in her mind as she walked back and forth across Paris between her rue de Fleurus home and Picasso's Montmartre studio, where she was posing for the famous portrait now in the Museum of Modern Art. "Melanctha," the most famous of the three lives, combines bits picked up by her eyes and ears during the Paris walks, with people and incidents recollected from her experience, as a Johns Hopkins medical student, in delivering Negro babies in the slums of Baltimore. Another of the lives relates the story of a servant she had while a student in Baltimore. Such stories should have resulted from clear and close observations; they should be moving, and they are. As Edmund Wilson says, one feels Gertrude Stein living in the minds of these three simple-complex women, reproducing the movements of their consciousness with an identification that seems almost perfect.

For all its excellence, Miss Stein herself seems not to have regarded her *Three Lives* very highly, despite the fact that it gave her her widest literary influence and her soundest critical esteem. She mentions it comparatively seldom, usually as the product of an imperfect, formative period. She seems vaguely and illogically ashamed of the book. What really bothers her, of course, is that it retains likenesses to the writing of the past. In it, as she says, she was "groping" for her true direction. The fact that her groping was better literature than her fully formed method should have contained a lesson for her, but it did not. The very things that made the fineness of the book are the things she carefully cut away as her style matured—the sense of complete emotional and intellectual involvement and the full use of the writer's common tools of observation and re-creation in language. Ultimately the artist as a sensitized human being is replaced by the artist as a recorder; all that remains of the early multiplicity of resources are the emergent moments of "reality" as they move past the lens of the camera artist.

Three Lives, as I have said, stands as Miss Stein's point of closest identification with the mind of a character, and it provides us with an important observation on her relation to the contemporary "stream of consciousness" technique. It should be recalled here that it was her teacher, William James, who coined the term. In this book Gertrude Stein, whether or not she knew it, was creating in an approximation of this style. The symptomatic thing is that this is the only instance in which it is the mind of the character whose stream is followed. After this single experience Miss Stein retains the stream, but she shifts the focus to the writer, to the flow of her "knowing." In one more of the many ironies that crop up with Miss Stein as she moves toward science and objectivity and forgetfulness of self, she is turned in upon herself. She did not forget self, but she forgot nearly everything else and again trapped herself in the multiple paradox of her theory.

For all its unlikeness to her later writing, *Three Lives* contains in embryo two tendencies that later became very important, indicating the fundamental orientation of her art to science. For one thing, she adumbrates here her disposition to classify people by types that are vaguely psychological, the interest that was soon to become the whole of *The Making of Americans,* containing as it does the germ of the attitude that finally turned humanity into "sheer phenomenon" for her. For another, she begins her pursuit of a kind of language that will be for her the scientifically accurate re-creation of her subject. In *Three Lives,* language is still largely under control; straightforwardly conceptual and communicative, it keeps the reader in mind, intending to share with him a finely realized experience. The language in *Three Lives* is, in general, intellectually and dramatically and poetically satisfying. Only in "Melanctha" does one see it begin to slip out of her grasp and begin to control her. The repetitions and ramblings and rebeginnings continue to the point where it becomes obvious that Gertrude Stein is giving birth, right under our eyes, to her fatal habit of ignoring the inevitable gap between the sensibilities of writer and reader. Large portions of the latter half of "Melanctha" cross the border of enlightenment and interest into that limbo of dullness and torpor in which Miss Stein soon becomes entrenched.

She is beginning to lose her sense of proportion in the egoistic excitement of arriving at the state of ideal "creative recognition." The deadly folding-in upon self, the constricting of the field of vision and depth of purpose, the noxious linguistic idiosyncrasy—all get under way. In her first book Gertrude Stein has already begun to insulate herself from her reader, but the book remains a fine one because the process is as yet imperfect.

Miss Stein's second book, *The Making of Americans*, three years in the writing (1906–1908), was not published until 1925. It was this book that Conrad Aiken called a "fantastic disaster." In it the movement away from art and toward science is far more complete than in the earlier work, and the effect is paralyzing indeed. But her aim in *The Making of Americans*, if not genuinely artistic, is genuinely, if wrongheadedly, humane. The book grew out of her experiments at Radcliffe in "cultivated motor automatism," or automatic writing, with a large group of men and women students as her subjects. She found that her experiments proved nothing, but she conceived a profound interest in what she saw as the revelations of character inherent in the reactions of the individual students to the testing process, and when her study appeared in the *Psychological Review*, it was significantly subtitled "A Study of Character in Relation to Attention." She had begun to see character revealed in every word and gesture, to see these symptoms grouping themselves into patterns indicative of basic personality types. When she came to the writing of *The Making of Americans*, which began as the history of her own family, she naturally found herself returning to this conception of human beings as types. Gertrude Stein then fantastically elaborated upon the purpose of the work until it came to be the history of "everyone who ever was or is or would be living."

Her motive, we repeat, was still idealistic and humane:

> I was sure that in a kind of a way the enigma of the universe could in this way be solved. That after all description is explanation, and if I went on and on and on enough I could describe every individual human being that could possibly exist.

Although this procedure promises little for the solution of the "enigma of the universe," it nevertheless suggests a great deal about the enigma of Gertrude Stein. Her first premise, that "description is explanation," gives prime evidence of the fixation of her mind at the shallow level of laboratory science. Miss Stein never really learned that describing human beings never explains them. The painters knew that the human being "essentially is not paintable," and she knew they knew it, but she did not know it herself. Her second premise, that it is possible by artful grouping to "describe every individual human being that could possibly exist," strikes one as equally invalid, testifying to the same disease indicated by her first error. Likeness among human beings is revealing to science, but the uniqueness of every human atom is the more profound truth and the thing that art most needs to concern itself with. The word "individual" is an anomaly as Gertrude Stein uses it. The individual is to her a classifiable phenomenon, hence not an individual at all. It is largely her mechanistic view of man that makes the "people" who inhabit her books after *Three Lives* seem so dun and protoplasmic.

At any rate, though her aim seems to be limited here by an extreme error in logic, it is interesting in that it marks almost the only point in her work where something like a moral purpose is visible. Her method, on the other hand, is pure, if eccentric, science. The heart of her theory lay in the shaky and curiously shallow doctrine of "resemblances." She observed her associates closely and watched for "resemblances" in their minutest gestures, in their "expressions or turn of the face." Then she traced likenesses and differences in presumably deeper aspects of character until she arrived at the classification of the "individual."

The child Stephen Dedalus at Clongowes Wood College noticed with astonishment that "every single fellow had a different way of walking," but the mature Joyce did not consider this observation sufficiently meaningful evidence for the determination of character. It is unfair to say that Gertrude Stein found "expressions or turn of the face" sufficient data, but in truth, her penetration of character does not go impressively deep. For example, witness her ultimate categories of personality in *The Making of Americans:*

> There are then always the two kinds in all who are or were or ever will have in them human being, there are then always to my thinking in all of them the two kinds of them the dependent independent, the independent dependent; the first have resisting as the fighting power in them, the second have attacking as their natural way of fighting.

Although this idea is vaguely promising, given elaboration and dramatization of the "kinds" through fully developed, interacting individuals, Miss Stein never really supplies the materials we need if the theory is to have life and meaning. But it does represent the ultimate in her realization of character in terms of personality types.

Scientifically enough, Gertrude Stein actually made enormous charts to record her researches into the "kinds" of human beings. In the process, people became for her the same kind of dun protoplasm they become for the reader when she transfers the results to the printed page:

> I got to the place where I didn't know whether I knew people or not. I made so many charts that when I used to go down the streets of Paris I wondered whether they were people I knew or ones I didn't.

But she still refused to be instructed by impossibility, and she wrote her book.

In *The Making of Americans*, Miss Stein was really pursuing what she called the "bottom being" of individuals, a phase of personality interestingly close to that "essence" of people and objects that became her constant and increasingly esoteric preoccupation. Her method, which at first glance seems intuitive and inspirational, is in fact nothing of the kind. It is the geared, oiled functioning of the artist who has made himself as nearly as possible a scientifically accurate recording mechanism. Edmund Wilson's metaphor describing Gertrude Stein as a kind of "august human seismograph" is by no means inapt. Miss Stein's apparatus includes a picture-taking eye, a sound-recording ear, and an occult attachment that "listens" seismically to the subtle vibrations of personality—all of it joining in the "listening to repeating" that constitutes the scientific apprehension of the "bottom being" of personality.

It is fascinating to watch the machine at work if one takes it in small, selective doses. One can feel the engine roar or falter or idle, according to the degrees of its current attainment, as it chugs along at the job of sorting and filing the punched and tabbed cards of categorized human beings:

> Alfred Hersland then . . . was of the resisting kind of them in men and women and now then I will wait again and soon then I will be full up with him, I am now then not completely full up with him. Now I am again beginning waiting to be full up completely full up with him. I am very considerably full up now with the kind of being in him, I will be waiting and then I will be full up with all the being in him, that is certain, and so then now a little again once more then I am waiting waiting to be filled up full completely with him with all the being ever in him.

Here we are fully in the presence of that process that strips the flesh from bones and rains the blood from veins of the human beings who are currently Gertrude Stein's object. Her people, like Prufrock, end up "formulated, sprawling on a pin." In the process of Miss Stein's coming to know them "scientifically," they are robbed of life for the reader. The people of *The Making of Americans* are not alive as are those of *Three Lives*. They begin now to be the "sheer phenomena" they later become completely—objectively and also subjectively unrecognizable, quantitatively weighed and calipered.

Note again in the above quotation the tendency to focus attention on the mind of the writer. The stream of consciousness is the writer's stream; the human character is grist for his mill.

Gertrude Stein assures us that she worked "passionately and desperately" on The Making of Americans, and there is no reason to doubt her. How pathetic that so much life went into the book and that so little comes out! The book that in its ideal and in its magnificent first pages promises so much becomes, in the process of scientific realization, phenomenally toneless and dull. Since the scientist can omit nothing, must record every instance of every "characteristic" gesture of "being," since he must record in chartable symbols, he passes on to us a record that is readable as any chart is readable, but that record is unreadable as art—hopeless, soporific, anesthetic. The Making of Americans, one of the longest books ever written, must also be one of the dullest: flat, featureless, incredibly repetitious, deadly.

In classifying Gertrude Stein's writings, apart from Three Lives, which must always be set aside as her best and least characteristic work, we can group them roughly into three divisions. It may be argued that in so doing we are committing Miss Stein's own sin of "classification," but we can advance in defense the need for compression, plus the fact that in the books there is very little warm life to be injured. In the first group we have the books that are largely autobiographical: The Autobiography of Alice B. Toklas, Everybody's Autobiography, Wars I Have Seen, and Paris, France. In the second group, the mass of her specifically "creative" works: The Making of Americans, Tender Buttons, Lucy Church Amiably, Matisse Picasso and Gertrude Stein, How to Write, The Geographical History of America or the Relation of Human Nature to the Human Mind, Ida, Four in America, Brewsie and Willie, Blood on the Dining Room Floor, the "forgotten" book, Things as They Are, and the various omnnibus volumes, Geography and Plays, Useful Knowledge, Operas and Plays, Portraits and Prayers, Last Operas and Plays, and the seven posthumous volumes. In the last group, Miss Stein's aesthetic and critical writings: Lectures in America, Narration, Picasso, and What Are Masterpieces.

The books I have called autobiographical are perhaps the best final index to Gertrude Stein's mind. They are, in the first place, in large degree parasitical and exploitative; while these traits are by no means the whole of her mind, they are a significant part of it. Of course, any autobiographical work is exploitative of its author's environment, but few environments have been mined more exhaustively than Miss Stein's. It seems, finally, that she capitalized on her name and on public interest in her circle of acquaintances to a point considerably beyond literature and almost beyond decency. One would at once suspect that Gertrude Stein is losing some of that integrity and obliviousness to "audience," courted so passionately in her ragged days, were it not for the fact that she palpably believes these books are good art and not mere exploitation.

The autobiographical books are singularly uneven. The one conviction they insist on, the thing the reader must accept if he is to find them of real value, is the pre-eminent genius of their author, the magic potency of her unique sensibility. Deny this and little remains. By and large they are chitchat—engrossing as the gossip of an alert and powerful personality who had made contact with many of the most creative people of her time. "Contact" is a distressingly accurate word here, and, if Miss Stein's own texts are to be taken as our evidence, it seems that she rarely penetrated these people and their ideas to a deeper than chitchat level. It is possible, of course, to mistake eccentricity for profundity, and it seems to me that this general error has added considerably to Gertrude Stein's reputation. In addition to being extremely interesting, her gossip is character revealing in a rather disastrous way, for it often proves to be grossly inaccurate, as Leo Stein and the authors of the "Testimony Against Gertrude Stein" have shown. The inaccuracies point to very fundamental and damaging aspects of Miss Stein's composition: her vast ego, for example, and the pathological cast of mind that allowed her memory to function in a Freudian way in order to "recall" events in those lights that always reflect glory on Gertrude Stein. Too often her accounts reveal a startling inability to comprehend the social milieu in which her own life developed.

When Miss Stein's autobiographical works attempt to probe deeply, they usually become even less satisfying. Prone to generalize widely and wildly, often without evidence or with mere eccentric shreds of fact, she almost never substantiates a theory with convincing supporting detail. Repeatedly we are asked to accept the bare ex cathedra statement and then find our own evidence in the magic of the pontifical name. Like most of her commentators, Gertrude Stein constantly begs the question.

One could cull scores of these exasperating pronouncements from her works, but her statement to a young American painter gives us a fair sample: "The minute painting gets abstract it gets pornographic." This meaningless generality she supports with the bull, "That is a fact." Then she drops it and runs. But the ramifications of such a contention are enormous, and, if she is to pretend to philosophy rather than dogma, she must explore them. A responsible thinker might have put it something like this: A painter must work with line, mass, color, light, and shade; if his work is abstract in the formal sense, it is probably true that he moves inevitably toward geometricity, working with forms—straight lines, angles, cones, cylinders, circles, ellipses—that may relate themselves subconsciously in the mind of the observer to male and female sexual equipment. If his work is abstract in its content, then he may deal primarily with the material of the subconscious, with its heavily sexual pigmentation. So far, Miss Stein's doctrine would seem to make rather good sense, although we have no way of knowing whether she arrived at it on these or better grounds.

Great questions remain. Whence comes the "pornography"? Is the prurience in the mind of the artist or in that of the observer? Mere presentation of sexuality does not constitute pornography—as Judge Woolsey fortunately ruled. If one thinks in Gertrude Stein's vein, can such a charge be leveled only at abstract art? To go to the opposite pole, how much of classical art is sex sublimated into the ideal stasis of beauty frozen or sex sublimated into the ideal kinesis of strength activated in warfare or the chase? If we are thoroughly serious, we must finally ask what proportion of the fundamental mythos of all art is sex urge. Finally, if this proportion is both large and inescapable, is it therefore pornographic? And so on. There is an unpleasant nasty-mindedness pervading this kind of thinking, an inexcusable irresponsibility in this kind of writing.

Gertrude Stein always works on the theory that being a genius relieves one of the burden of logical coherence. One need not know the mental processes of a genius; one need only accept the verbalism that results. When, however, she bares the process itself, as she occasionally does, the pattern often strikes one as startling indeed. The following lines from *Everybody's Autobiography* exemplify some of her more spectacular logic:

> . . . the most actively war-like nation the Germans always could convince the pacifists to become pro-German. That is because pacifists were such intelligent beings that they could follow what any one is saying.
>   If you can follow what any one is saying then if you are a pacifist you are a pro-German. That follows if any one understands what any one is saying. Therefore understanding is a very dull occupation.

The autobiographical works share the common faults of Gertrude Stein's writing—the formlessness, the unselectiveness, the ramblings, the repetitions, the tendency to review and record all experience as unweighted "sheer phenomenon," the insistence on the value of the genius sensibility—but these matters are less painful here. They are relieved by the great liveliness of the life she lived and recorded with comparative objectivity, by much that is genuinely funny, and by the fact that she writes with a reader in mind in her noncreative—hence comprehensible—language. To adapt Miss Stein's own terms, she is serving mammon, not god, in these books; we can be grateful for her sin and follow her with understanding, if not with great profit or complete belief.

Still, if the autobiographical books record Gertrude Stein's mind at its normally functioning level, the record is one of fascinating eccentricity rather than of profundity. Hers is a mind that ranged widely and alertly, but not deeply. Here, though in less offensive degree than in her so-called creative books, the recording technique is still basically mechanical, photographic, scientific—not artistic. She records with the camera's attention to surface and with the scientist's concern for inclusiveness. The writing lacks the artist's selectiveness, his attention to drama and meaningful detail, his sense of reality rearranged into organic form. The philosophical component, though often suggestive, never develops fully; it is embryonic and thin. Stylistically, these books, too, are predominantly flat. In them we find more modeling, a higher relief, but viewed topographically, they present an absence of light and shade that is arbitrary, illogical, and symptomatic of something that once more seems very near pathology in Miss Stein's mind. The stream of reality is laid on the page exactly as it impresses the camera artist, largely unshaded and unweighed.

Gertrude Stein pursued the laboratory technician's omnivorousness and refusal to discriminate to the point where it became solidified as thinking and as technique. It may be termed pathological, and certainly it is inartistic. When experience becomes mere phenomenon, it no longer presents material for art. It is finally just to say that Gertrude Stein's true position is antiliterary, anti-intellectual, and often antihumane and antimoral. Her whole orientation is ruthlessly egocentric. Although she has defined her own ego as creative of art, she has not spoken the truth. In the market place of art, where all of us who read must work, her definition has no meaning. . . .

When we turn from the autobiographical works to the specifically creative ones, those in which she is "serving god," we find ourselves in an even more barren country, the true desert. Here we are made to feel the full consequences for art of her aesthetic theories: the doctrines of spontaneous creation; the "search for immediacy" and the "whole present"; the faith in the eye rather than in the intellect, in the eye rather than in the imagination; and the progressive constricting of subject matter and technique to rule out beauty, emotion, morality, association, the subconscious, the past, all the life context surrounding the object seen—to rule out form, narrative, drama, movement, meaning; to demolish, in a word, everything not presently visible to the conglomerate eye of the camera-artist-scientist-genius and to include literally everything visible after this manner. What we get, clearly, is a drastic, almost total delimitation of the province of art; we are compensated by a multiplication of uninterpreted minutiae in the field of vision that is the artist's point of observation. This vastly elaborated triviality must then be cast in the form it stumbles into, in the unique language proper to the uniqueness of the insight.

This quick overview of the general aesthetic position of Gertrude Stein has the merit of letting us see quickly her cardinal sins: first, her attempt to revitalize the art of writing reduced itself to a destruction of all the accumulated resources of the art; second, her substitute was really no more than the narrow resources of the idiosyncratic self. The most appalling single fact about her "art" is that everything in it returns to the tinseled fiction of the pre-eminent value of the genius sensibility. The whole direction of Gertrude Stein's writing is the narrowing from public to private art, from multiplication to subtraction, from much to little.

The real content, the root matter of communication in Gertrude Stein's creative writing, may be said in general to be pathetically thin. For a writer of her supposed stature, it is quite unbelievably thin. I except, as always, *Three Lives*, written before she became Gertrude Stein. A thin but still perceptible content persists in *Ida*, *The Making of Americans*, *Things as They Are*, and *Brewsie and Willie*, but this list leaves a score of volumes, the great bulk of her creative work, that have, one feels, very nearly nothing to say. When we are confronted with this fact, it is very difficult for us to understand the quantity of admiration that has been tendered Miss Stein. The truth is, one suspects, that the great mass of those who profess to admire the writings of Gertrude Stein, as apart from the personality of their creator, are unconsciously testifying not to the excellence of these writings, but to an abstract ideal, to their commitment to the civil liberty of the artist, to the premise that the artist has the right to be as eccentric as he pleases. They do not really understand what she is saying, but they wish to make very sure she is not denied the right to say it.

Few critics today would deny this right. But the reader has civil liberties, too. He has the right to deny the title of art to work that remains, after long and sympathetic immersion, unknowable and unpleasurable. There is degree in all things, including idiosyncrasy. Art moves ahead by idiosyncrasy. The strangeness of a Shakespeare, a Donne, a Coleridge, a Rabelais, a Swift, a Melville, a Proust, a Joyce—this strangeness enriches and advances literature. The strangeness of a Gertrude Stein debilitates and paralyzes. When art turns in on its creator, it may still be creation, but it is not art.

If one accepts every premise of Gertrude Stein, beginning with the great parent premise of her genius, "in english literature in her time the only one," and acquiescing all the way down through the corollaries of her complex aesthetics, there still remains the bar of language. This barrier remains final and fatal because it is the medium she has chosen, the only one through which we can apprehend her. Like her subject matter and her form, but to an even greater degree, her language is private. Gertrude Stein chose words by two main criteria: they had to have for her "existing being"—they had to be privately alive and exciting—and they did not need to be words that in general possessed objective application to the subject at hand in order to be the words that "described that thing." All of this means, practically, for the reader a vocabulary of impenetrable, esoteric abstractions. Miss Stein clearly hopes to inaugurate an art uniquely possessed of accuracy and sensitivity, evoked by words stripped of their received meanings and laid bare and new on the page—a language as new as Homer's.

It is almost incredible that a woman of Gertrude Stein's intelligence could fail to see the fallacy inherent in this position. Yet she does fail to see it, and it is this colossal blind spot that ultimately condemns her to a stillborn art. Just as her "insistence" is to us inevitably repetition, so this abstraction that she looks upon as a bright new concretion seems to us a concretion foreign to hers, based on the received meanings of the words rather than on the meanings she arbitrarily and privately assigns them. The matter is as simple as this: the words do not mean the same things to us that they mean to her; she is writing in one language, we are reading in another.

Gertrude Stein could never bring herself to see that words are the least amenable to abstraction of all the artistic media. To a far greater degree than the musician's medium, sound, or the painter's medium, color, line, and volume, words are unseverably connected in our minds with things. When we see or hear the word, we see an image of the thing, and there is not much Miss Stein can do to make us see something else. That is why, when we read a characteristic Stein page and find that it relates itself to nothing we know, we find it easy to assume the truth of the superstition that she is aiming at abstract painterly or musical effects. Because she was inept at painting and music and because she was convinced that it was her mission to create a great abstract art—concretion by divinely inspired abstraction—she was driven to attempt an impossible degree of abstraction in the only medium left to her. She died believing she had succeeded.

The pathos and paradox of all this, as I see it, lies in the fact that the whole preoccupation with an abstract language is really unnecessary. Our language is not the abject, inadequate vessel Gertrude Stein found it to be. The real innovators—Joyce, Proust, Kafka, Hopkins, Virginia

Woolf—all are constantly making the language perform new acrobatics of color, nuance, and intelligibility by sensitively exploiting with new virtuosity its ancient resources. Very fundamental questions about the quality of Miss Stein's mind therefore arise. We can dismiss her distortion of language, as Leo Stein does, as compensation for a root inadequacy with language at its everyday level, but this solution seems oversimple. There is a more complex pathology inhabiting a mind that could pursue so long and so blindly a course so pointless and so perverse.

But even if we surrender entirely, if we go not only the second mile with Gertrude Stein, but the third as well, if we grant the possibility of struggling through her words to a vague approximation of her meaning, or, failing that, of closing upon some other poor literary remnant such as "mood" or "tone," there nevertheless remains the utterly insuperable barrier of her repetition. Gertrude Stein is a ruminant animal, not with the four stomachs of the cow, but with four hundred. Committed to the doctrine that the artist must record his ongoing present knowledge of his subject, she lays each moment's perception on the page, endlessly repeating or minutely varying that of the previous moment. To say that this becomes tiresome is the grossest understatement; it is deadly, it is not art, and it is not fit fare for a sane reader.

When Gertrude Stein's votaries are forced to face the rudimentary critical question of exactly what and how much of her intent is passed on to a reader, they are generally not very enlightening in their comments. They are likely to answer with large generalities that contain what the Maine parish clerk called a flux of words and a constipation of ideas, or, if they are trapped into being specific, the consequences are sometimes amusing. Julian Sawyer, for example, in his confident exegesis of the famous "rose" line, saw a yellow rose. It must have been embarrassing to have his yellow rose become, in Miss Stein's own explanation of the line, "red for the first time in English poetry for a hundred years." The initiated Mr. Sawyer is no better off than the carping critic who sees only the same old limp pink rambler he always sees when he hears the word "rose." W. H. Gardner read Miss Stein's "Susie Asado" as a portrait of "an amiable, slipshod, canary-bright spinster," but Carl Van Vechten, who should know, says that the piece is a portrait of a Spanish flamenco dancer. How mistaken can one be?

What usually happens, it would appear, is that Gertrude Stein's readers find something emerging to them and seize it thankfully and assume in self-defense that it is the thing she meant them to receive; otherwise, all is chaos. But the uncomely truth is that all, or very nearly all, *is* chaos.

Very little that is real or tangible passes from Gertrude Stein to the reader. Actual meeting of minds or sensibilities rarely takes place. The single weighable, measurable function of her most characteristic works is their service as a simple irritant. They say, in effect, "Think about this thing I have named"—little more. Generally, if value accrues, it develops in the reader's variation on the theme, not in Miss Stein's.

If Gertrude Stein would only admit the poverty of her content and admit that its essential quality is vague suggestion, she would be a great deal more respectable. But she would confess neither. Because the content of her writing was the content of the genius vision, it was to be considered always dense and ponderable. She stubbornly insisted that her object was always concretely present on the page; if communication was imperfect, that was the fault of the reader. So she grumbles, "Mostly those to whom I am explaining are not completely hearing," and, more heatedly, "But what's the difficulty? Just read the words on the paper. They're in English. Just read them. Be simple and you'll understand these things."

The amazing thing is that this is perfectly honest mystification and outrage. Gertrude Stein seems never to have understood certain elementary facts: that it is impossible to be "simple" with English words because they are loaded with meaning; that she is speaking one language, we another; that it is never possible for one mind to know another really well, impossible for one to know another at all without help. Therefore, it is accurate to say that throughout her creative life, Gertrude Stein practiced a kind of cultivated schizophrenia. By an act that may have been will, or stupidity, or some curious pathological quirk, she convinced herself first of the inevitable rightness of her position and then of the inevitable communicability of her vision through the chosen language. Willfully, or stupidly, or pathologically, she blinded herself to the crusted connotativeness of language and to the insularity of sensibilities foreign to her own. She sealed these unpalatable truths in a compartment of her brain that she never again entered. She takes an idea that could be made clear and cold in expository prose, or clear and warm in narrative-dramatic prose, or warm and vaguely— perhaps more meaningfully—clear in intelligible abstraction, and makes it cold and unclear—dead—in unintelligible abstraction. So I see the matter.

I am inclined to contend, then, that Gertrude Stein's creative writings are undernourished in intrinsic matter, that even this poverty fails of communication by being cast in a foreign language, and that her works are therefore practically worthless as art.

Since we have already discounted Miss Stein's autobiographical works as largely unselective chitchat, taking their principal value from their revelation of eccentricity, we are left with only her critical-aesthetic writings. The best of Gertrude Stein appears in these lectures. In them she tries her best to be serious and philosophical and plainly intelligible, and, with some reservations, she succeeds. She is wholly serious and genuinely, but not always deeply or originally, philosophical. The degree of her intelligibility depends on the reader's patience and the quantity of his previous exposure to Miss Stein's thinking and linguistic habits; with some experience and much patience, the reader can know her in all her lectures.

I have already discussed the content of the lectures [elsewhere], and there is no need to go through it all again. Here we need only make the point that in them Gertrude Stein shows a mind that is not great, but it is good enough to point up by contrast the pathos of her failure as an artist. The texts of the lectures often dramatize this failure in a very interesting and conclusive way: the occurrence there of the phenomenon in which Miss Stein, after making an eloquent and intricate presentation of one of her theories, pauses to read from her creative works to demonstrate the art that follows from the theory just expounded. The result, generally, is not enlightenment but blank mystification. The thing that had seemed interesting and worth while as theory has become perfectly opaque as art.

The best of her lectures are "Composition as Explanation," "What Are Masterpieces," "How Writing Is Written," "Plays," and "Poetry and Grammar." Her "Narration" lectures at the University of Chicago deal heavily in trivia and contain much that is repetition of earlier material. Of the four lectures in addition to "Plays" and "Poetry and Grammar" that are collected in Lectures in America, "What Is English Literature" and "Pictures" are almost completely unrewarding, casting serious doubt, as I have said, on the depth of Miss Stein's critical perceptions in the arts generally. "The Gradual Making of The Making of Americans" and "Portraits and Repetition," unevenly interesting, have value largely as exposition of Miss Stein's private literary practices.

These lectures, in contrast to the creative writings, hold more gold than dross, but we need not pretend to agree that the gold in them entitles Gertrude Stein to the title of genius she claims and in which she is supported by her admirers. But certainly enough may be found to defend her from the charge of being a fool and a charlatan, charges that have been leveled by her vilifiers. There is no point in vilifying Gertrude Stein. She is the victim of her pathology rather than her villainy. Her powers as an aesthetic theorist seem considerably better than mediocre, considerably less than first rate. Whatever its idiosyncrasy, her system is perfectly coherent. Against much that strikes one as mistaken or merely trivial must be set much that is interesting as theory and potentially fruitful for others, if not for herself. In her aesthetics Miss Stein is no more derivative than in her artistic practice, and one can almost always trace the maturing of an idea through her own thinking rather than through another's. Whatever Gertrude Stein is, she is self-made.

The two most interesting attitudes that emerge from the lectures are her passionate concern for the integrity of the artist and her doctrine of the necessary "presentness" of the ideal creative state. Nothing shows more painfully the drastic disparity between Gertrude Stein's aesthetics and her art than an examination of the product of these doctrines in her practice. When she moves to translate them into art, her schizophrenia goes to work and she blinds herself to proportion, to the necessity of compromising the ideal and the real. To maintain integrity, Miss Stein felt that she had to make herself not merely honest but unique; being unique, she is unknowable, and her creation is stillborn. To maintain the "presentness" of the creative vision, she threw away the archives, closed her mind and her conscience, fixed her lens in a static position, photographed reality as a still-life succession, and then ran the film through a warped projector onto the standard screen of the printed page. The result is a flawed art by subtraction and abstraction.

Gertrude Stein is not alone, of course, in being concerned with the illumination of the present moment of consciousness. This might with justice be called the characteristic preoccupation of prose writers in our time. The greatest of her contemporaries devoted major portions of their careers to its solution. Compared with them, she is pathetic—no other word suffices. To her pathetic narrowing must be compared their burgeoning inclusiveness; to her fortuitous form, their organic form; to her art-for-art insulation from life, their hot immersions in it; to her drab, cacophonous emptiness, their proliferation of the possibilities for beauty, meaning, and passion in the language. Gertrude Stein is right, as the others are right, in believing that it is important that art illuminate the "complete actual present," but in her method she is terrifically, fatally wrongheaded. Joyce once suggested that readers should devote their lives to his works, and his suggestion is less than absurd. But the feeling that remains after reading Gertrude Stein is not one of illumination and profit, but one of darkness and waste.

After writing *The Making of Americans*, Gertrude Stein should have made the great confession and begun anew. Instead, she burrowed blindly, molewise, deeper into a cul-de-sac. Now, reading her books, one lists the good things of literature and crosses them off one by one: her works possess no beauty, no instruction, no passion. All that is finally there is Gertrude Stein mumbling to herself. Everything in her writing returns upon the self for value. All that is left of literature is its function as delight to its creator—which perhaps justifies its writing, but not its being put in print.

Gertrude Stein, it seems to me, is already effectively dead as a writer. Nobody really reads her, but everybody continues to talk knowingly and concernedly about her. Her "importance" is a myth. She is enormously interesting as a phenomenon of the power of personality and as a symptom of a frantic, fumbling, nightmare age—our present—and it is as such that she will live. Later ages will gather about the corpus of her work like a cluster of horrified medical students around a biological sport.

RICHARD BRIDGMAN

"Things As They Are" and "Three Lives"

In spite of her awareness of Mark Twain as a writer and in spite of her being frequently placed in his camp by critics, it was in Henry James that Gertrude Stein found her original stylistic impetus. In her lecture, "What Is English Literature," she made a significant comment about what she saw in James. "The thing to notice," she said, was that "his whole paragraph was detached what it said from what it did, what it was from what it held, and over it all something floated not floated away but just floated, floated up there." All of Gertrude Stein's experiments with language are no more than explorations of what floated up there and how it was sustained.

When Adele, the character in *Things As They Are* with the closest resemblance to Gertrude Stein herself, was asked, "Haven't you ever stopped thinking long enough to feel," her answer was

> Why I suppose if one can't think at the same time I will never accomplish the feat of feeling. I always think. I don't see how one can stop it.

This perceptive self-analysis goes a long way to explain Gertrude Stein's stylistic course. Her active interest in the mind and its workings had begun at least as early as 1894 when with a fellow student, Leon Solomons, she had carried on a series of experiments with automatic writing in the Harvard laboratory of Hugo Munsterberg. In September 1896 they published an article describing their results, "Normal Motor Automatism," in the *Psy-*

From *The Colloquial Style in America.* Copyright © 1966 by Richard Bridgman. Oxford University Press.

chological Review. Gertrude Stein retained this experimental and objective point of view throughout most of her writing career. Even when she was recounting what were apparently severe personal emotional traumas in both *Things As They Are* and "Melanctha," the emotion was filtered and stylized in its passage through her mind. It is ironic that a writer often accused of permitting the pen to follow free associations should be one who placed so much importance on intellectual control.

To return to the exchange from *Things As They Are* quoted above: As important as the admission that Adele can not stop thinking was the way in which the thought was expressed. The question mark has vanished because it was superfluous. (As Gertrude Stein commented years later, "A question is a question, anybody can know that a question is a question and so why add to it the question mark when it is already there when the question is already there in the writing.") The anticipated comma following "why" has disappeared too, as has the possible one separating the two clauses between "time" and "I." Dropping punctuation is the opposite of James's normal practice, but curiously this technique, which Gertrude Stein later pushed toward its limit, produces much the same result as does excessive punctuation. Both methods isolate thoughts in a series of units, although by different means.

Here usage is made to conform to the evidence supplied by a sensitive ear coupled with the demands of a logical mind. If there is no good semantic reason for a question mark, neither is there one for separating "why" from "I suppose." That phrase can be delivered in two ways: either with a deliberate, thoughtful pause after "why," in which case the comma is obligatory; or by running the words together, with "why" becoming no more than a mannerism, an automatic verbal addition used for the sake of delay. With the sanction of psychological accuracy behind it, Gertrude Stein could then (only occasionally and cautiously here) deny the reader's expectations, give him a slight shake by changing the direction of her prose. By gradually increasing the incidence of novelty, she worked out her unique and often opaque style.

Gertrude Stein was quite willing to locate herself in the Jamesian fold. She once referred to her Radcliffe period saying, "It is rather strange that she was not then at all interested in the work of Henry James for whom she now has a very great admiration and whom she considers quite definitely as her forerunner, he being the only nineteenth-century writer who being an American felt the method of the twentieth century." She went on, "Oddly enough in all of her formative period she did not read him and was not interested in him. But as she often says one is always naturally antagonistic to one's parent and sympathetic to one's grand-parents." In support of this Robert McAlmon reported in 1925 that Gertrude Stein had said to him, "Nobody has done anything to develop the English language since Shakespeare, except myself, and Henry James perhaps a little."

The phrase "perhaps a little" can be glossed usefully by an examination of Gertrude Stein's first work, *Things As They Are*. Only eighty-eight pages long, the book describes a triangular relationship among three women. Each one is intended to represent a "civilization" and an ethical attitude. The whole is methodically divided into three sections, and it ends with no issue: " 'I am afraid it comes very near being a deadlock,' she groaned dropping her head on her arms." An overt reference is made to *The Wings of the Dove* when Adele says to herself, "I know there is no use in asking for an explanation. Like Kate Croy she would tell me 'I shall sacrifice nothing and nobody'."

John Malcolm Brinnin thought the book "naïvely colored by touches of Henry James," and Donald Sutherland believed that "in its way it is a Jamesian study or demonstration." Both critics deduce the influence of James upon Gertrude Stein from the two writers' shared interest in "the endless resources of the mind when it is moved to make interpretations of events or to register the climates of emotional situations." But the enduring significance of Gertrude Stein's apprenticeship to James lies in her assumption of his stylistic mannerisms. It was her elaboration of them that showed Ernest Hemingway how similarities in the styles of Twain and Ring Lardner could be utilized in order to organize colloquial language.

Both the dialogue and the narrative of *Things As They Are* make use of the rhetorical patterns of repetition that we have seen in James. The mannerism happened to be especially useful for the "mathematical proof" Gertrude Stein proposed to make. As soon as the trio of women are introduced, conscious rhetoric and unconscious alliteration emerge in the prose.

> All three of them were college bred American women of the wealthier class but with that all resemblance between them ended. Their appearance, their attitudes and their talk both as to manner and to matter showed the influence of different localities, different forebears and different family ideals. They were distinctly American but each one at the same time bore definitely the stamp of one of the older civilizations, incomplete and frustrated in this American version but still always insistent.

The women share a single aspect (they are of the wealthy educated class) but they are differentiated in three ways (appearance, attitudes, and talk).

These three ways are in turn divided into two more (manner and matter). This division is determined, Gertrude Stein says, by three more distinctions (locale, ancestors, and family ideals). The urge here is clearly toward charting, toward the establishment of fixed relationships, in short, toward extreme formalization.

Adele sets up a similarly rigorous rhetorical pattern in a letter whose essential structure is this:

```
My dear Sophie . . .
        Either . . .              or . . .
        If the first . . .        then . . .
        If the second . . .       then . . .
        If you don't . . .        then . . .
        If you do . . .           then . . .
```

Such structural repetition provides an appropriate support for the carefully objectified account Gertrude Stein had undertaken. However, when phrasal repetition occurs in the dialogue, then an important link is being established between James and Hemingway. These examples suggest the continuity.

> "Dear WE ARE NEITHER OF US SORRY that we know enough to find it out, are we?" "No," Helen answered "WE ARE NEITHER OF US SORRY."
>
> (capitals added)

> "I CERTAINLY NEVER EXPECTED TO FIND YOU one of the most gentle and considerate of human kind," she commented quietly and then Helen made it clearer. "I CERTAINLY DID NOT EXPECT THAT YOU WOULD FIND ME SO," she answered.
>
> (capitals added)

> "SHE IS QUEER AND WILL INTEREST YOU and YOU ARE QUEER AND WILL INTEREST HER. Oh! I don't want to listen to your protests, YOU ARE QUEER AND INTERESTING even if you don't know it and YOU LIKE QUEER AND INTERESTING PEOPLE even if you think you don't and you are not a bit bashful in spite of your convictions to the contrary, so come along."
>
> (capitals added)

Gertrude Stein also employed repetition as thematic reinforcement. For example, accused of selfishness and a lack of restraint, of indulgent egocentricity, Adele launches into a defense of herself that, in the reiteration of "I," reveals the accuracy of the criticism.

> "(I) do not admit," she said, "that (I) was wrong in wanting to know. (I) suppose one might in a spirit of Quixotic generosity deny oneself such a right but as a reasonable being, (I) feel that (I) had a right to know. (I) realize perfectly that it was hopelessly wrong to learn it from Sophie

instead of from you. (I) admit (I) was a coward, (I) was simply afraid to ask you." Helen laughed harshly. "You need not have been," she said. "I would have told you nothing." "(I) think you are wrong, (I) am quite sure that you would have told me and (I) wanted to spare myself that pain, perhaps spare you it too, (I) don't know. (I) repeat (I) cannot believe that (I) was wrong in wanting to know."

(parentheses added)

Sometimes the repetition of a word is joined with associative rhyme, as in " 'I honor you for being honest.' 'Oh honest,' returned Adele lightly. 'Honesty is a selfish virtue. Yes I am honest enough'." Sometimes sounds are unconsciously counter-posed one against the other. "Her ACCUSTOMED DEFinite resignation and the tremendous DIFficulty of ACCOMPLISHMENT" (capitals added). And sometimes a word unexpectedly crosses the boundary between narrative and dialogue in order to be repeated. "SUDDENLY she stopped and dropped heavily on a bench. " 'Why' she said in a tone of intense interest, 'it's like a bit of mathematics. SUDDENLY it does itself and you begin to see,' and then she laughed" (capitals added). I can hardly explain the source of these examples, but they need pointing out, for they are not normally found in nineteenth-century prose. Although I doubt that they are consciously composed, they do seem to be deliberately retained. I then take them to be an important part of the colloquial tradition which retains evidences of extemporaneity that had been formerly eliminated in revision as blemishes.

On several occasions in *Things As They Are* Gertrude Stein openly indicates her understanding of how the mind operates. Thought gathers to a verbalization.

ADELE CONTINUED A LONG TIME TO LOOK OUT ON THE WATER. "I wonder" SHE SAID TO HERSELF AGAIN. FINALLY IT CAME MORE DEFINITELY. "Yes I wonder. There isn't much use in wondering about Helen. I know no more now than I did last night and I am not likely to be much wiser. . . ." AND SHE RELAPSED ONCE MORE INTO SILENCE. HER MEDITATIONS AGAIN TOOK FORM. "As for me is it another little indulgence of my superficial emotions or is there any possibility of my really learning to realise stronger feelings. If it's the first I will call a halt promptly and at once. If it's the second I won't back out, no not for any amount of moral sense," and she smiled to herself.

(capitals added)

On another occasion the same idea is even more clearly expressed. " 'Was I brutal this afternoon?' SHE THOUGHT IT IN DEFINITE WORDS 'and does she really care?' " (capitals added).

If one thinks in words, then one hypothesis will hold that the original, the primal statement represents pure truth. This belief was to influence Gertrude Stein's stylistic progress. Evidence of the mind operating by associations of sound already can be found in the narrative prose of her first novel. Even as Henry James fell into fits of alliteration—the more so when he began to dictate his work as an expression of confidence in controlled spontaneity—so Gertrude Stein this early displays similar signs of associational workings in the mind. Such moments are still infrequent and obscured by the narrative movement, but the seeds are planted. As here:

> The two were left settled down again quietly but somehow the silence now subtly suggested the significance of their being alone together.

> There would be no need of recognizing their existence, but these two people who would be equally familiar if they were equally little known would as the acquaintance progressed, undoubtedly expose large tracts of unexplored and unknown quantities, filled with new and strange excitements.

Finally there are phrases determined as "the feat of feeling" was; they present an equally odd sound and appearance, as "and so she lay there quite quiet, quite dulled."

II

Gertrude Stein made one more attempt to deal with love. This time she further increased the distance between herself and her material. In "Melanctha," the second of her *Three Lives*, she outlined the history of a heterosexual love affair. Using personal experience acquired when she was a medical student at Johns Hopkins, she transferred the action from the white upper-middle class to the Baltimore negro. She also reduced the affair from a triangle to a psychological tug-of-war between Jeff Campbell and Melanctha Herbert. Essentially, however, much of the emotional climate and motivation of "Melanctha" are identical with those of the earlier story. The Adele of *Things As They Are*, whose resemblance to Gertrude Stein herself has been noted by B. Reid, becomes Jeff Campbell, while Helen is changed into Melanctha. Other figures are added to or erased from the cast, but the main contest between the two intelligent members of the triangle in *Things As They Are*, between the mind-heart and the mind-conscience, is retained.

Just how and when Gertrude Stein decided to transform the material of *Things As They Are* into "Melanctha" is not clear, for we possess differing accounts of the genesis of the later work. At least a superficial connection with Flaubert's *Trois Contes* is obvious. Since Henry James had been a qualified admirer of Flaubert, having called him in his preface to *Madame Bovary* in 1902 "the novelist's novelist," Gertrude Stein's interest in him is understandable. Flaubert stressed those aspects of writing congenial to her, objectivity and accuracy in content, rhythm and harmony in treatment. But whatever his effect upon her writing, the important consideration here is the link between *Three Lives* and *Things As They Are*. Was the shift sudden, abrupt, and absolute, or a gradual, clear extension of learned principles?

The most accomplished of the three histories, "Melanctha" contains an abundance of materials related to *Things As They Are*. Two sentences in particular are useful guides to the stylistic reorganization Gertrude Stein imposed on her old material. Each sentence appears first in *Things As They Are*, and is then amplified in "Melanctha."

> "Tell me how much do you care for me." "Care for you my dear," Helen answered, "more than you know and less than you think."

> I certainly do care for you Jeff Campbell less than you are always thinking and much more than you are ever knowing.

> "You have no right to constantly use your pain as a weapon" Adele flashed out angrily.

> "You ain't got no right Melanctha Herbert," flashed out Jeff through his dark, frowning anger, "you certainly ain't got no right always to be using your being hurt and being sick, and having pain, like a weapon. . . ."

The epigrammatic concision of the original sentences is sacrificed to a programmatic conception of style. The elements emphasized by Gertrude Stein are familiar by now: repetition, punctuation and its lack, and numerous present participles, all of which are intended to produce local emphasis, immediacy, and a noticeable rhythmic effect.

"Melanctha" is a conglomeration of such eccentric and apparently uncontrolled effects. Although a close reading can demonstrate the relevance of many of the author's experiments to the story's thematic development, quite as many instances seem to be no more than inexplicable fussing, distortion for the sake of distortion. A simple example of this is Gertrude Stein's random hyphenation, reminiscent of Mark Twain's fondness for varying his punctuation of compound words. If on page ninety-one of the Modern Library edition Melanctha is said to have "break neck courage," then on page ninety-five it becomes "breakneck," and shifts back again on page ninety-seven to "break neck." Inconsistent as the technique may be it still makes a distinct impression of innovation.

The diction of "Melanctha" is considerably simplified. By using a carefully restricted vocabulary Gertrude Stein was able to point up patterns of language, rhythms, and verbal combinations. Her ironic juxtaposition of words, her shifting meanings, and her dislocation of syntax depended on simplicity of diction in order to be noticed. In the following passage the fact that few words are used emphasizes the distinctions gradually established between being "bitter" and "a little bitter," and between "beauty" and "real beauty."

> Now Jeff had come to where he could understand Melanctha Herbert. Jeff was not bitter to her because she could not really love him, he was bitter only that he had let himself have a real illusion in him. He was a little bitter too, that he had lost now, what he had always felt real in the world, that had made it for him always full of beauty, and now he had not got this new religion really, and he had lost what he before had to know what was good and had real beauty.

"Melanctha" still contains a few instances of word play: the desire of two lonely people to "talk low some," "real religion," "your kind of kindness," "patient doctor." But their frequency is low, as is that of rhyme, alliteration, assonance, and other instances of aural association. Gertrude Stein steadily drew away from puns and portmanteau words; although evidence of the volatility of language as well as accidents of syntax were often left in her early work, neither were of much interest to her. She weeded them out and made her prose answer to that monstrous, often comic, internal logic that was her specialty.

Gertrude Stein generally arranged and punctuated her narrative in three ways. Rarely employing subordinate conjunctions or the semi-colon, she often relied upon a series of short declarative sentences, in the manner of Henry James, begun on a repeated or slightly varied phrase. Or she used commas to do the work of the stronger signals of pause, which gave her prose something of a run-on effect. Or she used polysyndeton, that is, the frequent repetition of the co-ordinating conjunction. No matter which method she used, her narrative moved methodically through a sequence of experiences, or if it sought to render a complex state in time, then each part of that state was laid on separately without any attempt at synthesis. The difference is, roughly, that existing between,

> Although she was smiling, her feet hurt.

and:

> She smiled. Her feet hurt.
> She smiled, her feet hurt.
> She smiled and her feet hurt.

The first example is synthesized, while the other three represent typical Steinian procedures.

Within this restricted set of structural patterns, Gertrude Stein executed endless verbal variations. Some were semantic (as in the distinction between "bitter" and "a little bitter"), some syntactic (as in the placement of the adverb in this example: "She didn't know how well now I know you"), and some rhythmic.

When her narrative was punctuated by commas, Gertrude Stein made it sound very much like an off-key product of Henry James.

> Then it came that Jeff knew he could not say out any more, what it was he wanted, he could not say out any more, what it was, he wanted to know about, what Melanctha wanted.

Such choppy rhythms are sometimes useful, as here in organically rendering Jeff's uncertainty, but they are derivative and annoying. Gertrude Stein soon dropped them, preferring plain, run-on sentences. In *Lectures in America,* composed and delivered in the 'thirties, she called the comma "servile," announcing cheerfully that "a comma by helping you along holding your coat for you and putting on your shoes keeps you from living your life as actively as you should lead it." The accumulation of a series of brief declarative sentences is more characteristic of Gertrude Stein's achieved style. "Jeff Campbell never asked Melanctha any more if she loved him," begins a typical sequence. "Now things were always getting worse between them. Now Jeff was always very silent with Melanctha. Now Jeff never wanted to be honest to her, and now Jeff never had much to say to her."

When on the other hand Gertrude Stein connected her narrative with a series of "ands," she departed from Mark Twain's example in *Huckleberry Finn.* He normally provided colloquial ease and untroubled clarity, but Gertrude Stein stirs the reader with bumps, blocks, and slight detours. Laid out in units the following sentence demonstrates how, on a monosyllabic base of the simple acts (and even of the clichés) of a distraught lover, a harmonic structure is built.

> All that long day,
> with the warm moist young spring stirring in him,
> Jeff Campbell worked,
> and thought,
> and beat his breast,

and wandered,
and spoke aloud,
and was silent,
and was certain,
and then in doubt and then keen to surely feel,
and then all sodden in him;

and he walked
and he sometimes ran fast to lose himself in his rushing,
and he bit his nails to pain and bleeding,
and he tore his hair so that he could be sure he was really feeling,
and he never could know what it was right,
he now should be doing.

Phrases such as "he bit his nails to pain and bleeding" and "wanted to be honest to her" are precisely what Donald Sutherland must have meant when he said that Gertrude Stein works out of "a version of the most popular phrasing." It is this "version" too that helps to explain John Peale Bishop's description of the style of *Three Lives* as "a curious formalization of the common speech."

As a complement to this kind of phrasal organization Gertrude Stein continued to expand her use of repetition. Near the end of "Melanctha" an instance occurs in which variations are played upon exactly the same kind of repetition Isabel Archer employed, "Osmond's beautiful mind, Osmond's beautiful mind." Here Melanctha, having broken almost altogether with Jeff Campbell, wants to move in with her old friend Rose Johnson. But Rose will not invite her.

IT COULD NEVER COME TO MELANCTHA to ask Rose to let her. IT NEVER COULD COME TO MELANCTHA to think that Rose would ask her. IT WOULD NEVER EVER COME TO MELANCTHA to want it, if Rose should ask her, but Melanctha would have done it for the safety she always felt when she was near her. Melanctha Herbert wanted badly to be safe now, but this living with her, that, Rose would never give her. ROSE HAD STRONG THE SENSE for proper conduct, ROSE HAD STRONG THE SENSE to get straight always what she wanted, and she always knew what was the best thing she needed and always Rose got what she wanted.

(capitals added)

Such repetition fulfills an organic purpose. It graphically expresses the difference between the "subtle, intelligent, complex" Melanctha and the "shrewd, simple, selfish" Rose. Melanctha's phrases shift slightly each time they are repeated, and periods isolate her thoughts in separate sentences. But Rose's mind goes straight to the point, three times saying exactly the same thing. As the paragraph ends it is abundantly clear why Rose always got what she wanted.

Sometimes, however, the repetition becomes playful. In the following instance, the seriousness is eased by the pattern of words.

> Dr. Campbell BEGAN TO FEEL A LITTLE about how she responded to him. Dr. Campbell BEGAN TO SEE A LITTLE that perhaps Melanctha had a good mind. Dr. Campbell was not sure yet that she had a good mind, but he BEGAN TO THINK A LITTLE that perhaps she might have one.
>
> (capitals added)

This repetition guides us to a recognition that Dr. Campbell's feelings, senses, and mind are all beginning to respond to the warmth of a woman. Yet the chilly shell of his caution is symbolized by the repeated professional title, "Dr. Campbell."

Other words are repeated not only locally but throughout the work. They often bear a symbolic meaning that only becomes partially clear through repeated use in separate contexts. "Wandering," for example, is an ambiguous term usually associated with Melanctha to suggest activity of a sexual nature. And if Jeff Campbell's steady verbal signal for sexual activity is "getting excited," then for him its opposite is "living regular." His ultimate accusation of Melanctha is that she cannot "remember right"—that is, she rearranges reality to fit her emotional needs. Melanctha in turn is proud that she never "hollers," that she can stoically bear both physical and psychical pain. These are all major terms in the central patterns of the story. Other words used less frequently but often enough to develop an aura of meaning that wavers and changes as each is placed in relation to the others are "summer," "tender," and "sunshine." Others like "sweetness," "patient," "decent," "good," "happy," "simple," and "suffer," although repeated frequently, do not become symbols but carry only the weight they accumulate through usage.

Two words, however, drone steadily throughout "Melanctha." "Always" and "certainly" recur in every possible combination to lend support to the epigraph of the book, which says that there is misery in the world, but neither human nor cosmic responsibility for it: "Donc je suis un malheureux et ce n'est ni ma faute ni celle de la vie." The characters in "Melanctha" move to an inexorable rhythm determined by the pulse of an apparently indifferent universe. With the repetition of these two words we are given ironic insight as we hear the characters qualify their words with absolutes just when they are losing control.

> I certainly do know . . .
> I certainly do understand . . .
> I certainly do see . . .
> I certainly do believe . . .

We know that Jeff and Melanctha are engaged in still another mathematical proof, in a "struggle that was as sure always to be going on between them as their minds and hearts always were to have different ways of working." But in the full light of our knowledge, even as we are slowly impressed by the menacing beat of inevitability we also pity these people in their blind certainty.

NORMAN WEINSTEIN

"Four Saints in Three Acts": Play as Landscape

What is drama for Gertrude Stein, and how does her definition mark a break from the definitions provided by our literary tradition? In her lecture "Plays," Miss Stein traces the roots of her interest in playwriting and supplies us with several highly individual views of the theatrical experience:

> Generally speaking all the early recollections of a child's feeling of the theatre is two things. One which is in a way like a circus that is the general movement and light and air which any theatre has, and a great deal of glitter in the light and a great deal of height in the air, and then there are moments, a very very few moments but still moments. One must be pretty far advanced in adolescence before one can realize a whole play.

Out of all the factors an adult considers when attending a theater the spatial dimensions of the play area are probably the most neglected. After all, why does one attend the theater? For the story of course. And the performance of the actors. And the insights into the human condition. And to laugh or cry or to "forget ourselves." But we are drawn into William James's perception theory again: what do we attend to most intensely in our perceptual field? Consciousness is always necessarily consciousness of something to the neglect of something else in the field. I believe that most of us attend plays with the plot primarily in mind. What we chiefly attend to is the direction of the plot, which, throughout our literary tradition,

From *Gertrude Stein and the Literature of the Modern Consciousness.* Copyright © 1970 by Frederick Ungar Publishing Co., Inc.

implies a dramatic movement toward resolution of action, cartharsis, cli-max. Needless to say, there are thousands of variations on this pattern of dramatic action. A dramatic climax for Aristotle is not the same for Racine or Shakespeare or Shaw. I am insisting only on the central reality of plays in our tradition as movement of character action. In the most elemental terms: things happen on stage in a progression toward greater disclosure of information. Eventually, sometime during the play's course of events, in-formation is given that allows the audience to synthesize earlier disparate bits of data. A key is given to the movement of the characters. A plot is discovered. The dramatic action is resolved. In this most simplified and skeletal view of theater we can consider most dramatic productions prior to the twentieth century.

In the twentieth century this elemental model breaks down. One of the primary model breakers was Gertrude Stein. Her attack upon this conventional notion of drama begins with her recollection of trips to the playhouse, quoted earlier.

She reminds us that all plays take place in a highly particularized space. A play is, first of all, that which takes place behind a curtain, on a stage frontally located apart from the audience. The play is something presented for the consideration of an audience. But considerably more may be presented for an audience's consideration than dialogue. Take for ex-ample the fact of the actors' presence, the setting, the lighting, the curtain. These elements are usually considered secondary and subordinate to the message. But must they be?

For Gertrude Stein the stage area is analogous to a circus ring. Things happen at a circus: clowns go through their paces, horses and bears prance, the ringmaster shouts. And yet ask a child who has attended a circus for the first time in his life what happened, what was it like? and his answer will probably follow Miss Stein's. We remember the atmosphere of the tent. We remember clowns and buffoons not merely for their slapstick but for their costumes, makeup, and postures. The circus is an area of magical possibilities sealed off from objective reality. It is a particularized area with "a great deal of glitter in the light and a great deal of height in the air."

"And then there are moments," Miss Stein reminds us. These mo-ments at the circus are when a fusion of atmosphere and action occurs, when the magic of the arena becomes actualized, when the clowns in costume enter the imaginations of the audience in suits.

I risk repeating the obvious to emphasize Gertrude Stein's concept of theater. Her theater turns away from naturalism to enter a realm of high fantasy or romance. Rather than attempting to simulate social reality on stage, she uses her talents to create an alternative, imaginative reality. This alternative reality is created entirely through verbal magic and setting.

Keeping this frame of reference let us consider *Four Saints in Three Acts.* Whatever else the play is it is a landscape—which implies the following: the area on stage is "Spain" (though certainly not in a naturalistic Spain grounded in history). There are the following objects in "Spain": saints—forty at my last count, in spite of the title—pigeons, magpies, fish. The title, the play notwithstanding, occurs in dozens of acts. In fact the conventional categories of acts and scenes serve as a parodying device much as the chapter divisions of Sterne's *Tristram Shandy* do. Not only is the play a conscious effort to seriously redefine drama but it is also a humorous thrust at the oldtime "well-made play."

The play became the text for an opera with music composed by Virgil Thomson. Although my remarks about *Four Saints* consider it primarily as a play, it is worth keeping in mind that this was a play sung by characters. That the entire cast of the opera was Negro was a most unusual facet to a play with absolutely no connections with Negro life. Virgil Thomson writes that an all-Negro cast was chosen "purely for beauty of voice, clarity of enunciation, and fine carriage." With due respect for Mr. Thomson's honesty another reason for an all-Negro cast might have been the spectacle created by their presence. There is something of a Barnum & Bailey flavor to a play about Spanish saints taking place on a stage with scenery composed entirely of cellophane, performed by an all-Negro cast choreographed to move like Balinese dancers.

Add to this spectacle Miss Stein's text:

> To know to know to love her so.
> Four saints prepare for saints.
> It makes it well fish,
> Four saints it makes it well fish.

The language of the play is a composite of Gertrude Stein's styles of the past three decades. Relatively straight-forward lines are combined with hermetic ones. For example:

Four saints were not born at one time although they knew each other. One of them had a birthday before the mother of the other one the father. Four saints later to be if to be if to be if to be if to be one to be. Might tingle.

One of the styles used widely throughout *Four Saints* is the "cut-up" method, which has not been previously discussed [here]. In Miss Stein's movement from an idiosyncratic but nevertheless naturalistic style to the cubistic lines of *Tender Buttons* an intermediary style arose. Snips, or cutups from everyday conversation were removed from their total speech flow and arranged architectonically. For instance, this brief section from a short prose composition of the 1920s:

> PAGE II
>> What did you say about women.
>> Were you angry.
>> Do you mind.
>> Can you feel a discrimination.
>> Can you be harsh.

Here each phrase makes perfect sense within itself but the accumulation of such phrases, often trivial in meaning, tends to render the cluster meaningless. Many of the cut-outs consist of selections from high society or ladies' tea parties, and are fascinating as exhibitions of the vapidity and mental sloth of such circles:

> Can a Jew be wild
>
> Can you speak.
>
> The dog.
> Can you bear to tear the skirt.
>
> I cannot find a real dressmaker.
> Neither can I.

Entire scenes of *Four Saints* consist of these cut-outs reproduced verbatim with an occasional reference to Spain or saints to keep some local color in the play:

> It is very easy to love alone. Too much too much. There are very sweetly very sweetly Henry very sweetly Rene very sweetly many very sweetly. They are very sweetly many very sweetly Rene very sweetly there are many very sweetly.
> There is a difference between Barcelona and Avila. What difference.

> (SCENE II)

The play does focus its attention between Barcelona and Avila in a spiritual sense: the two chief characters in the play are Gertrude Stein's favorite saints: Saint Therese of Avila and Saint Ignatius Loyola. The two saints have much in contrast with each other: male, female; passive suffering, active suffering; humility and grandeur. But within the play we are not dealing with the historical saints of the Church tradition. We are faced with saints that are Miss Stein's personal creations:

In Four Saints I made the Saints the landscape. All the saints that I made and I made a number of them because after all there are a number of things in a landscape all these saints together made a landscape . . . A landscape does not move nothing really moves in a landscape but things are there. . . .

Saint Therese and Saint Ignatius are stage props: talking stage props. Their importance to the play is simply that they do most of the talking. There are dozens of saints that are silent for the duration of the play. Their appearance is justified by what they contribute to the set, the landscape. Here we see a possible reason for Miss Stein's choice of saints as a play subject. Donald Sutherland writes: "A saint, whether he does anything or not, exists in and with the universe and shares its life, sustained in existence by the general miracle of the present world." I find Sutherland's remark directly to the point. A saint need not do anything but exist in order to create an aura, an atmosphere about himself. A saint is defined by the quality of his presence, his ability to be within the world and at the same moment transcend it:

If it were possible to kill five thousand chinamen by pressing a button would it be done.
Saint Therese not interested.

This saintly mixture of worldknowingness and otherworldliness can be found plentifully in Gertrude Stein. Having lived through two world wars she writes about war with the same naïveté and lightness as she does about an Alice B. Toklas dinner. This quality of absolute indifference toward the world of political and social responsibilities infuriated many of her fellow writers. But perhaps they failed to realize how closely Miss Stein kept the saint figure as an ideal.

A saint is a traveler between two worlds: earth and heaven. One result of traveling both kingdoms is that a saint learns to speak both with the languages of men and angels:

Tangle wood tanglewood.
Four saints born in separate places.
Saint saint saint saint.
Four saints an opera in three acts.
My country 'tis of thee sweet land of liberty of thee I sing.

From this most American-jargonized saint talk we move to the grand, mysterious sounding litanies of:

All Saints. Any and all Saints. All Saints. All and all Saints. All Saints. All in all Saints. All Saints. All Saints. All Saints. Saints all in all Saints. All Saints. Settled in all Saints. All Saints.

What does all this mean? . . . . I believe that *Four Saints* can be set apart from Miss Stein's other creations in the following manner. *Four Saints* is a circus. We are confronted not by performing clowns but by talking saints. As clowns are run through their paces so these saints unleash their bag of verbal games and plays. What is presented to the play's audience is a set of verbal games and musical statements that the spectator might enter into and play for himself. Valéry's remark that someday literature will exist only as entertaining games comes to mind. The audience is presented with a landscape to gaze upon ("the glitter in the air") and words to dazzle, to confuse, to delight. Among the games presented are:

ILLOGICAL REPETITIONS:
> Four saints are never three.
> Three saints are never four.
> Four saints are never left altogether.
> Three saints are never left idle.

COUNTING GAMES:
> One two three four five six seven all good children go to heaven some are good and some are bad one two three four five six seven.

GRADUATED SYNTACTIC DISPLACEMENT:
> To be interested in Saint Therese fortunately.
> To be interested in Saint Therese fortunately.
> Saint Ignatius to be interested fortunately.
> Fortunately to be interested in Saint Therese.

PHONEMIC PLAY:

Saint Therese.	When.
Saint Settlement.	Then.
Saint Genevieve.	When.
Saint Cecile.	Then.
Saint Ignatius.	Men.

Pigeons on the grass alas.
Pigeons on the grass alas.

All of these verbal structures are woven into a larger fabric for a most surprising reason. Miss Stein distinguishes this play from the conventional, naturalistic drama in this manner:

> Your sensation as one in the audience in relation to the play played before you your sensation I say your emotion concerning the play is always either behind or ahead of the play at which you are looking and to which you are listening. So your emotion as a member of the audience is never going on at the same time as the action of the play.

The issue of dramatic presentation for Miss Stein involves the synchronization of dramatic movement with audience passional response. This issue of synchronizing actor action with audience response is not considered by most playwriters as a problem. Indeed, what is usually called "dramatic tension" in a play by Shakespeare or Shaw is the very want of synchronized action Gertrude Stein complains about! The actors in such plays are always one step ahead of the audience, which implies the possibilities of surprising the anticipations of the audience. But such a lack of synchronized action and audience response also gives the conventional drama an aura of the past. The play is reenacted, implying that the actions of the play actually occurred in one stretch of past time and they are being acted *again* in present stage time.

Gertrude Stein sought to infuse her plays with the same state of presentness and immediacy that informed all her other compositions. How could a play exist totally in the present consciousness of the audience? The first step would entail the elimination of plot. If nothing happens but talking there is no worry about distinguishing past from present. If the play is nothing more than landscape, landscapes change little over long stretches of time, particularly if they are landscapes grounded in the Spanish countryside. In a setting with minimal change and movement there is an atmosphere of timelessness. Into this timeless arena saints speak. What the saints say is also timeless. Games and riddles, verbal melodies and textures, need no precise temporal or spatial context in which to exist. It is when words are considered primarily for their semantic carrier that they seem dated. The words "one two three four five six seven" formed a melody for Shakespeare as well as for Gertrude Stein. Although the period from Shakespeare to Miss Stein has witnessed the variation or loss of the original meaning of thousands of words, the ability of the words to be sounded as musical tones has remained constant. There is nothing iconoclastic in Miss Stein's use of verbal games and music in drama. How different is Shakespeare's "Hey nonny, nonny, no" nonsense refrain from Gertrude Stein's "pigeons on the grass alas"? The issue is one of emphasis. Gertrude Stein chooses to create entire plays composed solely of these constructs.

So the effort to involve the audience in *Four Saints* focuses upon the audience's willingness to enter the author's consciousness through her verbal games: a three-ring circus of saints' singing games. Yet, while listening to the recording of the opera, I discovered that parts of the play seem to "move" faster than others. How is this possible in an actionless play? An answer might be that some verbal games are denser, more for the audience to ponder than others. Anyone can follow the counting games.

But the plays with word positioning through long sequences are slower to adjust to. So the conventional categories of accelerated or decelerated dramatic action are replaced by games of lesser and greater verbal density. Dramatic tension is created by the contrasts between different verbal masses. Some scenes consist of only one word repeated three times. Others comprise scores of lines filled with the most intricate varieties of verbal embroidery. Set in contrast with each other they create tensions analogous to the color of painted masses in Kandinsky or Pollock.

One final comment is in order concerning *Four Saints*. Like any circus it is great fun. The whimsy and nonsense of much of the play is handsomely complemented by Virgil Thomson's simple and popular-sounding score. There is something basically absurd about the play, absurd in terms that are congenial to such contemporary absurdist playwrights as Samuel Beckett and Eugene Ionesco. The lack of character movement, the play as static landscape, the nonsensical talk, and the verbal, gamelike qualities with which Gertrude Stein shocked 1934 audiences have become commonplaces to 1970 audiences accustomed to *Waiting for Godot* and *The Bald Soprano*. But Miss Stein prophesied this direction for the theater, and prophesied her own role as an artist bringing about this revolution:

> This is the reason why the creator of the new composition in the arts is an outlaw until he is a classic. . . .
> For a very long time everybody refuses and then without a pause everybody accepts.

JUDITH P. SAUNDERS

Gertrude Stein's "Paris France" and American Literary Tradition

Paris France is not primarily a portrait of a nation, though it has usually been mistaken for one. Janet Flanner, one of the earliest reviewers of the book, informed readers of the *New York Herald Tribune* in 1940 that "what [Stein] talks about, better than any other American has ever done in print, is the pattern of the French mind . . ." This view of the book has remained essentially unchallenged, as Richard Bridgman echoes Flanner in 1970 with small variation: "Its real subject is the French character, especially as represented by the solid virtues of the agricultural provinces." However, to define the subject of Stein's book so literally in terms of geography and nationality is to underestimate profoundly its purpose and scope. France is Stein's subject in approximately the same sense that the countryside of Concord, Massachusetts is the subject of Thoreau's *Walden*. Like Thoreau, who describes his pond, his fields, and his woods in loving detail, Stein introduces us to French agriculture, custom, and fashion. But both Thoreau and Stein present an environment primarily for the sake of the Self which that environment nourishes. Paris, France, like Walden woods, provides a retreat for self-preservation, an escape to freedom.

Stein defines her France in abstractions, and in terms of paired opposites. Apparently trivial anecdotes concerning French dogs, French

From *South Dakota Review* 1, vol. 15 (Spring). Copyright © 1977 by *South Dakota Review.*

hats, or French servants function as small epiphanies and provide kernels of insight into the special polarized perspective which Stein calls "French." She opens emphatically, defining her theme with a sweeping oxymoron: "Paris, France is exciting and peaceful." This assertion of duality, set apart as a paragraph unto itself, provides the kind of impetus and suspense which might otherwise be created by a storyline. Piqued by a seemingly paradoxical description (exciting *and* peaceful), the reader looks to the anecdotes of French life which follow to discover how Paris, France can evoke two contradictory feelings simultaneously. Repeating her opening phrase at intervals as a kind of running leitmotif, Stein reinforces its significance as a structural and thematic focus in the book. The experience of reading quantities of casually arranged anecdotes receives shape and direction as our attention is drawn repeatedly to the underlying concept of peace-and-excitement. Even the most seemingly banal stories can shed light on Stein's meaning: "At the Cafe Anglais their pride in French cooking expressed itself in the perfection of simple dishes, a saddle of mutton so perfectly and so delicately roasted that in itself it became peaceful and exciting." Instantly we perceive how the simpleness, the ordinariness of the dish render it "peaceful" at the same time that its perfection makes for a breathtaking "excitement." The anecdote enables us to see Paris, France as a place where opposites remain opposites, yet belong together and enhance each other.

From her very first sentence Stein introduces us to a place characterized by co-existing contradictions, a place suspended in delicate balance between equal but opposite poles of feeling. After her initial definition of France as "exciting and peaceful," all her important perceptions continue to fall into pairs of linked opposites. Her notion of expatriation, to name a prime example, assumes a need in writers and artists for two countries: "the one where they belong and the one in which they live really." Determined to live "inside themselves," they require a certain distance from the everyday social and political goings-on outside themselves. The advantages of the second, adopted country are that it demands no involvement, deflects no energies away from an interior life. One enjoys familiarity, yet retains a sense of separateness. This state of being at home while remaining a perpetual stranger represents, again, the establishment of an equilibrium which is based on contradictions.

Poised perfectly between surface familiarity and essential foreignness, Stein discovers the precious free space: "that other country that you need to be free in." Introducing her private world apart in the 1936 essay "An American and France," she echoes Melville's advice that we "live in this world without being of it." She extolls the creative freedom which she finds in France, asserting that "everybody was there and everybody and anybody did what they did *in it not being of it.*" Drawing her foreignness around her like a protective garment, Stein resembles Melville's whale in its insulating coat of blubber:

> Like man, the whale has lungs and warm blood. Freeze his blood and he dies. How wonderful is it then—except after explanation—that this great monster, to whom corporeal warmth is as indispensable as it is to man: how wonderful that he should be found at home, immersed to his lips for life in those Arctic waters! . . . It does seem to me, that herein we see the rare virtue of a strong individual vitality, and the rare virtue of thick walls, and the rare virtue of interior spaciousness. Oh, man! admire and model thyself after the whale! Do thou, too, remain warm among ice. Do thou, too, live in this world without being of it. Be cool at the equator: keep thy blood fluid at the Pole. Like the . . . great whale, retain, O man! in all seasons a temperature of thine own.

"At home" in a strange land, Stein maintains "strong individual vitality" and discovers the secret of "interior spaciousness." Cherishing her dichotomous position as an inhabitant of "that other country," she lays claim to the traditional American literary Eden: Hawthorne's "neutral territory, somewhere between the real world and fairy-land, where the Actual and the Imaginary may meet," and where the individual self is both independently separate and communally connected. Like Whitman, to name another obvious predecessor, she aspires to be "both in and out of the game." In "Song of Myself" Whitman assumes this stance, merging with the life around him while at the same time preserving individual identity; "out of the dimness opposite equals advance . . . always a knit of identity, always distinction . . ." Stein, too, frames her identity between "opposite equals," withdrawing to Paris, France to establish her own version of a typically contradictory American pose.

Her description of her adopted country as "not real but . . . really there" (another version of the foreign-but-familiar paradox), sets up a polarity between different kinds of reality, and that polarity is further explored in connection with art. We learn that Stein's first significant aesthetic experience occurred at the age of eight when she was taken to see the Panorama of the Battle of Waterloo: "all around you on every side was an oil painting." The effect of this attempt to extend the single flat surface of a painting was to impress upon her all the more forcibly the irreconcilable differences between "a painting" and "out of doors." In a sudden flash of intuition, she tells us, she perceived that experiential reality is three-dimensional, while painting is one-dimensional. She embraces the distinction which she sees so clearly, forevermore assured that art and the world are two different things, never to be confused, and each—for that very reason— illuminating the other. Representational art ("painting that imitates air") is uninteresting, since aesthetic pleasure stems from our perception of the *unrealness* of human designs. Like "the other country," art offers us a liberating separateness from ordinary reality.

Once the reader has grasped that "Paris, France" is a state of being— that Stein's subject is the discovery of fruitful tension between opposites— the apparent jumble of anecdotes sorts itself out quite reasonably. Stein's childhood aesthetic awakening in San Francisco is relevant, for example, not because the Panorama of the Battle of Waterloo was painted "by a Frenchman," but because her perception of art and the world as two distinct things is an important recognition of duality. Things come in pairs: two countries (one to live in and one to belong to), two realities (painting and "out of doors"), even, as we learn, two languages. French is a spoken language, while English is a written language, she informs us. The context she has set up saves this assertion from being merely absurd; as another example of complementing opposites, it serves as a gloss on the two-country theme. Insisting that French is a spoken language only is a whimsical way of underlining the retreat into inwardness which expatriation permits the artist. Writing in English while hearing French spoken daily all around her, Stein sees a sharp dividing line between her own creative inner world and an outside world of ephemeral, mundane affairs. To return to Melville's whale image, the functional distinction she makes between the two languages is part of the insulation necessary to maintain optimum interior temperature.

Paris, France becomes an increasingly magical place as we learn more about its power to contain opposites. Even those eternal opposites, male and female, can be combined without loss of their individual qualities: "It always pleases me that French boys are often called Jean-Marie . . . it hallows the male name to add the female name to it." In France, too, "the city and country and country and city are not separated." The deliberate repetition in reverse of the double subject is typical, as Stein positions the words on the page to mimic her point concerning turnabout movement between two distant places. She renders her special world with epigrammatic succinctness: "not real . . . but really there"; "it is not a secret but one does not tell it"; "facts should be known but not remembered." Such teasingly paradoxical declarations operate like a combination of folk maxim and sphinx riddle. Enjoying her role as wise naif, Stein concocts phrases rich in repetition, antithesis, parallelism, and inversion, demonstrating how the world can be two, yet one.

It is, above all else, their unique apprehension of reality which enables the French to sit between stools without falling. "France has scientific methods, machines and electricity, but does not really believe that these things have anything to do with the real business of living. Life is tradition and human nature." Here we find "tradition and human nature" at one end of the spectrum, with "scientific methods, machines and electricity" at the other. The way to enjoy scientific knowledge and conveniences without forfeiting cultural traditions is to have the new things without "believing" in them. (The French have a "profound conviction" that "science is interesting but does not change anything"). This particular dichotomy is a central one in the book. In place of "tradition" Stein sometimes substitutes "logic," "the family," "the soil of France," or "civilization"; in place of "science" she occasionally inserts "progress" or "fashion." No matter which terms she employs, her point is the same: the French observe the changing surfaces of life—science, progress, fashion—against a background of permanence: a permanence rooted in the earth, in human nature, and in cultural inheritance. Stein likens changing "fashion" to the seasons. One knows the earth itself is always there and so one accepts the mutability which continually alters its outward aspect: "the earth has its seasons and the people who live on that earth have fashions and that is all." In tune with natural laws of cyclicity, the French "change completely but all the time they know they are as they were."

Stein is suggesting here a view of reality in which human cultural behavior has an inevitability and permanence. She rejoices in her observation that in France patterns of familial interaction and social custom are seemingly as real and as changeless as natural processes: "All the contact between them [i.e., the French] is so fixed and inevitable, so definite and so real that there is no question of either nature nor choice nor mistake. There can be no mistake and they cannot be mistaken." She clearly relishes the eccentricities of the French, their stubborn adherence to their own inherited "logic." Her anecdotes present in loving detail behavior which often appears absurd, but the more odd their national quirkiness proves, and the more tenaciously they cling to it, the better Stein likes the French. There are several reasons why this is so. Perhaps the most important reason is that she increases her freedom from involvement in the daily life of her expatriate home if she can stand aside and comment on its peculiarities with benign and almost anthropological objectivity. There is nothing to prevent her from retreating into herself and her work, for if relationships are fixed and formalized, one need expend no energy thinking about them. "Intimacy"—a *bête noir* in the book—is a more spontaneous, unpredictable interaction, and hence wasteful of time and inner resources ("with tradition and freedom one cannot be intimate with anyone").

She renders even the course of history predictable (and thus less disrupting) by adopting the "French" theory of periods of human life: after a conservative childhood and an adolescent stage of revolt, a man settles down to a "civilized" and family-centered maturity. Stein applies this pattern of growth metaphorically to the "lives" of centuries, reasoning in 1939 that World War I was clearly the adolescent revolutionary period for this century and that it is thus not "logical" to expect another war. Literally and historically, of course, Stein was wrong. War—no matter how illogical—did come. She has been criticized for her naive and unrealistic thinking regarding the approach of World War II, but *Paris France* is not primarily concerned with literal and historical reality. By emphasizing the fixed and predictable nature of human social and political facts, Stein preserves necessary psychological distance from them.

There are still other reasons why Stein glories in the on-going eccentricity of French cultural tradition. If there is security in perceiving cultural behavior as predictable, there is also freedom in realizing that this very predictability is a product of human invention. As usual, Stein is making paradoxical claims: in security there is freedom, in whimsy there is inevitability, and in artifice we find reality. No matter that the customs handed down to us are a collective creation whose sources and *raison d'etre* are largely forgotten—each prescribed social pattern bears witness to the continuing power of human constructs to shape our experience. In the very arbitrariness and occasional absurdity of French traditions, Stein sees evidence of human creative strength. Even if the reality we have devised is sometimes silly or destructive, we at least retain the capacity to change or suspend it. "War," she muses, "is more like a novel than it is like real life," for "it is a thing . . . invented." Indications of the coming war "might only be a fire drill, it might only be a make believe." In comparing war to a novel, a "make believe," Stein reminds us that what man has invented, man can alter. Gifted with a "sense of reality," the French appreciate man's potential control over collectively created ideas and institutions. When, for example, a girl goes off to an isolated village to be a school teacher, the French suspend their usual assumptions about a young girl's need for care and protection: "it is understood, and if it is understood to be so nothing happens that should not happen." Thus they acknowledge that their social world is of their own making.

Viewing cultural patterns as a collective invention allows Stein to compare them with art, to insist that there is great value in all manifestations of human creativity. The French, capable of suspending their agreed-upon notions about young girls, understand the proper relationship between life and art. They know that "nobody really lives who has not been well written about." Contending that life derives from art (instead of the other way around), they corroborate Stein's special definition of "reality": The real world—the world outside the human imagination—exists only insofar as it is reflected and interpreted in the unreal world of human consciousness. Hence we have no choice but to conclude that the unreal is somehow more "real" than the real. In her carefully balanced contradictions, Stein does not ask us to choose one reality over another. We need no ignore the world in favor of art, nor renounce the land where we "belong" in favor of an adopted country. Just as excitement can be experienced only in the context of peacefulness, so the value of human designs first emerges when we hold them up against the backdrop of the experiential world. Our uniquely human ability to structure and interpret our experience represents control over that experience and, ultimately, freedom from it ("once a thing is completely named it does no longer worry them [the French]"). Stein agrees with Wallace Stevens that "life consists of propositions about life." Things are the way we think they are, and thus our imaginative and intellectual constructs take on unarguable reality.

Stein's *Paris, France* is itself an imaginative construct; it is a created fiction, a spiritual rather than a literal place, where apparent contradictions are the source of wholeness. This wholeness finds metaphoric expression in her confident assertion, repeated several times in the course of the book, that "the world is round." Roundness is Stein's term for the ideal reconciliation of opposites which Paris, France represents ("exciting and peaceful"); roundness is a state of ultimate equipoise. She gives us crucial insight into the concept in an anecdote about the death of her dog, Basket. A French friend advises her, "Get another [dog] as like Basket as possible call him by the same name and gradually there will be confusion and you will not know which Basket it is." Picasso, however, recommends that she get a different kind of dog entirely: "No, never get the same kind of a dog again never . . . . supposing I were to die, you would go out on the street and sooner or later you would meet a Pablo, but it would not be I . . . ." Eventually she combines the two contradictory suggestions:

> So we tried to have the same and not to have the same . . . at last we
> found another Basket, and we got him and we called him Basket and he
> is very gay and I cannot say that the confusion between the old and the
> new has yet taken place but certainly le roi est mort vive le roi, is a
> normal attitude of mind.

Trying to have "the same and not the same" is to strive for Whitman's
position "both in and out of the game"—perfect equilibrium between city
and country, tradition and progress, fact and fiction. With the single phrase
"le roi est mort vive le roi" the French show what it means to live on a
round world, to embrace change within a pattern of continuity. Though
its leaves fall, a tree lives on; though the King die, his office continues.
We observe a human institution imitating natural cyclicity, and in the
chiastic symmetry of the deliberately unpunctuated phrase "le roi est mort
vive le roi" we see stylistic "roundness" as well.

In fact, Stein suits her method to her subject, structuring and narrating her book on the principle of circularity. She proceeds by means of
apparently spontaneous association and digression, frequently returning to
a topic begun earlier, developing it further and then abandoning it, only
to pick it up yet again and again. Each time she returns to discussion of
an abstract topic such as "art" or "civilization," she elaborates on it with
more anecdotes, fleshing out a concept with concrete detail. With repeated
references she establishes connections among diverse topics until finally we
recognize them as aspects of a single, larger subject. Much as if her book
were a musical composition, she announces a theme—art, war, science,
hats, dogs, cooking—then introduces variations, eventually weaving it
firmly into her main melody. She circles around her subject, following her
own prescription for narration, "using everything by beginning again and
again." Continually discovering new perspectives and interconnections,
she demonstrates structurally and stylistically—as well as thematically—
"the inevitability of resemblances and continuations." She recreates the
experience of living on a round and rotating world, poised between stasis
and motion, between peace and excitement. It is not accidental that critics
have selected such descriptive metaphors for her writing as snowballing,
circling, and orbiting. Her narrative method mimics organic cycling, rein-
forcing her presentation of the fictive Paris, France as a place where opposite
poles rest in balance.

In inventing a world apart "to be free in," Stein allies herself with
a quintessentially American myth of escape. Her withdrawal to her own
special "other country" is the twentieth-century counterpart of Thoreau's
retreat to Walden or Huck Finn's flight to raft and river. Even more than

her literary predecessors, Stein recognizes that the new paradise, the Great Good Place, is not identifiable with any particular geographic location—certainly not with the American West or "the Territory." In *Paris France* her metaphoric and psychological move back across the Atlantic Ocean suggests a logical conclusion to the original European westward quest. She discovers the new world in the context of the old, and personal freedom in the context of cultural restraint. Consistently she interprets the universe in terms of Whitman's "opposite equals," or Emerson's concept of "bipolar unity"—"that polar, paradoxical, ironic, ambiguous monism" which, as Edwin Fussell observes (*Frontier: American Literature and the American West*), "remains to this day the signature of American thought and expression." In its affirmation of possibilities of escape and renewal, in its insistence on unity-in-duality (i.e., roundness), Stein's book represents a resurgence of deepest American longings. Not since the mid-nineteenth century has an American writer asserted with such optimism our ability to shape our own destiny and to balance "somewhere between . . . the Actual and the Imaginary." Going far beyond a literal portrayal of place, Stein celebrates in *Paris France* her own self-made reality.

CATHARINE R. STIMPSON

The Mind, the Body, and Gertrude Stein

I wish to outline a phenomenon I call the feminization of the mind/body problem. By that I mean certain social and psychological questions that women had to confront about the relationship of their minds to their bodies; I do not mean a peculiarly female or feminine analysis of an old, complex philosophical question. Though my phrase may prove to have a wider use, I will apply it to the life of Gertrude Stein (1874–1946) during the first decade of the twentieth century. She was a genius, whom I honor, but one with several disagreeable traits.

The feminization of the mind/body problem was and is a modern event. Historically, the sexual ideologies of Western culture have assigned intellectual and aesthetic prowess to men. For the most part, men have also controlled institutions such as the church and university that help to shape public consciousness. However, by the end of the nineteenth century, the woman who both used her mind and employed it to structure a career was a member of a recognizable minority. Even if the majority of women could not construe a professional, intellectual, or imaginative life as a serious possibility, some did—enough to be a group.

Access to higher education, helpful for such careers, had been achieved. If, in 1900, only 4 percent of all Americans between the ages of eighteen and twenty-one were undergraduates, 35 percent of them were women. They took 19 percent of the bachelor's degrees. If women were

From Critical Inquiry 3, vol. 3 (1977). Copyright © 1977 by Critical Inquiry.

awarded only 6 percent of the doctorates, they comprised 19 percent of higher education faculties. Indeed, for Stein's generation of undergraduates, higher education was as much a freedom to be exercised as a freedom to be won. Though Stein's retrospective constructions of reality may lack fine precision, a comment she made in 1935 is suggestive:

> For some years now college students good college students tell me they want not to go on going to college and this has surprised me because we we [sic] liked going to college and I asked them why. I said perhaps they had had freedom too soon, that is before they went to college and college was for us freedom physical and mental freedom.

If the use of women's minds was changing, the use of women's bodies, a combination of social and sexual behavior, was still immersed in past practices and in the fiats of biology. In brief, consciousness was more liberated than the flesh. As a result, a problematic gap existed, particularly for elite women, between what they might do with their minds and what they might do with their bodies. One ideological solution was to project an ideal woman. She would not abandon sexual functions, particularly maternity, for the mind. Rather, she would add a disciplined and agile intelligence to these traditional functions. The synthesis would be the all-round woman: a sturdy, healthy, interesting wife, mother, and worker.

Stein, in the late 1890s, though unmarried and childless, enthusiastically endorsed the concept of the superwoman who would unite the new mind and old body. So doing, she explicitly acknowledged the influence of "Charlotte Perkins Stetson." The role of women, Stein proclaimed, had to change. Women were "over-sexed" economic dependents, a betrayal of the past, a danger to the future. As if "No more Gwendolen Harleths" were her rallying cry, she announced that education would help women expand their lives. Insouciant in her class bias, she gave some case histories of the New Woman, the intellectually competent housewife. She spoke approvingly of a woman who took in lodgers, taught three times a week, took care of the baby, did original lab research, and "type writed [sic] the whole of her husbands [sic] books." Moreover, the woman did all this with "only one servant and the remarkable part of it is that it was all well done."

The feminization of the mind/body problem describes a second gap as well: between what women might do with their bodies and what they might say about it, especially in public. The history of modern literature proves that men as well as women were punished if they broke through the limits both respectability and law had set on written descriptions of the body in general and erotic activity in particular. Dreiser, as well as Kate Chopin, was penalized for ignoring certain repressive restraints. However, for women, the right to speak or write, in public, as professionals, was both newer than that of men and more restricted. Perhaps members of neither sex could fully play with the First Amendment, but women had more limits placed upon them.

The response to such dissonances was a multiplicity of private solutions. For some, the active professional pursuit of consciousness would prove impossible. Will and ambition faltering, they would turn from a "career" to more "traditional ideals" of womanhood. Others tried for both. Still others devoted themselves wholly to a career. Still others worked and nurtured psychological liaisons with other women, an apparently necessary condition of productivity and creativity for many. Of the sixty-seven women listed in Stein's cohort of authors in *Notable American Women,* thirty-seven were married, though a number were without children; fifteen were single; ten were single, but their entry mentions a friendship with another woman; three were married, but after a significant link with a woman; and two were single, but lived with a female relative.

To try to understand both the nature and the nuances of these private solutions, one must presume nothing and expect anything. The women exemplify the complexities, inventiveness, and contradictions of behavior that occur during periods of change. Mary Douglas, the anthropologist, offers a concept that might apply to them: that of the anomaly. She says that every culture has categories that are

> public matters. They cannot . . . easily be subject to revision. Yet they cannot neglect the challenge of aberrant forms. Any given system of classification must give rise to anomalies, and any given culture must confront events which seem to defy its assumptions. It cannot ignore the anomalies which its scheme produces.

Living out the feminization of the mind/body problem, Stein and her contemporaries were anomalies in the process of being integrated, if only marginally, into their culture and its categories. However, not all anomalies can be handled. Some, the pollutants, must be rejected. "Uncleanness or dirt," Douglas writes, "is that which must not be included if a pattern is to be maintained."

Much about Stein is atypical, even for her cohort. A Jew who became more and more hostile to Jews, she had the privileges of an independent income, the advantages of as much education as she wanted, and her singular brains, temperament and talent. She was also, after struggling against her own puritanical distrust of passion, a practicing lesbian. However, because of that very cluster of characteristics, particularly her sexuality, she is representative—of the anomaly who floats, sometimes beyond, sometimes within, the boundary that separates manageable from "polluted" behavior.

During the period from 1900 to 1920, I suggest, she came to terms, if in inconsistent and spasmodic ways, with that status. She was well into chronological maturity. *The Making of Americans* is a massive novel in which she narrates the history of herself as writer, of her family, of America, and of the human passage from birth to death. In it, Stein labels the age of thirty as the genesis of adulthood and a sense of fitness for serious labor.

> It happens often about the twenty-ninth year of life that all the forces that have been engaged through the years of childhood, adolescence and youth in confused and sometimes angry combat range themselves in or- dered ranks . . . uproar and confusion narrow . . . down to form and purpose and we exchange a dim possibility for a big or small reality.

She made two linked, irrevocable choices: of home and of vocation. The home, a signal of the ability to give and to receive love, erected a stable defense against the painful, "weakening" loneliness to which she thought women might be more susceptible than men. It also vigorously supported the vocation. In turn, the vocation may have helped to justify the sexuality of the home and to drain it of some of its anxiety-provoking power.

Stein's education had been eccentric. It is unclear whether she, or her influential older brother Leo, graduated from high school in Oakland, California, where they spent much of their childhood and adolescence. With or without that degree, Leo went to Harvard in 1892. She followed him to the Harvard Annex in 1893, chartered as Radcliffe the next year. She did well, particularly in psychology. However, she received one "C" in English, and another "C" in a junior psychology class studying "con- sciousness, knowledge, and the relation of the mind to the body." After Leo went to Johns Hopkins to study biology, she joined him in 1897 as a Hopkins medical student. Baltimore, called Bridgepoint, was later to appear in much of her early fiction.

For Stein and others, college and professional school were a source of female friendships and a site of female networks. Such relationships were adaptations of those Carroll Smith-Rosenberg has pictured. They were also novel. Their location, away from home, promised a measure of indepen- dence and privacy. Next, their commitments and rituals were those of study and work, not of family. Higher education also offered a chance for private trials; for strenuous testing of personality; for proof of self-reliance. Stein, in medical school, said:

> . . . in the four years away from home with no one to protect you or be fond of you unless you earn it . . . it is here for the first time that you

are thrown wholly on yourself with out any aid of family or heretary [sic] friends and if there is anything worthy in you it must come out for here you must earn whatever you get and through that discipline you become a selfrespecting human being.

However, in the spring of 1902, Stein left medical school. She either failed or did badly in four courses. Her official excuse was professorial rigidity about her work habits and her "boredom" with the materials. As the word boredom may mask other emotions, so may low grades signify stress. Stein's were in obstetrics (though not gynecology); laryngology (the study of the larynx); rhinology (the study of the nose); ophthalmology and otology (the study of the ear); and dermatology. Such courses concern childbirth, the orifices and openings of the body, and the skin. Overtly or symbolically, they are sexual. Moreover, during the year, Stein had become emotionally entangled with Mary (May) Bookstaver, who was also at Hopkins and who was involved with a third woman, Mabel Haynes.

Stein's triangular affair was to torment her for several years. In 1901–2, she stayed in Baltimore to do brain research. That, and her earlier scientific training, probably helped her to evolve a modern mimetic literary theory that proclaims the limited possibility of consciousness accurately apprehending the external and internal realities of the historical moment in which it finds itself. In the fall of 1903, after some traveling, she settled with Leo in Paris at the famous 27, Rue de Fleurus. In October 1903, she wrote her first full novel, Q.E.D. ("Quod Erat Demonstrandum"). In 1904 she visited America, to which she would not return until 1934, as a celebrity. Between 1905 and 1906, she finished Three Lives: two stories about immigrant German servants, one story about a black "wanderer." In 1907, while in the middle of The Making of Americans, she met Alice B. Toklas, who learned to type during the next year in order to transcribe the manuscript. In 1909, Toklas moved in with the Steins. By 1913, Leo had left. Stein's transition—from endogamous to exogamous mate, from male mentor to female companion, from one who was, at best, indifferent to her writing to one who was utterly supportive—was complete.

During the decade of choice, Stein, consciously or unconsciously, devised several strategies that might enable one to live as a possibly tainted anomaly. First, she appears to have had at least two groups of friends. They might all meet each other, but only some would know about her sexuality, while others would not. Those who were aware did not have to be homosexuals themselves. The sorting principle between the groups was less sexual preference than the ability to absorb knowledge; less sexual experience than free-wheeling sophistication. If necessary, the initiates protected their shared secret through tact, discretion, and silence.

For example, Stein told some people about her unhappiness because of May Bookstaver. She spent the painful winter of 1902–3 with a few of them in New York, in a house at 100th Street and Riverside Drive. One of Stein's chattier biographers writes:

> Here the friendships and conversations of student days were resumed, but there was a difference. These young women were now in their late twenties and all but Gertrude were absorbed in their professions and their young men. She was unattached and so a little out of it, but she lived with vigour, walking, reading and writing letters.

However, others were apparently ignorant of her sexuality. Miss Etta Cone, a Baltimore friend close enough to type the manuscript of *Three Lives* in Europe, was one. Her nephew says of her:

> To my sister she once mentioned something that had been troubling her for some time. "You know, Frances, people say that there was something *between* Gertrude and Alice, but I never believed it. After all, what can two women *do*?" On this point Frances [her niece] wisely professed ignorance.

A second strategy was to deploy a number of conventional and heterosexual terms to describe her life, as if language might sweepingly both name and legitimize the unconventional and then the homosexual. A passage in *Q. E. D.* points to such a practice. As one lover says goodbye to another, she remarks: ". . . in you I seem to be taking farewell of parents, brother sisters my own child, everything at once. No dear you are quite right there is nothing pleasant in it." With Toklas, Stein was "Baby." In a long-standing friendship, Carl Van Vechten was "Papa Woojums"; Fania Van Vechten "Empress" or "Madame Woojums"; Toklas "Mama Woojums"; and Stein "Baby Woojums." In fact, Stein had been the last of the five children that had survived in her blood family, two having passed away before Leo and she were born. Early deaths haunted her adolescence as well: her mother's in 1888; her father's in 1891.

Consistently, the language of self was male and masculine. Stein was "husband" to Toklas' "wife." Sometimes, others applied male terms to her. In 1897, for example, a friend, who also discouraged her from going to medical school, wrote: ". . . I know a good many women pretty well. As a rule so much sensuous intellectuality as you have is found in men." She certainly applied them to herself. Speaking of the female as male/masculine, she reverted to old patterns to meet the new dilemma of the feminization of the mind/body problem. In 1908 she read that dreary classic of male supremacy disguised as science: Otto Weininger's *Sex and Character.*

She apparently praised it, for in 1909, a friend wrote to tell her that it was lunatic, even if Stein did say it "exactly embodied" her views.

That Stein would approve of Weininger points to some confusion and ambivalence. For Weininger despises both women and Jews, who are, to him, womanly. He asserts that no woman ever has been or will be a genius, an exalted status to which Stein aspired. On the other hand, Weininger's cranky ideology could offer Stein some support and consolation. He believes that everyone is bisexual, not just a contaminated few. He also claims that the homosexual woman is better than the rest of her sex. Actively partaking of male elements, she may aspire to those aesthetic and intellectual pursuits that are otherwise a male province. Weininger announces:

> My law of sexual affinity . . . [applied] to the facts of homo-sexuality showed that the woman who attracts and is attracted by other women is herself half male. . . . Sappho was only the forerunner of a long line of famous women who were either homo-sexually or bisexually inclined . . . homo-sexuality in a woman is the outcome of her masculinity and presupposes a higher degree of development.

Stein was already projecting herself, if more defiantly, as an exception. To think of one's self as special has several functions: to justify loneliness; to glamorize the role of anomaly and to remove it from the realm of social movements and politics; to help scour pollution. In an introductory passage to *Fernhurst*, a short, jagged novel written around 1904–5, Stein bursts out about her generation of educated women. They have stripped away the illusions of their immediate predecessors, the heroic women who fought for education. So doing, they have learned that sex equality is a farce. If Stein is explicitly repudiating M. Carey Thomas, she is also implicitly repudiating the younger Stein who celebrated the new woman who would be wife, mother, and economic boon. Instead of identifying herself with the new woman, she now sharply separates herself from her sex in order to assail and herself enter a male world too strong for most women. She writes:

> Had I been bred in the last generation full of hope and unattainable desires I too would have declared that men and women are born equal but being of this generation with the college and professions open to me and able to learn that the other man is really stronger I say I will have none of it. And you shall have none of it says my reader tired of this posing, I don't say no I can only hope that I am one of those rare women that should since I find in my heart that I needs must.

A passage in *The Making of Americans* condenses that shift from some solidarity with women, particularly of her class, to aloofness from nearly all of them. Within two sentences, Stein goes from thinking about women as a sex she knows to thinking about women as a sex that may only be easier to know than men:

> I like to tell it better in a woman the kind of nature a certain kind of men and women have in living, I like to tell about it better in a woman because it is clearer in her and I know it better, a little, not very much better. One can see it in her sooner, a little, not very much sooner, one can see it as simpler.

However, Stein's self-images are more than appropriations of a male identity and masculine interests. Several of them are irrelevant to categories of sex and gender. In part, Stein is an obsessive psychologist, a Euclid of behavior, searching for "bottom natures," the substratum of individuality. She also tries to diagram psychic genotypes, patterns into which all individuals might fit. Although she plays with femaleness/maleness as categories, she also investigates an opposition of impetuousness and passivity, fire and phlegm; a variety of regional and national types; and the dualism of the "independent dependent," who tends to attack, and the "dependent independent," who tends to resist. In part, as she puzzles her way towards knowing and understanding, she presents herself as engaged in aural and oral acts, listening and hearing before speaking and telling. That sense of perception as *physical* also emerges in a passage in which she, as perceiver/describer, first incorporates and then linguistically discharges the world: "Mostly always when I am filled up with it I tell it, sometimes I have to tell it, sometimes I like to tell it, sometimes I keep on with telling it."

If the presentation of self, as person and writer, varies, the dramatization of homosexuality is paradoxical. During the decade of choice, Stein both stopped resisting her sexual impulses and found domestic pleasure in them. However, during the same period, if often before the meeting with Toklas, she takes certain lesbian or quasi-lesbian experiences and progressively disguises and encodes them in a series of books. I would speculate that she does so for several reasons. Some of them are aesthetic: the need to avoid imitating one's self; the desire to transform apprentice materials into richer, more satisfying verbal worlds. Other reasons are psychological: the need to write out hidden impulses; the wish to speak to friends without having others overhear; the desire to evade and to confound strangers, aliens, and enemies.

Whatever the motive, the literary encoding does what Morse Code does: it transmits messages in a different form which initiates may translate back into the original. However, it also distances the representation of homosexuality from its enactment in life. Curiously, the books written under the immediate influence of the May Bookstaver relationship are refreshingly free from *The Well of Loneliness* syndrome: the conviction that lesbianism is a disease, no less sinful for being fatal. Stein finds the will towards domination, ignorance, and corrupt character more immoral than homosexuality. But, during the process of encoding, what were lesbian experiences become, if possible, sadder and sadder. Accompanying this is a subtheme of *Three Lives* and *The Making of Americans*, the pathetic frustrations of women's feelings for each other: Good Anna for her employer, Miss Matilda, a character based on Stein; Good Anna for her "romance," Mrs. Lehntman; Gentle Lena for other servant girls; Melanctha Herbert for Rose Johnson; Mrs. Fanny Hersland for a governess, Madeleine Wyman.

One process of encoding takes place in the shift from *Q.E.D.* to "Melanctha," the second and most complex section of *Three Lives*. Both proven fact and inference suggest that *Q.E.D.* more or less transcribes the Stein/Bookstaver/Haynes history. The figure of Adele is surrogate for Stein; Helen Thomas for May Bookstaver; Mabel Neathe for Mabel Haynes. In *Q.E.D.* the affair between Adele and Helen symbolizes a conflict between the person who believes in control, reason, and middle-class virtues and the person who believes in action, passion, and experience. During its course, Adele abandons easy moral and intellectual formulae and grows into moral and erotic knowledge. The affair ends because the lovers' physical and emotional appeals to each other are not synchronized. As one advances, the other resists or retreats. Mabel, behind a pose of decorum and friendship for Adele, also fights to keep Helen. She is devious, brittle, jealous, and successful. That she has some money and Helen has little helps her. *Q.E.D.*'s last scene shows an isolated Adele, wondering "impatiently" why Helen refuses to "see things as they are . . .": " 'I am afraid it comes very near being a deadlock,' she groaned dropping her head on her arms."

"Melanctha" rewrites the affair between Helen and Adele in a racial context. Helen becomes Melanctha Herbert; Adele, Dr. Jefferson Campbell. Although Stein no longer explores the psychology of the rigid triangle that must break, she has several figures serve as Jeff's rivals: a black woman, Jane Harden (Stein wrote, but did not publish, *Three Lives* under the name of Jane Sands); a black man, Jem Richards; anonymous men, white and black, among whom Melanctha wanders. If the final words of *Q.E.D.* are about Adele, lonely but alive, those of "Melanctha" poignantly show Melanctha lonely and dead: "Melanctha went back to the hospital, and there the Doctor told her she had the consumption, and before long she would surely die. They sent her where she would be taken care of, a home for poor consumptives, and there Melanctha stayed until she died." It might be tempting to suggest that Stein, as she revised her experience, exorcised it through the death of the surrogate of her difficult lover. However, the pattern of *Three Lives* as a whole, which each of the three stories reduplicates, is the movement of life's guiltless, unfortunate victims from a moment of happiness to death.

"Melanctha" does reveal two clear kinds of coding. First, female homosexuality is masculinized. Stein/Adele becomes Jeff. Wish fulfillment or irony, Jeff is the medical doctor Stein refused to become. Next, problematic passion among whites is transferred to blacks, as if they might embody that which the dominant culture feared. The facts that Stein disliked raw racial injustice and that a black author, Richard Wright, praised "Melanctha" itself must be balanced against the fact that racial stereotypes help to print out the narrative. Not only does white blood breed finely-boned blacks, but the primitive darker race, especially in the South, embodies sensuality: ". . . wide abandoned laughter . . . makes the warm broad flow of negro sunshine."

Though Stein did not abandon the dramatic materials of *Q.E.D.*, she ostensibly hid the manuscript. Stein has Toklas artlessly give out the public version of the manuscript's history in *The Autobiography of Alice B. Toklas*, which Stein wrote about thirty years after *Q.E.D.*

> The funny thing about this short novel is that she [Stein] completely forgot about it for many years. She remembered herself beginning a little later writing The Three Lives but this first piece of writing was completely forgotten, she had never mentioned it to me, even when I first knew her. She must have forgotten about it almost immediately. This spring just two days before our leaving for the country she was looking for some manuscript of The Making of Americans that she wanted to show to Bernard Faÿ and she came across these two carefully written volumes of this completely forgotten first novel. She was very bashful and hesitant about it, did not really want to read it. Louis Bromfield was at the house that evening and she handed him the manuscript and said to him, you read it.

Even after the manuscript was "discovered," it was not listed in the 1941 Yale catalogue of Stein's published and unpublished work, with which she helped. Finally, in 1950, under Toklas' copyright, *Q.E.D.* was published by the small Banyan Press as *Things as They Are*. A few textual emendations (for example, Adele's brother becomes her cousin) made the book slightly less autobiographical.

Stein's motives, I believe, were less to suppress public knowledge of her own homosexuality than to protect her private relationship with

Toklas. Toklas was sensitive enough, as late as 1932, to burn Bookstaver's letters to Stein. In 1947, Toklas, in a letter, said about Q.E.D.: "It is a subject I haven't known how to handle nor known from what point to act upon. It was something I knew I'd have to meet some day and not too long hence and to cover my cowardice I kept saying—well when everything else is accomplished." She adds that she would not want Q.E.D. read while she was alive. "Gertrude would have understood this perfectly though of course it was never mentioned." Despite such silences, May Bookstaver retained at least a peripheral relationship with the novel. After five commercial publishers had turned Three Lives down, a vanity press, Grafton, issued it in 1909. Among the people who acted as Stein's agents in the transactions was Bookstaver, who had married Charles Knoblauch in 1906 and who continued for years to serve as a medium between Stein and potential readers.

If the passage from Q.E.D. to "Melanctha" represents one process of encoding, the passage from Fernhurst to the Martha Hersland section of The Making of Americans embodies a second. Like so much of Stein's work, Fernhurst draws on real people and events. The title itself comes from the name of an English town where Stein and her brother spent some of the unhappy summer of 1902. She used a Bryn Mawr College scandal, of which she and her friends were aware. The college president, M. Carey Thomas, had lived with an English professor, Mary Gwinn. In 1904, after several years of intrigue, Gwinn ran away with and married Alfred Hodder, who had come to Bryn Mawr as a married professor of philosophy.

Fernhurst, the name of the women's college in New Jersey in which Stein's fiction is set, encodes M. Carey Thomas as Helen Thornton; Mary Gwinn as Janet Bruce; Alfred Hodder as Phillip Redfern; and Mrs. Hodder as Nancy Talbot Redfern. Helen Thornton has a second friend as well, Miss Wyckoff, who gives the college financial help, a narrative detail that had a Bryn Mawr equivalent. The relationship between Dean Thornton and Miss Bruce has more to do with power, principle, sublimation and habit than erotic love. Stein writes:

> The Dean never suspected in this shy, abstracted, learned creature a desire for sordid life and the common lot. It was not that she did not see the passionate life in this reserved nature but she who knew in herself how abstracted ecstasy could be never once thought that this passionate life could desire a concrete form. She watched her and delighted in her— appreciating her quality as an object and satisfied with her usefulness as a subject.

When the Redferns arrive, he and Miss Bruce complement, attract, and educate each other. When Dean Thornton finally discovers their affair, through overhearing the gleeful gossip of some students, she acts. Bluntly, even crudely, she orders Mrs. Redfern "to keep Mr. Redfern in order." Mrs. Redfern, already isolated from her husband, cannot. The marriage breaks up. As she vainly tries to become worthy of him and waits for him to return, he becomes a "hopeless inextricable mess." Eventually, Dean Thornton retains Miss Bruce. The last paragraph of *Fernhurst* has a little of the bleak misery of a James novel in which the powerful possess the powerless, in which the mediation of love seems remote:

> Patiently and quietly the dean worked it out and before many years she had regained all property rights in this shy learned creature. . . . Fernhurst was itself again and the two very interesting personalities in the place were the dean Miss Thornton with her friend Miss Bruce in their very same place.

Although *Fernhurst* goes into the *The Making of Americans* with many passages intact, Stein does some trivial changing: Dean Helen Thornton becomes Dean Hannah Charles; Janet Bruce, Cora Dounor, a more exotic name; Nancy Talbot Redfern, Martha Hersland Redfern; Fernhurst College, Farnham College. Phillip Redfern, though he keeps his name, may take on some of the features of Leon Solomons, Stein's mentor, collaborator, and friend at Harvard, who had died as a young man. More important for the tracing of codes, Stein also alters *Fernhurst* in significant ways. Martha Hersland is a far richer figure than Nancy Talbot. Indeed, she embodies many of Stein's own experiences, especially as a child. Stein now projects herself as a worthy, if narrow, woman, who becomes a rejected wife. Moreover, in *The Making of Americans*, after the two couples collide and shatter each other, their four individual members remain alone: Dean Hannah Charles to administer her college; Dora Dounor to disappear; Phillip Redfern to die; and Martha Hersland Redfern to study, to become a feminist, and eventually, to return to her father. In *Fernhurst*, no matter how ambiguously, two women remain together. Now, neither two women nor a man and a woman do. Stein dissolves, into sorrow and loss, any anomalous sexuality, be it quasi-homosexual or adulterous.

Not all of Stein's writing about anomalous or "unclean" sex during the decade of choice is unhappy. In 1908 she began to experiment with her "portrait" form. Among the first was "Ada." Lovely and loving, it apparently pictures the coming together of Toklas ("Ada") and Stein ("Someone" or "this one"). Ada, after a flurry of tender letters, leaves her father. She comes "to be happier than anybody else who was living then. . . . Trembling was all living, living was all loving, some one was then the other one." "Ada" symbolizes the beginning of a new writing about sexuality that can be more joyous and erotic in mood, domestic in setting, and modern in linguistic style. Nevertheless, "Ada" exists in a context in which unconventional private acts, subject to social judgment of differing degrees of severity and contempt, emerge in literary artifacts that display conventional moral and narrative patterns. Throughout her career, Stein continued to be generally reluctant to write about sexuality in obviously open forms. The job of rendering her forms accessible, like the larger task of clarifying the totality of her achievement, remains unfinished.

In general, the consequences of the feminization of the mind/body problem were mixed. On the one hand, it became less anomalous, less peculiar, for women to assume the role of professional writer, artist, or intellectual. On the other hand, the mere assumption of the role entailed living through certain pressures and stresses. Their form varied. For example, it demanded greater rebellious energy for a woman such as Kate Chopin to describe sex in a culture in which femininity signified a defense against nastiness and animal vulgarity than in a culture in which that linkage was less pervasive. Ironically, the fact that Woman has also symbolized nature/the body/the flesh/sexuality was of little or no help to real women. Not only did many of them feel that the symbol was imposed upon them, but their very writing itself defied a dictate of the symbol: that Woman was nothing but nature/the body/the flesh/sexuality.

Whatever the precise configuration of tensions, they affected both private experience and the presentation of work to public scrutiny. If a woman was living with another woman as a domestic precondition for writing, as Stein was, the risk of being labelled a pollutant might hamper the authentic revelation of experience. If a woman was living with a man, though often in complex ways, as Woolf was, the conflict between the desires of the mind and the demands of the body, be that conflict conscious or unconscious, might inhibit the transformation of physicality into any public speech other than letters or gossip. Asymmetries between the mind (or spirit) and the body can provide rich subject matter. It has certainly given Christians a literary field day. However, for modern women, the possibilities for the public exercise of consciousness were still fresh enough to breed anxiety, the nervousness of the historical novelty. The texts such women generated were often coded rather than open; sublimated rather than straightforward; hazy with metaphors and silence rather than lucid. Women are now far more exuberantly expressive. Such a capacity is the result of many forces, among them the struggle of the women who first exemplified the feminization of the mind/body problem. They left for contemporary women the consolation that it could be endured, even transcended, and, if inadvertently, a warning of the penalties of one sort of solution.

Scholarly investigations have a life of their own. Propelled by their own inertia, they may not stop until they have met, not the boundaries of their subject, but the needs of the spies, explorers, critics, and cataloguers who have begun them. So it may be with our interest in the ways in which writers, among them Stein, have used language to consume the body and sexuality. In 1947, Alice B. Toklas, though perhaps for reasons of her own, warned against placing too much emphasis on sexuality in the interpretation of Stein's work. She wrote to a correspondent:

> You will understand I hope my objection to your repeated references to the subject of sexuality as an approach to the understanding of Gertrude's work. She would have emphatically denied it—she considered it the least characteristic of all expressions of character—her actual references to sexuality are so rare. . . . Gertrude always said she did not like private judgments.

One must wonder if future scholars will not ask about us, "Why were they so interested in sexuality? What did the fascination with sexuality itself encode, disguise, and hide? For what was sexuality their metaphor?"

WILLIAM H. GASS

Gertrude Stein and the Geography of the Sentence: "Tender Buttons"

Buttons fasten, and because tender buttons are the buttons we unbutton and press, touch and caress to make love, we can readily see why they fasten. These extraordinary pieces of prose, which Gertrude perversely called poems, do much more than simply resemble the buttons she liked to collect and sort, though they are indeed verbal objects, and their theoretical affinity with the paintings of advanced cubism is profound. Like many of the canvases of Cézanne, Matisse, and Braque, each piece is a domestic still. They employ many of the methods of collage, too, as well as those of Dada disassociation.

Thematically, they are composed of the implements, activities, colors and pleasures of home life, its quiet dangers, its unassertive thrills: cooking, cleaning, eating, loving, visiting, entertaining, and it is upon this base that the embossing of these buttons takes place. Plates are broken, pots and tables polished, meat sliced, food chopped, objects are repaired, arranged, contained. The highest metaphysical categories of sameness and difference, permanence and change, are invoked, as are the concerns of epistemology, of clarity and obscurity, certainty and doubt.

Like a cafeteria tray, *Tender Buttons* has three sorting sections (Objects, Food, Rooms), but it is also built with three floors, so that its true shape is a cube. Objects are things external to us, which we perceive,

From *The World Within the Word.* Copyright © 1976 by William H. Gass. Nonpareil Books.

manipulate, and confront. Next are the things which nourish us, which we take into ourselves: information, feeling, food. Finally, there are things which enclose us as our body does our consciousness, like a lover's arms, or as people are embraced by rooms. If the X-axis is divided as I've described, the Y-axis is marked off into Work, or household chores, Love, or the complicated emotional exchanges between those who spend their daily life together, and Art, or in this case, the composition of odd, brilliant, foolish, accidental, self-conscious, beautiful, confused, or whimsical sentences.

For example, clinging to objects and dulling their glitter is *dirt.* . . . That is, objects are either clean, so that they shine and glitter, gleam and dazzle, or like the tarnish on copper pots, the grayness of dusty glass, the dinginess of soiled pillows, they are dull and dirty, as our lives become when we are left unloved and unemployed.

Throughout, the crucial word is *change.* Some processes, like cleaning and mending, are basically restorative. They remove the present in order to return to and conserve the past. Others, like sewing, decorating, and cooking, principally through operations which alter *quantity* (by shaping, enlarging, reducing, juxtaposing, mingling, and so on), create *qualities* which have not previously existed. Many times these qualities are positive, but naturally not always. In the human sphere, to which these activities are precisely proportional, similar consequences occur. Finally, both these areas are metaphorically measured against the art of writing and found to be structurally the same. Words can be moved about like furniture in their sentences; they can be diced like carrots (Stein cuts up a good number); they can be used in several different ways simultaneously, like wine; they can be brushed off, cleaned and polished; they can be ingeniously joined, like groom and bed, anxiety and bride. Every sentence is a syntactical space (a room) in which words (things, people) act (cook, clean, eat, or excrete) in order to produce quite special and very valuable qualities of feeling. Cleaning a room can be a loving or a vengeful act, a spontaneous tidying, mere routine, or a carefully planned Spring Scrub, and one's engagement to the task can be largely mindless or intensely meant. Similarly, not a few of these buttons are as accidental as kicked stones (my typewriter writes "spoiled cushions" instead of "soiled" and I wonder whether I shouldn't leave the phrase that way), others are painfully self-conscious and referential, as planned as a political coup, while a few seem wholly momentary whims whose consequences have been self-indulgently allowed to stand.

Although the "poems" do not avoid nouns, as their author suggests she was trying to do, and have nice tasty titles ("SINGLE FISH," "SAUSAGE,"

"CELERY," "VEAL"), they avoid naming. Picasso's hermetic *The Clarinet Player,* for instance, painted during the same period *Tender Buttons* was being composed, offers no comment, visual or otherwise, on clarinet playing, players, or the skill of playing. After the motif has been analyzed into its plastic elements, these are modified and recombined according to entirely abstract schemes in which colors and forms predominate and respond solely to one another. The world is a source of suggestions, nothing more, and every successful work supersedes its model and renders the world superfluous to it.

Yet we are already in a tangle of terminology, because Gertrude Stein was always doing "descriptions," and she furthermore felt that naming was the special function of the poet. *Tender Buttons* is, she insists, a book of poems; poems are based, she claims, on the noun; and tender buttons are portraits, as she puts it, not of living people like Mabel Dodge and Sherwood Anderson, but of ordinary objects and common processes and simple spaces. Naming and not naming, describing and not describing, subject or sign: can we straighten this out?

In the first place, nouns are full of remembrance since they represent collections of past experience, and although it may seem reasonable to encounter the present well-padded by the past, this tends to give to every meeting of bell and clapper the same dull clonk: ah, there you are again, Socrates. We cease to listen, cease to see. So we must rid ourselves of the old titles and properties, recover a tutored innocence, and then, fresh as a new-scrubbed Adam, reword the world.

> I began to wonder at at about this time just what one saw when one looked at anything really looked at anything. Did one see sound, and what was the relation between color and sound, did it make itself by description by a word that meant it or did it make itself by a word in itself . . .
>
> I became more and more excited about how words which were the words that made whatever I looked at look like itself were not the words that had in them any quality of description. This excited me very much at that time.
>
> ("*Portraits and Repetition*")

When she did her portraits, Gertrude Stein spent a great deal of her time listening, because each of her subjects was, as we all are, a talking machine, and of course what she listened to was in part a response to herself, to her talking. Now she wanted to stress seeing, because, of course, though frying pans speak and one might mutter to one's knitting, objects mainly spangled space with color and reflection.

We have bought a poodle. What shall we name it? We can, of course, confer upon it a name we idly like, and force it to conform, or we can study the beast until it says "Basket." Yet the poet seeks the names of things because she loves the names. Al-ci-bi-a-des, we call out. Ai-e. Ai-e. Alcibiades.

> . . . you can love a name and if you love a name then saying that name any number of times only makes you love it more, more violently more persistently more tormentedly.
>
> *("Poetry and Grammar")*

To denoun and undenote, then to rename, and finally to praise the old world's raising of the new word out of the monitoring mind:

> Poetry is concerned with using with abusing, with losing with wanting, with denying with avoiding with adoring with replacing the noun. It is doing that always doing that, doing that and doing nothing but that. Poetry is doing nothing but using losing refusing and pleasing and betraying and caressing nouns.
>
> *("Poetry and Grammar")*

Suppose then that I have a carafe of wine in front of me. My aim is to peel language from it like a label, and I shall then allow these words, put in attractive proximity, to draw other senses, sounds, and sentiments, from one another. A CARAFE, THAT IS A BLIND GLASS is the name of the first Object (if these titles indeed are names), and we observe at once (1) that, although the Object is an occasion for these words, it is the author who accounts for their singular character; and (2) that the heading possesses a maliciously ambiguous structure. The single comma is a kind of curiosity, and only one will appear in the first sentence of text which lies beneath it. Shall we read: "A carafe, that is to say, a blind glass," as if we were being given a definition; or shall we think of it as a carafe which happens to be a blind glass, in which case its blindness is not defining; or is it an exclamation, and should we come down hard as a hammer on 'that': "A carafe, wow, is *that* a blind glass!"? Obviously the order runs from exclamation back through accident to necessity like a wound which leaves a scar.

The rest of the button is finished off as follows:

> A kind glass and a cousin, a spectacle and nothing strange a single hurt color and an arrangement in a system to pointing. All this and not ordinary, not unordered in not resembling. The difference is spreading.

Not every decanter is made of glass, but this is one of the glass kind. (The word 'kind' will reappear.) Its opaqueness makes it a cousin to the clear. Blind people wear dark glasses because they do not desire us to see they cannot see and be disconcerted by rolling pupils or the glaze of a sightless eye. Thus this glass is not made for seeing but for being seen: it is not a pair of spectacles but a spectacle. A spectacle is normally something grand and extraordinary, however here there is nothing unusual, nothing strange.

A bruise varies in color from purple through pale green and yellow, and as it ages, fades. I cannot say directly which of these colors the glass is, but each hue is one which wine has: apple clear or straw or ruddy. The blind person's tinted glasses signify a hurt too, and it is of course an irony when glasses are used to say that someone cannot see. Everything in a carafe flows up the neck like a pointing finger or a fountain. As we shall see. Words, as well, appear to point or fountain. Though these poems do not point, they have one. As asparagus.

Now I (the poet, the perceiver, the namer, the praiser) reflect: not upon the Object but upon the pattern I've made of my words and how they space themselves, for their space is inside them, not openly disposed upon the page as poetry normally is. I notice that my verbal combinations are, on that account, unusual (I shall brag about it), and that, although they resemble nothing else which passes for poetry, they are nevertheless not without their own system and order . . . these sentences which form tri-angles, crowds, or squares, go verbless as one goes naked, or which wind around Being like a fateful spindle.

A kind   in glass   and a cousin,
a spectacle   and nothing strange
a single hurt color   and an arrangement

          in a system

                    to pointing.

Gloss 1: These poems are like a wine-colored glass carafe. Their most common shape is that of a truncated hour-glass (an anticipatory interpretation).
Gloss 2: The carafe is like a blind person's glasses.

So these poems are opaque containers. They have been made to fasten us through pleasure together, as indeed wine does . . . and most household objects and the acts which center on them: pots, pans, pillows, cooking, cleaning, love. The difference between these buttons and other swatches of language is going to deepen, she says, and there are going to be more and more of them, not only because the book will pour them out on us, but because the principles of their composition will be widely imitated.

The next button, GLAZED GLITTER, continues the theme of change with a first line which is immediately followed by a commentary:

Nickel, what is nickel, it is originally rid of a cover.

The change in that is that red weakens an hour. The change has come. There is no search. But there is, there is that hope and that interpretation and sometime, surely any is unwelcome, sometime there is breath and there will be a sinecure and charming very charming is that clean and cleansing. Certainly glittering is handsome and convincing.

Let us attempt to answer that initial question. Responses rise like hungry fish. Many household utensils are nickel-plated because the metal they're made of may wear, rust, redden, or otherwise become unwholesome to use. Nickel is naturally shiny and easy to maintain (i.e., is a benefit without labor, a sinecure). Nickel has, in short, an impermeable surface, a glaze, which has a glitter.

But had the question been: nickels, what are nickels? we might have replied: small change.

However, if we listen intently, we shall hear inside the word two others of woeful association: 'Nick,' the name of the Devil himself, and 'Hell,' his hot location. Our license for following this procedure is, first, that Gertrude Stein regularly requests us to find other words within her words in exactly this way; second, that a little research into the history of the term tells us that the original nickel was a German coin called *Kupfernickel* because, although it was a copper color, it yielded none of the metal, and for this deceit, like fool's gold, was accused of being the devil's ore; and third, that the lines which immediately follow, as well as all of the remaining poems, require it.

Snuffling at roots gives us another method for finding words in words, as well as another fundamental sense of what a tender button is: a swollen, underground stem or bud, a truffle. That is, these poems are buds based on hidden roots. The fourth poem, A BOX, is explicit about this.

She often permits 'this,' 'there,' 'they,' and 'it' to float free of any single reference because she wants so many. These terms are like holes in buttons through which the threads pass. And in the opening line that bewildering 'it' stands for all original nakedness and exposure. Stainless steel souls, one imagines, need no cleansing, no catharsis, no cover. They are the ultimate solution to the problem of sin. . . .

Having lost our innocence and put on knowledge with our leaf, we had to earn our keep, labor, sleep, and learn to wash. Like Alcibiades to the cloak of Socrates, cleanliness crept next to Godliness and made itself beloved by health and hospitals equally. Coverings grew grand and hid our weaknesses. We covered sculpture's plaster glands, legs of pianos, tables too, and all our thoughts with discretions. These poems are themselves excessively discreet.

To red up is to rid oneself of whatever is extraneous and out of place (a small change, 'e' for 'i'), and the uppermost meaning here is how the work of tidying tires out both time and ourselves. Still we cannot forget that red is the past tense of reading, the color of blood and wine, of Jezebels, the suit of Satan, and the cent it takes five to make a nickel of. And any reader who observes Stein's sly small small-change in this passage (to mention but one of so many), must begin to be of different mind about her alleged subconscious methods of composition.

We hope of course that one day we shall be able to take it easy, draw an idle breath, purify ourselves the way we polish hardware and pots, clear tables, or better yet, cure sin, and cook without dirtying a dish. Cleaning, like confession, is a rite, and the spells it casts are effective, because a tidy house does seem for a time to be invulnerable.

There is no gratitude in mercy and in medicine. There can be breakages in Japanese. That is no programme. That is no color chosen. It was chosen yesterday, that showed spitting and perhaps washing and polishing. It certainly showed no obligation and perhaps if borrowing is not natural there is some use in giving.

The medical theme (one thread: hurt-spreading-rid-red-weakens-hope-interpretation (diagnosis)-breath-cure-clean and cleansing) is joined by the sacramental (another thread: "wine"-"Satan"-"the Fall"-hope-interpretation (hermeneutics)-breath-sinecure-cleansing) to become momentarily dominant. We do not receive mercy from God because He is grateful to us, nor does the physician feel he is discharging a debt.

"The change has come." If the change has come (unlike the coming of the Kingdom, to be sure, but love has been made with Alice for some time, and Leo has been replaced), it has come without our fumbling for it (reds, nickels, dimes, quarters, halves). One may borrow a nickel (after all, what is a nickel?) without any obligation to repay. Actually one rarely asks for the loan of such a small sum, and indeed a nickel is easy to give away. Later one learns how these little daily things add up, for a dollar contains ten dimes the way loving is made of lots of light caresses. . . .

GLAZED GLITTER is a "poem" with a subject: roughly, the price of change and restoration, repairs and healing, the charm of coming clean.

A SUBSTANCE IN A CUSHION

The change of color is likely and a difference a very little difference is prepared. Sugar is not a vegetable.

Callous is something that hardening leaves behind what will be soft if there is a genuine interest in there being present as many girls as men. Does this change. It shows that dirt is clean when there is a volume.

I have quoted only two of this important section's ten paragraphs, yet these, and the two poems already so cursorily examined, make the fundamental moral and metaphysical issues apparent: the contrast between surface and depth, for example, the relation between quantity and quality, permanence and change, innocence and knowledge, giving and receiving, art and life, in and out.

Sugar cane, of course, is a vegetable, a grass, but the process of refining it transforms the juice of the stalk. Sugar is often a surface addition, as on cereal; it sweetens our coffee, for which we may be grateful; it enhances, but it does not nourish.

Again: if we multiply dust until it becomes earth, it is no longer dirt, and so long as Gertrude lived with her brother there was no suspicion, but when Alice moved in to form, in effect, a *ménage à trois*, or after Leo left, the whispering began. One must become hardened.

So sometimes work, sometimes writing, sometimes love, are uppermost; sometimes one metaphorical carrier (cooking, cleaning) rises above another; key words are obsessively repeated, not only in particular paragraphs, but throughout; sometimes the sentences look over their shoulders at where they've been, and we are not always prepared for the shifts.

Although the text is, I think, overclued, the language plain, and the syntax so Spartan as to be peculiar, naked as a Dukhobor whose cause we cannot yet comprehend; nevertheless, the "total altogether of it" remains cryptic, and we are likely to feel that our interpretations are forced unless they are confirmed by readings from another direction. Some knowledge of Gertrude Stein's daily life and obsessive concerns is essential, as well as familiarity with the usual associations she makes among words, and the in-common subjects of her works. Then, not only must we fasten ourselves to Webster, as Empson chained himself to the OED, and avail ourselves of slang dictionaries too, we must go to Skeat or Partridge as eagerly as a cat for cover on a cool day.

Thus this is certainly not an airtight text. It leaks. But where? and why should we care? It will not tell us what day the bridge is to be bombed, the safe rifled, or buck passed. We must set to work without reward or hope of any, and submit ourselves to the boredom of an etymological narrative.

A BOX

Out of kindness comes redness and out of rudeness comes rapid same question, out of an eye comes research, out of selection comes painful cattle. So then the order is that a white way of being round is something suggesting a pin and is it disappointing, it is not, it is so rudimentary to be analysed and see a fine substance strangely, it is so earnest to have a green point not to red but to point again.

A box protects and conceals. It is frequently wrapped and tied. It is usually of wood or paper. Ribbons are found on it. A box contains surprises. Gifts. Pandora had one. Although a box is something one can get caught in, it is also something one can get out of. A jack is often in a box. A word is a box out of which we can draw other words. A woman has a box into which penises are put and from which babies are taken. To have such a box in our world, certainly in Stein's, is to be in a box (*hemmed* in). And so the passage assumes the structure of a series of Biblical begettings. Or are we listening to a recital of the pedigrees of prize stock? Etymology affirms everything at once, for the root of 'box' is tree (the boxwood). A FAMILY TREE. THE TREE OF KNOWLEDGE.

The *manifest* text invokes two *covert*, or, in Stein's terms, covered, colored, or red, texts: a main one, the Old Testament tale of Adam and Eve, which establishes the linear order of ideas in advance of any other expression which may be placed on top of it, and whose verbal character is relatively *fixed*; and a second, subordinate one—the story of Pandora and the box of Prometheus—which is not fastened to any single formulation, and so *floats*. The *alignment* of the two covert texts is parallel, and the *relationship* between them is one of structural identity, thus the *function* of the secondary tale is to interpret and heighten and universalize the first. God makes Adam out of clay, for instance. Zeus shapes Pandora out of the same substance. Both are seen as vessels into which the breath of life is blown, and thereafter they hold that life like a liquid: wine or water. Clearly the two texts are accompanied by sets of traditional *interpretations*. For example, it is often supposed that Adam took a carnal interest in Eve only after the Fall. Both tales are anti-feminist tracts. Both involve disobedience to the chief. Both are about revenge. Both explain why mankind must live in sorrow and die in delusion. And both invoke male saviors.

The principal covert text manifests itself immediately in two ways: through a *key* word or phrase—in this case, 'box'—and by means of a *mirrored* rhetorical *form*, the Biblical begats. The key in the latter case, of course, is the phrase 'out of.' Even more darkly mirrored, with a parallel alignment and the same key, is the form of the livestock pedigree. Eventually the proportion: as men are to the Lord, so are women to men, and cattle to their owners, will control our understanding of the argument. Both forms, because of their associations, contribute substantially to the meaning of the passage. They are, that is, *significant forms*.

The manifest text contains a *coded commentary* on the covert texts. Each word must be regarded as standing for many others, the title A BOX referring to a blow as well as a container. Not only is *Tender Buttons* a *polytype* text, it is frequently *polytokenal* too (see the formation of 'kindred' in the first line). There is evidently a *metatextual metaphor* operating here. The paragraph before us is a box containing words which are also regarded as boxes. In short, the passage does not describe some object which the title designates as much as the title describes the passage. *Tender Buttons*, itself, is a metatextual metaphor.

The meanings we discover when we open these boxes are, like the covert texts, both floating and fixed; that is, certain associations are general: with the 'red' which comes out of 'kindness' we may connect a blush of pleasure, but we are not confined to exactly these words, as we shall not be to 'shame' and 'embarrassment' later. However, when we extract roots, such as 'recircle' from 'research,' we are. These meanings have no serial order. They are *clustered* like grapes, and the way they are eventually fitted together depends not upon the order of words in the manifest text, but upon the way each illuminates various aspects of the covert text. At first we may want to think of 'kindness' as kindness, but it is difficult to continue in that vein. Digging down we find a few roots. We might favor 'inborn' first, but 'kind' seen as 'nature' snaps into '-ness' understood as 'state,' with a satisfying certitude. We must not abandon 'kindness' as kindness, though, because it is in fact the complaisance of the woman which leads to sin and kinning; but the incorporation of this surface sense into the total interpretation of the passage has to come later, after most of the ground floor has been built. Thus there is no preestablished order. We must wait until a place to fasten the meaning to the emerging sense can be found.

Except for the fact that the manifest text hides Adam and Eve like a leaf, the text is not *layered*. Certain themes or threads can be continuously followed, but sometimes one will be more obvious or dominant than another, so it is more accurate to describe the text as *woven*. Since the text often looks at itself, it is *reflexive*, and since meanings which emerge rather late in the manifest text must often be sent back to the beginning like unlucky players, the *presentation of meaning is spatial*, not temporal the way, for example, 'John hit Jack' is temporal. It is temporal, that is, until we decide that 'John' is Jack and 'Jack' John. Then the sentence spatializes, swinging back and forth. . . .

The entire passage is held together by underlying meanings which are greatly akin and often simply repeat one another—a familiar characteristic of Stein's manifest texts—and the passage is pushed forward as much by the progressive disclosure of these deep meanings as by ordinary linear onset. There is a cluster around what might be called the idea of an early state; there's one around gestation, blood, and pain, as well as punishment and judgment; there's still another around resistance, repetition, and property. There is finally a solution expressed in the dimmest imagery of all: the target with its black bull's-eye.

I recall particularly that Zeus, desiring to punish Prometheus for stealing fire from the gods and giving it to man, fashioned a beautiful woman out of clay, clothing her like a queen and, with the help of the Four Winds, breathing life into her according to the customary recipe. This done, he sent his glittering clay creature to the brother of Prometheus as a gift, but Epimetheus, warned not to accept any favors from Zeus (as though to "beware of gods bearing gifts"), politely refused her until Zeus frightened him by chaining his disobedient brother to a pillar high in the mountains where a vulture ate by day the liver which grew heedlessly back by night (just as waking life was to be ruinous for us ever afterward). Pandora, of course, capricious and willful and curious, opened the box in which Prometheus had bottled all the evils which might beset man, among them delusive hope whose sting keeps us from suicide and still alive to suffer the bites of the others.

Similarly, Satan ('red'), speaking through a serpent and by tradition from a tree ('box'), tempts Eve in Paradise ('kindness') to pick ('selection') and eat the apple ('box,' 'red'). A whole set of derivations indicates that we should interpret this act as a case of praiseworthy resistance. (No time is wasted on Adam.) *Kindness is thus reduced to rudeness.* God soon ('rapid') seeks out ('research') the impure pair ('rudeness') and holds an official investigation ('question'). He finds that their eyes ('eye') are now open; they see ('research') that they are naked, and are consequently full of shame ('red'). His judgment ('question') is that Eve shall belong to her husband like a chattel and bear her children ('kindred') henceforward in pain and labor ('painful cattle'). At the point of the first full stop, there is a definite break in the text. In order to go on, we must go back.

And who are "we" at this point? Not even Gertrude would have read this far.

Without the myths of Eve and Pandora I should have no sounding board, no principle of selection, nothing to paste my conjectures to, however remarkably I imagined them. So far what have I been made to do? I have been required to put roots and shoots and little stems and tendrils together much as their author did, to wander discouraged and confused as Hansel and Gretel through a dark wood of witches, to strike the hot right way suddenly, but just as suddenly to mire, to drag, to speed, to shout Urreek! to fall asleep, to submit to revelations, certainly to curl a lip, to doubt, unnose a disdainful snort, snick a superior snicker, curse, and then at some point not very pleasantly to realize that the game I'm playing is the game of creation itself, because *Tender Buttons* is above all a book of kits like those from which harpsichords or paper planes or model bottle boats are fashioned, with intricacy no objection, patience a demand, unreadable plans a pleasure. So I am pulling a poem out of this BOX. The words on the page do not contain it, but their conundrum does.

Adam and Eve now beget children who, though innocent infants for a time ('rudeness') have the same in-born impulses ('kindness'), so that shortly ('rapid') they manifest the same lusts and suffer the same punishment as their parents ('rapid same question'). The cycle ('research') of generation ('kindness') is viciously continuous ('redness'), and soon ('rapid') women are being picked ('selection') as Eve once was ('eye'), and bred ('rapid') like cattle.

So God's command ('order') is that the common way ('round,' 'way') is a repetition ('round') of that first fornication and painful multiplication ('something suggesting a pin'). There is, in effect, a second break in the argument here, so with a little help from the final lines I shall loop back over these still unclear combinations. The Virgin Mother was spared both sin and pain, shame and copulation. Her child was engendered by the prick of light from a star (see the section, A WAIST). While gloomily researching 'point' (whose 'disappoint' deprives the 'pin' of its pain), I come upon the phrase *'de pointe en blanc'* (from a point in the white of a target), and everything rattles into place like iron gates. But will it rattle for you unless you labor? Something fired point blank is fired from the outer white toward the bull's-eye; that is, from a point so close that an arrow needs no compensatory arc in its travel to the target. Its path ('way') is straight (as a pin). So the chaste way of becoming pregnant is through that gleaming straight arrow of light from a star, while the common way requires mating with a bull.

The consequences of our investigation of this basic and traditional myth, reducing it to small rubblelike bits ('rudimentary'), the paragraph goes on to say, is not disappointing because it shows how the penis may be removed ('disappointing'), and how the woman's struggle ('substance,' 'earnest,' and so on) to escape male domination ('analysis') can be won ('fine'). She ('a green') must turn not to her complementary, the male ('red'), but to his opposite, her own sex ('to the point again').

In sum, A BOX is an ironic argument (the jest in 'suggesting') for lesbianism on the ground that such sexual practices preserve virginity, avoid God's punishment, and do not perpetuate original sin.

Now that A BOX has been broken down, we can look back at the CARAFE, THAT IS A BLIND GLASS, with eyes from which the scales have fallen. Fitzgerald's Omar, among others, testifies to the commonness of the metaphor which, on Old Testament authority, pictures man as a clay vessel containing a gaseous spirit or liquidy soul.

> Why, if the Soul can fling the Dust aside,
> And naked on the Air of Heaven ride,
> Wer't not a Shame—wer't not a Shame for him
> In this clay carcase crippled to abide?
>
> (XLIV)

Mankind, before eating from the tree, was a blind glass, a carafe (an object and a word of Spanish and Arabic origin). Women were also a "kind," in-born, cousin to man, taken out of his side by caesarean; thus neither sex was a stranger to the other, and both were designed from the first for copulation. Nevertheless, as time passes and people disperse and multiply, the differences between men and women aggravate and widen.

The techniques at work here do more than allow Gertrude Stein to disguise her drift. They permit a simply astonishing condensation. The word 'difference' alone contains *to carry apart, delay, disperse, to bear (as fruit)*. And this inner economy facilitates the interweaving of contradictory strands of meaning within a single sentence.

When we try to grasp the significance of these truly peculiar pieces, it helps to remember that their composition was stimulated by a trip Gertrude and Alice made to Spain in 1912; that Robert W. Service brought out *Rhymes of a Rolling Stone* the same year; that Gertrude's household was breaking up and her affections had been rearranged; that not a line of Joyce or Eliot had appeared, though there'd been some Pound and a little of the greater Yeats; that Havelock Ellis had been arguing for the equality of women with great reasonableness and little effect, though the suffragettes were out in strength; that Rilke's thing-poems, in print, quite miraculous, quite beautiful, quite other, were in effect as invisible as the spirit of the vagina'd Spanish saints, although everywhere both writers saw sanctity's black battledress and the southern region's austere landscape redolent with renunciation like a vine; that in fifteen years *The Well of Loneliness*, genteel, inept, and as unlibidinous as beets, will still cause a scandal; that the Dadaists haven't uttered their first da yet, let alone their second; that a play can be driven from the boards because it shows one woman giving another a bunch of violets, and that when Colette kissed Missy on the mouth in one such there was a howl of rage; that in those Andalusian towns where Jewish, Muslim, and Catholic cultures came together with a crash, their ignorant collision created buildings—rather than rubble—whose elastic functions, dubious faith, and confusing beauty, were nearly proofs, even to a Jew, of a triune god; that people in the United States are really reading Rex Beach or James Oliver Curwood; and that only Apollinaire might have preceded her in her aims, a few methods, and some effects.

Words, of course, were tender buttons, to be sorted and played with, admired and arranged, and she felt that language in English literature had become increasingly stiff and resistant, and that words had to be pried out of their formulas, freed, and allowed to regain their former Elizabethan fluidity, but it is now evident, I think, that she had other motives, indeed the same ones which had driven her into writing in the first place: the search for and discovery of Gertrude Stein, and the recording of her daily life, her thoughts, her passions.

One does not need to speak in code of Adam and Eve, though if you are going to take Eve's side against the serpent, God, and Adam—all—you had better begin to dip your tongue in honey; but what about the pleasures of cunnilingus or the dildo, of what she was later, as she grew more frank, to call "lifting belly"? Even Natalie Barney was less bold in print than in the dalliance and dance and undress of her notorious salons. And Gertrude had Alice to contend with, a reader who was not as eager as she was to see their intimacies in print, and who could coldly withhold her favors if she chose.

> This must not be put in a book.
> Why not.
> Because it mustn't.
> Yes sir.
>
> ("Bonne Annee,"
> in *Geography and Plays*)

She might have to disguise it, but she was damn well going to write about it: "Suppose a collapse in rubbed purr, in rubbed purr get," for instance, a line which explodes, upon the gentlest inspection, into a dozen sexual pieces. There is 'suppose,' which means *to place under,* followed by the neck and lap of 'collapse,' which contains the French 'col,' of course (the next line begins, "Little sales ladies . . ." a phrase I construe as "little dirty girls"). 'Collapse' also yields the root, *to fall* (sin) *together,* immediately after which we must deal with 'rub,' 'purr,' 'get in bed,' 'rub her,' 'rubber,' and Gertrude's pet name for Alice, which was Pussy.

Here is the third to last button in the box labeled Objects:

PEELED PENCIL, CHOKE
Rub her coke.

Remember those paper pencils you sharpened by peeling? Don't Jews do the same to the penis? Oral sex with such will make you choke. Certainly the writing instrument is one of Stein's household gods, as Penates are, gods of our most interior and secret parts. It's what we reach when we peel off the leaves of an artichoke: the hairy center. But isn't this a joke? The pencil has an eraser and a graphite core. A woman's core is her clitoris, which one rubs to please her. With what? a rubber cock. It *is* a joke.

Let's push the culminating button and see what buzzes.

THIS IS THIS DRESS, AIDER
Aider, why aider why whow, whow stop touch, aider whow, aider stop the muncher, muncher munchers.
A jack in kill her, a jack in, makes a meadowed king, makes a to let.

This poem contrasts male and female love-making. There is disgust for the former, joy in the latter. The word 'aider' is not only a sound shadow for *aid her* and a muffled form of 'Ada,' one of Gertrude's code names for Alice, it is also the original Old French root, meaning *to give pleasure to.* I have already claimed that we must read the title as THIS IS DISTRESS, AID HER, but the distress is partly explained by the twice-hidden 'his,' by the fact that 'distress,' itself, gives us 'strain,' which immediately yields 'stretch,' as in the various expansions consequent to begetting. 'Dress,' in turn, has its roots in the Latin *directus* and the French *drecier,* and these extend toward 'make straight,' or 'put in proper position,' 'prick up.' Hence, we have (1) Ada, help me take off this dress (dis·dress), and give me pleasure, for I am in sexual need, and (2) it is his doing, this stress and strain of begetting, save her from him. In short, Gertrude is to save Alice from men, while Alice is to save Gertrude from sexual want. In this passage, the square-off of male vs. female, and the balance of pleasure and pain with rescue and reward, is perfect.

Stein now imitates, perhaps too predictably, the stop/don't stop alternation of sexual excitement, but this allows her, at the same time, to render the resistance of the female and the painfulness of male penetration.

(1) Ada, why what are you doing? wow, how, wow, stop, oh touch, Ada, wow, Ada stop . . . and Ada, of course, is grazing, a cunnilingual metaphor.
     (2) Help, help, ow, ow stop ouch, help, ow, stop the muncher . . .
     (3) Aid her. Why aid her? how to stop the touching and help her,
how?

The relation of 'how' and 'cow' (hence 'munch' and 'meadowed king') is not infrequent in Gertrude Stein. "A Sonatina" (written in 1921) is only one poem which makes the connection explicit:

A fig an apple and some grapes makes a cow. How. The Caesars know how. Now.

A similar ambivalence governs the construction of the final sentence. Shadowing 'A jack in kill her' are at least three other Jacks: Jack the Giant Killer, Jack and Jill, and Jack in the Box. Jack is normally any male, a knave, a jakes or john, and a penis, both real and artificial, while 'a jack in' imitates the pump and rock of sexual stimulation. The dildo imagery, which some readers may wish to resist, becomes increasingly explicit. For instance, in "A Sonatina" again:

Do you remember that a pump can pump other things than water . . .
Yes tenderness grows and it grows where it grows. And do you like it.
Yes you do. And does it fill a cow full of filling. Yes. And where does it
come out of. It comes out of the way of the Caesars.

So: (1) if a man gets hold of her, he can kill her as a consequence of rape or pregnancy, to say nothing of the pain, the shame and humiliation. When Jack and Jill go up the hill together, Jack falls down and breaks his crown, but Jill comes tumbling after. Men merely rent the body anyway, and make the woman a toilet for their secretions; (2) when there is a dildo in her, however, she will know pleasure (die), and this jack will kill the giant one, and let in instead the meadowed king (the bull). 'Let,' which means both *permit* and *hinder*, perfectly represents the alternating currents here. The same toy and toying sound which seduces Ada pleasantly when she is mastered by the meadowed king, would turn her into a toilet bowl if she were jacked by a man.

Strong stuff. *Not* a joke.

In 1951 Edmund Wilson conjectured

. . . that the vagueness that began to blur [Gertrude Stein's writing] from about 1910 on and the masking by unexplained metaphors that later made it seem opaque, though partly the result of an effort to emulate modern painting, were partly also due to a need imposed by the problem of writing about relationships between women of a kind that the standards of the era would not have allowed her to describe more explicitly. It seemed obvious that her queer little portraits and her mischievously baffling prose-poems did often deal with subjects of this sort . . .

but he later felt he might have overestimated the motive of sexual concealment. If the reading I have given the Object section of *Tender Buttons* is even somewhat sound, however, Wilson will have been right the first time.

Evasiveness, of course, becomes a habit, a style, a method which overreaches its original excuse and must seek another justification, just as the quadriplegic, who must paint with his teeth, will eventually find reasons why the bite is superior to the squeeze. Although, in a few works—the popular public ones like Alice's and Everybody's autobiographies, *Brewsie and Willie*, and *Wars I Have Seen*—Stein's style is as simple and open and even giddy as we might imagine the letters of a young girl to be, much of her work is written, like *Tender Buttons*, in a kind of code, even when, as in *How to Write*, the subject does not appear to require it; and there is no question whatever that the coding dangerously confounds the surface; for even if a passage effects a concealment, as when a body is covered by clothing, from the artistic point of view, those clothes had better dazzle us as much as the truth would, unless the concealment is only gestural and temporary, and we are expected to penetrate it at once, because the object of art is to make more beautiful that which is, and since that which is is rarely beautiful, often awkward and ugly and ill-arranged, it must be sometimes sheeted like a corpse, or dissolved into its elements and put together afresh, aright, and originally. Stein is painfully aware of the problem. Coming clean is best. "Certainly glittering is handsome and convincing."

The manifest text of *Tender Buttons* is only one segment of its total textual surface. That CHOKE is 'joke' is a surface phenomenon, as is AIDER's 'aid her.' In a swirl of lines a horse's head may be hidden, some clouds do in fact look dragonish, and a drawing may turn itself inside out before our very eyes; thus 'get in bed' lies disguised in 'rubbed purr get,' and an unseen 'i' will fit between the words 'to let.' The problem is that in *Tender Buttons* the unconcealed surface usually makes no sense. AIDER, for instance, is not an active English verb, and might as well be a word in the *Wake* or in "Jabberwocky." Occasionally, instead of the word being wounded, the syntax will be: "Please a round it is ticket." Most often, however, the confusion in the surface is semantic. "This is no authority for the abuse of cheese," she will suddenly say severely, and we think we are listening to the Red Queen. "Suspect a single buttered flower," we are warned, but what is the warning? In contrast, the other segments of the surface are usually fairly clear. "Aid her" is plainly what we are being asked to do.

Some covert texts are hidden like the purloined letter, others are concealed the way the family portrait hides the safe, still others the way the safe contains its money. That 'color' is a cover, or that 'cow' is cunt or that 'a white way of being round' refers to immaculate conception, is nothing that can be read directly off the page. Since many of the meanings of *Tender Buttons* are etymological, the covert text can be said to be sometimes *inside* the surface text. We have only to enter the word on these occasions. However, the idea that the innocent dust which makes up Adam and Eve is a 'blind glass' can be safely said to lie *beneath* its covering phrase. . . .

The manifest surface of A BOX is represented by the idea, container. There is a covert surface, too, that of contest or blow. Each such covert text adds to the *width* of the surface, just as its *length* is determined by the basic unity of the verbal series chosen for examination (A BOX, in this case, rather than merely BOX). In this [piece], we have a surface two words long and two texts wide. *Inside* A BOX is its root, 'tree.' *Behind* it is the slang meaning, womb or vagina. Pandora is *beneath*, while hovering *above*, though not like an angel, is its characterization as the label of a button. Because A BOX is set up as a title, it has no *immediate* before or after; there is to be imagined, before the opening of each book, an endless preceding silence, just as an equally endless one follows its close; but these are the silences of one text alone, not the quiet of all texts, for the whole of literature surrounds every work like water.

Here, then, is a notable explosion of language out of time into space. Although the button which follows A BOX makes sense, and is even funny (if the labor of reaching the punch line does not itself supply the reel which should result), it is, by and large, without the swift sensuous intake which is essential, since our response, as readers, must always run even with, if not ahead of, understanding. Basically, our knowledge of a poem serves simply to explain why we were shaken. It will never, alone, do the shaking.

In *Tender Buttons* the conflict between concealment and expression is especially intense. This kind of contest can sometimes lead to the most beautiful and powerful of consequences, so long as the victory of concealment remains incomplete, so long as the drapery leads us to dream and desire and demand the body we know it covers, so long as passion speaks through rectitude, so long as impulse laughs with the lips of duty. We can, of course, rip the clothing off anyway, as I have; but it is the promise of the nipple through the slip, the tender button, which matters to us here, and is the actual action of art; it is the hint of the hollow which holds us, and the way a stone arm encircles nothing but atmosphere so loving we want to believe in our being there, also surrounded, and only then as alive in our life as that stone.

MARIANNE DeKOVEN

Melody

Stein's styles no longer progressed strictly chronologically in the twenties. Instead, she developed several styles concomitantly through most of the decade. Generally, however, "melody" dominated the early and late parts of the decade, and "landscape," the most important style after "lively words," dominated the middle.

The various forms of "melody" are the result of interesting but often fruitless experiments which Stein performed on the surface of language, primarily investigating the possibilities of writing as a form of music. Speaking of the early twenties in *The Autobiography of Alice B. Toklas*, Stein says "She also liked then to set a sentence for herself as a sort of tuning fork and metronome and then write to that time and tune." (She also liked simply to sit in her beloved Ford car, Godiva, and listen to the street sounds, which "greatly influenced" her.) One of the first of the resulting poems is "Polish," 1920:

> Poling poling the sea into weather along.
> Poling poling dogs are pretty who have such a song.
> Girls and boys tease the seas.
> We are capable of this ease.
> Not so the Poles and their brothers the foals.
> They are the ones that made the Huns, do what.
> Be sick at their guns.

Perhaps the organization on the page of the late "voices" fragments suggested the idea of poetry to Stein, and certainly it is the *idea* of poetry as musical language she is pursuing here: the possibility of using poetry to

From *A Different Language: Gertrude Stein's Experimental Writing*. Copyright © 1983 by The Board of Regents of the University of Wisconsin. University of Wisconsin Press.

engulf writing in patterns of sound. Whether or not the reader can discover possibilities of meaning in this work (Virgil Thomson says it is "about Poland and current events") is finally irrelevant. Whatever connections of meaning there may be among the words are overwhelmed by connections of sound and rhythm. Playfully, but arbitrarily, Stein is filling in words to a preestablished "time and tune." As in the unsuccessful late "insistence" and late "lively words," meaning is submerged beneath the linguistic surface.

"Mary" is extreme but characteristic of 1920–21:

> Mary Minter and Mary P.
> Mary Mixer and Esther May.
> Henriette Gurney and Mrs. Green can you see what
> I mean.

"Mary" is unabashedly trivial, giving us only rather crude internal prosody and a singsong nursery meter. But nonetheless its failure to offer meaning is less disturbing than the "senselessness" of a work like *Tender Buttons*, where meaning is present but multiplied, deranged, shattered. Since meaning is clearly and simply absent here, one needn't feel frustrated or inadequate at not being able to find it, nor need one condemn the work for obscuring something it never pretends to offer.

"Mary" is completely unresistant, transparent, pliable. These qualities make it not only inoffensive but also, to some, appealing: it is easy, light, happy work by a notoriously "difficult" writer. With the laughing bow and scrape of the court jester, Stein seems voluntarily to renounce the power she acquired over the reader through the unsettling disruptions of her earlier work.

These poems are often pleasing in a more conventionally sophisticated way as well: "Henriette Gurney and Mrs. Green can you see what I mean." Of course we cannot see what she means, or rather we can see that she means nothing. This type of joke is a variation of Stein's characteristic verbal dissonance: "the Poles and their brothers the foals," or this sequence from "A Hymn" of 1920:

> Indeed an account knows
> Which way they rub their woes
> And in the middle Christmas
> There is butter.

Juxtapositions such as "account knows," "rub their woes," and "middle Christmas" might well be found in *Tender Buttons*, but submerged as they are here beneath the time and tune, they spark only a mild sense of comic incongruity rather than the powerful realignment of language and meaning they might effect in the "lively words" writing. Such comic incongruity, as in the "voices," appears at many levels in these poems: not only in individual juxtapositions and in a vocabulary ludicrously mixed of sophisticated and childish words, but also, and perhaps primarily, in the dissonance of the mock-serious, lecturing, assertive tone and syntax on one hand and the nursery rhyme sing-song on the other.

But beyond its absolute accessibility and its verbal wit, this work offers a more significant kind of pleasure as a primary, visceral, presymbolic language. As its nursery rhyme meter signifies, it returns us to the infant's state of linguistic experience, where all we absorb of language is sound and rhythm. As Julia Kristeva argues, the melodic and rhythmic patterns of our language form part of the intense, primal, undifferentiated sensation of infancy, when we are still merged in omnipotence with the outer world, with the "mother's body." The process of acquiring or entering patriarchal culture is concomitant with the gradual transformation of language as sound to language as sign. But that transformation represses, rather than destroys, our connection with the mother's body and with presymbolic language. The initial impact of language as internal/external sensory event, as melodic and rhythmic pattern, is submerged but not obliterated by the culturally ascendent language of the Father, which is exclusively a tool for ordering and communicating meaning. The dominance of time and tune to the exclusion of meaning in Stein's early twenties writing allows us to reexperience, as a return to that intense sensation of infant pleasure, an alternative, nonpatriarchal state of language.

I dwell on the nature of the appeal in these minor poems because they represent an important option for experimental writing. Until the early twenties, writing of Stein's which failed to articulate meaning also failed to offer any sort of access to the reader, still less any interest or pleasure. Here is writing that offers both ready access and also a wholly different kind of pleasure, unrelated to the presence or absence of readable meaning (in some poems, such as "A Hymn" or "Polish," there are connections of meaning among the words; in others, such as "Mary," there are not).

The appeal of these poems also comes from the relief they provide both from the difficulty of Stein's other work and from the alienating difficulty of the increasingly complicated uses of symbolic language in twentieth-century writing. But most important, this writing represents the fullest possible liberation of Kristeva's repressed female *jouissance:* an assertion of the freed "magic of the signifier" (Barthes) over the repressed, hierarchical order of the signified.

However, it is difficult to attach such significance to the verse we have seen so far, . . . which seems to have been written mechanically, without the concentration, commitment, and powerfully original invention that characterize Stein's best work. These poems do not have sufficient force to restore to language, or restore language to, the magic of the signifier. Later . . . we will see a much less compromised, more successful form of melodic writing.

Not all of Stein's early twenties poetry submerges meaning entirely beneath the linguistic surface. Though time and tune still govern the composition in a work like "Sonnets That Please," meaning also functions in the text in an interesting way:

SONNETS THAT PLEASE
I see the luck
And the luck sees me I see the lucky one be lucky.
I see the love
And the love sees me
I see the lovely love be lovely.
I see the bystander stand by me. I see the bystander stand by inside
   me.
I see.

Another Sonnet That Pleases
Please be pleased with me.
Please be.
Please be all to me please please be.
Please be pleased with me. Please please me. Please please please
   with me please please be.

These "sonnets" do not "please" through comic dissonance: they contain no incongruous juxtapositions, no mixed vocabulary, no mock-earnest assertion. Like the other 1920–21 poems they "please" through pure sound, but here the simple pleasure of time and tune is also reinforced by the simple pleasure of sentiment. Many conventional love lyrics, particularly in popular music, have little more content than these poems, and it is precisely the popular love lyric that Stein parodies here and at the same time emulates.

Both "Sonnets That Please" and popular love songs operate through an appeal to reflex sentiment. What any particular love lyric actually says is irrelevant to its effect: "I love how he loves me" calls up the same mass fantasy, with all its predictable ecstatic yearning, as "I'll be true to you" or "love me tender love me sweet," different as the contents of those statements seem. Stein draws her vocabulary in "Sonnets That Please" from the cliché horde of that popular fantasy, recognizing that all one needs in order to evoke the pleasurable reflex associated with the love lyric is any reasonable combination of words like "love" and "please," set to an appropriate time and tune.

Calling these pieces "sonnets" is not a reference to their prosody but rather, I would imagine, an announcement that they are intended as love poems. Stein's approach to genre here is characteristically abstract. Just as she wanted to make her first play "the essence of what happened," she is attempting in "Sonnets That Please" to render the essence of the love lyric. But while her abstract approach to plays yielded powerful dramatic forms, her abstract aproach to the love lyric—a form the word "sonnet" would suggest she takes seriously—arrives only at its most banal component.

However, at the same time that they imitate the popular love lyric's appeal to automatic sentiment, the "Sonnets That Please" also parody the genre precisely by revealing the irrelevance of the coherent sense the conventional lyrics make. As far as emotional impact is concerned, "I love how he loves me" might just as well be "I see the lovely love be lovely." But there *is* a difference at the level of linguistic surface: the puns and other verbal play separate Stein's work from popular cliché and give it the appearance of a more sophisticated, or at least literary, kind of writing. That difference allows us to read "Sonnets That Please" as parody or verbal wit or pure musical language without sacrificing our enjoyment of the pat sentiment which is the strongest element of its appeal. That combination of formal invention and banal sentiment makes "Sonnets That Please," and Stein's other early twenties work like it, typical of a good deal of popular avant-garde literature and therefore inimical to the project of experimental writing, which is to provide culturally alternative modes of signification in literature, not to conceal pat, conventional themes beneath a deceptive surface of unconventional language.

It is this kind of spurious experimentalism that allows Norman Holland, in *Dynamics of the Literary Response*, to claim that the appeal of *all* avant-garde or "difficult" art is only in the distraction or defense the unconventional form provides from the enjoyment of threatening or forbidden fantasy content. According to Holland, when we think we are fitting together the fragments of an avant-garde work to organize it into a large thematic statement about modern life, what we are actually doing is distracting and defending ourselves from the knowledge that we're basking in forbidden sexuality. This argument is useful in its recognition that form and content can have wholly divergent impact, but it falsely discredits the formal preoccupations of avant-garde art by making the impact of form seem entirely subservient to the impact of the content. Again, Holland is able to make his argument categorical because there is a large class of avant-garde art in which the fragmented form does conceal or distract from, without complicating, fairly banal, straightforward, or conventional content—content which is often the raw sexual fantasy which Holland discovers in his analysis of contemporary film.

Stein's poetry of the late twenties and early thirties avoids banal content, but not banality. In her best known poem, "Before the Flowers of Friendship Faded Friendship Faded" of 1930, Stein employs for her metronome not the singsong of nursery rhyme but, entirely at the other end of the poetic spectrum, the free, largely iambic rhythms of serious modern poetry. In "Before the Flowers," and also in most of the book-length "Stanzas in Meditation" of 1932 (some of "Stanzas" is like "Polish" and "Mary"), Stein seems to be trying to capture the structural and emotional essence of poetry itself. Unfortunately, she seems to equate the essence of poetry with the way many poems sound, and instead of illuminating abstraction she achieves only travesty:

In the one hundred small places of myself my youth,
And myself in if it is the use of passion,
In this in it and in the nights alone
If in the next to night which is indeed not well
I follow you without it having slept and went.
Without pressure of a place with which to come unfolded folds are a
    pressure and an abusive stain
A head if uncovered can be as hot, as heated,
to please to take a distance to make life,
And if resisting, little, they have no thought,
a little one which was a little which was as all as still,
Or with or without fear or with it all, . . .

"Before the Flowers" has an added liability: it was meant to be a translation of a fairly conventional poem by Georges Hugnet (Stein's title refers to the consequences of his reading her version). Much of the painfully unassimilated "poetic" diction in Stein's poem is the trace of the French original. "Stanzas in Meditation" is not as oddly interspersed with hackneyed, melodramatic language ("use of passion," "nights alone," "abusive stain"), but it too attempts to realize the essence of poetry by imitating, ingeniously enough, its rhythms and seriousness of tone:

I have not heard from him but they ask more
If with all which they merit with as well

If it is not an ounce of which they measure
He has increased in weight by losing two
Namely they name as much.
Often they are obliged as it is by their way
Left more than they can add acknowledge
Come with the person that they do attach
They like neither best by them altogether
For which it is no virtue fortune all
Ours on account theirs with the best of all
Made it be in no sense other than exchange
By which they cause me to think the same
In finally alighting where they may have at one time
Made it best for themselves in their behalf.

Though this verse, typical of the "Stanzas," does not have the pretentious patches which are the mark Hugnet left on "Before the Flowers," it does contain diction ("obliged," "acknowledge," "attach," "altogether," "virtue," "fortune," "alighting") which Stein had banished from her earlier experimental vocabulary as weak, abstract, or pompous. One can only assume that Stein considered such language a necesssary concession to "serious" poetry.

Unlike "Polish" or "Mary," this work invites no return to a powerful presymbolic linguistic bliss. But like "Sonnets That Please," it is premised on an appeal to reflex reading, not through the mawkish fantasy of Romance but through the brooding seriousness of Poetry. Stein tries to put us in an elevated spiritual realm without doing the difficult work required to get us there. The result, to this ear, is just plain silly. It is unlikely that Stein intends comic travesty in either "Before the Flowers" or "Stanzas." This work represents a genuine attempt to realize the essence of poetry, which fails because Stein is no longer in the safe, simple realm of popular cliché or fantasy. Her method is simply too superficial for the complex uses of language it attempts to assimilate.

It may seem impertinent to give these works, particularly "Stanzas in Meditation," such short shrift. Other readers have found and no doubt will continue to find in them qualities to value. However, we do not fail in respect for Stein by remaining faithful to our actual experience of reading her. If a work, however long it is or however substantial in the canon it appears, fails to offer anything to a reader, there is no point in pursuing a reluctant analysis.

There is an important exception—a mode of early twenties "melody" based entirely on rhythmic repetition of a few words:

A Very Valentine

Very fine is my valentine.
Very fine and very mine.
Very mine is my valentine very mine and very fine.
Very fine is my valentine and mine, very fine very mine and mine
is my valentine.

This section of "A Valentine to Sherwood Anderson" is similar to "Sonnets That Please" in its poetic line structure and in its playful appeal to conventional sentiment. But not only is the repetition more concentrated here, the rhythm has a subtly different quality. While "Sonnets That Please" used the simple nursery rhythm that we saw in "Polish" and "Mary," the more complex rhythm of "A Very Valentine" is a function of the sounds of the words themselves as they are repeated and recombined rather than of an externally imposed, preestablished pattern.

In his book *Roots of Lyric*, Andrew Welsh makes a very useful distinction, mainly via Frye, Valéry, and Pound, between what he calls song-melos and charm-melos. Charm-melos is related to Welsh's third root of poetic sound, speech-melos, in that both derive from sound and rhythm patterns internal to a language, while song-melos is an externally imposed musical pattern. Charm-melos is essentially a heightening or concentration of the natural, internal sound patterns of speech-melos. Together, these three roots form "melopoeia," which, along with Pound, Welsh distinguishes from "phanepoeia": "Phanopoeia in poetry drives toward precision of image and thought, the clear, precise seeing and knowing that is needed for a good riddle or a good Image poem. Melopoeia, on the other hand, is a force that leads poetry away from precisions of word and meaning, but that may be, as Pound said, a bridge to a non-verbal consciousness." It is easy to recognize in this distinction the idea that Stein's experimental writing is an anti-patriarchal exploration of a literary language prior to, and cut loose from, coherent sense.

Within melopoeia, it is charm-melos that has been most overlooked by poetry:

New books of poems appear each year with the word "songs" on their title pages [song-melos], . . . Similarly, each generation of poets reaffirms the spoken language as a source of the rhythms of poetry [speech-melos] . . . The third root—less well recognized, perhaps, but no less fundamental—lies in the mysterious actions of the closed, internal rhythms of language, the echoing reflections of sound we have called charm-melos.

It is in the dense sound patterns of charm-melos that Stein finds another powerful means of reinventing literary signification. As Welsh points out, charm-melos is primarily concerned with power, both in the primitive cultures where it originates and in the subsequent uses to which it has been put (Welsh gives examples from Shakespeare, Blake, Poe, Valéry, and Pound): "The language of the charms is a language of power, and that power comes primarily not from lexical meanings, archaic or colloquial, but from other meanings hidden deep in the sounds and rhythms." Those "other meanings" are precisely what I have been calling presymbolic signification. Their power, so often called magic, is the power of experimental writing.

We are beginning to see how complex an effect the seemingly very simple writing of "A Very Valentine" has. Unlike "Polish" and "Mary," "A Very Valentine" does not use the shortcut of childish rhythms to take us back to presymbolic language. By avoiding that shortcut, "Valentine" also avoids the negative connotation of the word "childish." The presymbolic language-state can be experienced as powerful magic—Barthes's "magic of the signifier"—which is where its value lies, rather than as regression to immaturity or infantilism—escape from the adult responsibility of making sense—which is where its danger lies; evidence "Polish" and "Mary."

Moreover, "A Very Valentine" demonstrates the close connection between language as music and language as incantation (Welsh considers incantation part of charm-melos). In "Valentine," in fact, it is difficult to differentiate the two, since both are a function of the repetition and recombination of the sounds of the words. But as we know from "insistence," it is quite possible for incantatory writing to be entirely unmusical, unmelodic. "Insistence" is musical only in its dependence on repetition in time. Its monotonous, droning sounds make no independent music; they merely support the incantation: "This thing that is such a thing, this thing that is existing, that is a frightening thing to one, is a way of living of very many being living . . ." ("Rue de Rennes").

By combining incantation with melody, "A Very Valentine" weaves together two experimental modes which define separate language-states, each of which opposes, from a different direction, the ordering, dominating mode of patriarchal-symbolic, sense-making language. The two are more effective combined than either is alone.

Writing in the style of "A Very Valentine" functions powerfully at the level of lexical meaning as well. "A Very Valentine" itself does not, because it uses the same kind of appeal to reflex emotion that "Sonnets That Please" uses: no reiterative recombination of "fine," "mine" and "valentine," particularly under the title "A Valentine to Sherwood Anderson," could undermine the pat, sentimental impact of the initial statement "very fine is my valentine." But in other instances of this style, Stein avoids that problem:

> Not only wool and woolen silk and silken not only silk and silken wool and woolen not only wool and woolen silk and silken not only silk and silken wool and woolen not only wool and woolen silk and silken not only silk and silken not only wool and woolen not only wool and woolen not only silk and silken not only silk and silken not only wool and woolen.

> If I told him would he like it. Would he like it if I told him.
> Would he like it would Napoleon would Napoleon would would he like it.
> If Napoleon if I told him if I told him if Napoleon. Would he like it if I told him if I told him if Napoleon. Would he like it if Napoleon if Napoleon if I told him. If I told him if Napoleon if Napoleon if I told him. If I told him would he like it would he like it if I told him.

> Shutters shut and open so do queens. Shutters shut and shutters and so shutters shut and shutters and so and so shutters and so shutters shut and so shutters shut and shutters and so. And so shutters shut and so and also. And also and so and so and also.
> ("If I Told Him. A Completed Portrait of Picasso")

What becomes of meaning in these passages? On one level, it is obliterated. Repetition this intense has the effect of cutting the verbal signifier loose, entirely, from lexical meaning—no longer merely submerging meaning beneath the linguistic surface, but bringing about a radical transformation of the reader's experience of the signifier. Through relentless repetition, Stein reveals the signifier in its utter arbitrariness, totally divorced from the signified—shattering, as Derrida does in *Of Grammatology*, the notion of an "organic" or "natural" or "necessary" connection between signifier and signified. Tellingly, children often play the game of repeating a word or a name until it becomes entirely a disembodied set of sounds. The function of this game is to reveal the wonder of the signifier, the wonder of language: language is a great power, which normally effaces itself as mere representation, tool, mediation of direct experience. Again, as with Stein's poetry of the earlier twenties, we temporarily reacquire the presymbolic order of language. However, in this writing, we reacquire it not as reminiscence which coexists with our subsequent knowledge of sense-making, but, in moments of vertigo, as return to the pure state itself, in which words simply have no lexical meaning. Unlike the unsuccessful writing in Stein's earlier styles, where meaning is lost beneath the linguistic surface, leaving nothing in its place to activate the text, this writing uses the obliteration of meaning to enhance its primary effect: the "mysterious actions of the closed, internal rhythms of language, the echoing reflections of sound" of Welsh's charm-melos, and the intense, primal sensation of presymbolic language.

Paradoxically, meaning is magnified as well as obliterated in this writing. Intense repetition can always obliterate meaning, but if the repeated words are chosen in a certain way, repetition can also—not simultaneously but alternatively—intensify meaning. In the passages quoted above, several facets of Stein's choice and ordering of words enable this intensification of meaning. First, the repetition is not uniform. As in "insistence," it involves slight variations; also, more than one (usually three or four) verbal element is repeated. If only one word were repeated, without variation in its form, obliteration of meaning would be an absolute, unmitigated effect, as it is in unsuccessful late "insistence."

Stein also generates that alternative effect of intensification of meaning by employing some of the techniques she used in the "lively words" style. In the above examples, she chooses words with visual or tactile strength ("wool and woolen, silk and silken"); or words which portray a vivid, simple action ("shutters shut and open"); or juxtapositions of bizarre suggestiveness ("so do queens"), and tantalizing near-intelligibility ("would [Picasso] like it if I told him [he was] Napoleon"). These techniques serve to fix the image, action, or idea in the reader's mind firmly enough so that repetition can emphasize rather than (or as well as) obliterate it. Obliteration and intensification of meaning oscillate for the reader: in separate readings, or sometimes in the course of a single reading, obliteration or intensification of meaning alternately emerges, becomes "visible," as the other disappears. This double effect of obliteration and expansion of meaning, coupled with the powerful presymbolic "magic" of charm-melos, makes this "melody" extremely effective. It becomes a mainstay of Stein's writing in the late twenties.

JAYNE L. WALKER

History as Repetition: "The Making of Americans"

As early as 1903, Stein had begun writing a novel based on the lives of members of her family. After completing "Melanctha" in 1906, she returned to this project and worked on it for the next five years. The final version of *The Making of Americans* was shaped by her increasingly radical commitment to presenting repetition as the "reality" that informs human history. The 1909 aesthetic credo that begins by invoking the "reality" of Cézanne and Caliban concludes with the declaration, "I believe in repetition. Yes. Always and always, Must write the eternal hymn of repetition." *The Making of Americans* began as a straightforward family chronicle, but it soon became Stein's "eternal hymn of repetition." Its complete title, *The Making of Americans Being a History of a Family's Progress*, seems to align the novel with the optimistic view of history as revelation of human progress that dominated most eighteenth- and nineteenth-century historiography. But its opening paragraph introduces an alternative paradigm that radically challenges this idea of history:

> Once an angry man dragged his father along the ground through his own orchard. "Stop!" cried the groaning old man at last, "Stop! I did not drag my father beyond this tree."

Repetition, not a linear sequence of discrete events linked in a chain of causality that manifests progress, is the form and force of history in Stein's text.

From *The Making of a Modernist: Gertrude Stein from Three Lives to Tender Buttons*. Copyright © 1984 by Jayne L. Walker. University of Massachusetts Press.

In 1843 Kierkegaard posited repetition as the "modern lifeview," the "new category which has to be brought to light." He was not mistaken. Writers as diverse as Nietzsche, Marx, Spengler, and Yeats explored patterns of repetition in history, while Freud established the repetition compulsion as a motive force in individual lives. Stein's 1908 notebooks reveal that, some years before, her initial confrontation with the idea of history as repetition had shattered her faith in historical progress and, at first, had left her profoundly depressed. By the time she began the final draft of *The Making of Americans*, however, she had come to see repetition as a positive force that resolves the apparent chaos of human history and of individual lives into reassuring patterns of orderly recurrence.

In *The Making of Americans*, "repeating in each one makes a history" of individuals and of family life as well. Characters repeatedly reveal what Stein calls their "bottom natures"; as they repeat themselves, they repeat variations of their parents' essential personality traits. The first chapter presents the Hersland and Dehning families as two closed sets of personality types which, in different "mixtures," pass from parents to children. These characters repeat themselves within a larger field as well, the "simple middle class monotonous tradition, . . . always there and to be always repeated, . . . worthy that all monotonously shall repeat it." In the early draft, these families are German. Shifting the focus away from particularized chronicle to collective history of "[t]he old people in a new world, the new people made out of the old," the final version leaves their country of origin unspecified. The Herslands and Dehnings are presented as "ordinary kinds of families" whose "repeating, common, decent enough kind of living" typifies the American middle class.

The story Stein's novel tells of the making of these Americans hardly supports the optimism of its title. After coming to America, the children of the immigrants make "substantial progress . . . in wealth, in opportunity, in education." Henry Dehning and the elder David Hersland both become rich. Their children are born with all the material advantages their parents' generation struggled hard to achieve. Early in the novel, Henry Dehning challenges his children, "[T]ell me exactly what you are going to get from all these your expensive modern kinds of ways of doing . . . I say you tell me just what you are going to do, to make it good all this money. Well what, what are all these kinds of improvements going to do for you." After the first chapter, the narrative focuses, in turn, on four members of the children's generation. As in many classic realist novels, business and marriage are the two major spheres of adult activity in *The Making of Americans*. But in Stein's text, circumstantial details are kept to a minimum, to emphasize the monotonous regularity of this middle-class tradition. In these spheres, none of the children's lives presents a striking record of continuing "progress." Martha Hersland's marriage fails; and the marriage of Alfred Hersland and Julia Dehning is not a happy one. Neither Alfred nor David Hersland continues the material success of their father's generation. David achieves a high degree of sensitivity and understanding, but he dies young, without having done much of anything. Even the elder David Hersland, the paragon of middle-class success, loses his fortune before the end of the novel.

The beginning of the novel is situated ambivalently between satire and celebration of this "monotonous middle-class tradition." The account of Julia Dehning's marriage satirizes bourgeois American tastes and attitudes "twenty years ago, in the dark age." The narrator proclaims her affection for this tradition, while announcing her geographical and personal separation from it, "here in the heart of a people who despise it." A reworking of the 1903 manuscript, this section is a kind of palimpsestic recapitulation of Stein's early narrative styles. It contains elaborate physical descriptions of characters and settings, the kind of circumstantial details Stein eliminated in the course of writing *Three Lives,* as well as traces of the archly archaic style she affected in the 1903 draft. Characters utter long speeches, in the rhythmically repetitive colloquial style of *Three Lives,* which is the dominant style of the surrounding narrative as well. As the text progresses, however, the characters' voices are soon silenced and the circumstantial details of their lives disappear; all that remains is the omnipresent voice of the author, composing her "hymn of repetition."

Early in the first chapter, the narrator warns the reader that her characters will lack "vital singularity" because America mass-produces its youth in a uniform mold:

> I say vital singularity is as yet an unknown product with us, we who in our habits, dress-suit cases, clothes and hats and ways of thinking, walking, making money, talking, having simple lines in decorating, in ways of reforming, all with a metallic clicking like the type-writing which is our only way of thinking, our way of educating, our way of learning, all always the same way of doing, all the way down as far as there is any way down inside to us. We all are the same all through us, we never have it to be free inside us. No brother singulars, it is sad here for us, there is no place in an adolescent world for anything eccentric like us, machine making does not turn out queer things like us, they can never make a world to let us be free each one inside us.

First identifying with this culturally determined uniformity, the narrator suddenly asserts her own alienated individuality. Halfway through the first chapter, however, the author begins to develop a theory of character that will swallow up all individualizing differences, including her own, in a universal typological system:

> There are many kinds of men, of every kind of them there are many millions of them many millions always made to be like the others of that kind of them, of some kinds of them there are more millions made like the others of such a kind of them than there are millions made alike of some other kinds of men. Perhaps this is not really true about any kind of them, perhaps there are not less millions of one kind of men than there are millions of other kinds of them, perhaps one thinks such a thing about some kinds of men only because in some kinds of men there is more in each one of such a kind, more in the many millions of such a kind of them, of an individual feeling in every one of such a kind of them.

Classic realist narratives create the double illusion that their characters are unique individuals and at the same time representatives of social types. When Balzac compares his inventory of social types in the *Comédie humaine* to the zoological species isolated by natural historians, he relishes the vast array of social types with their multitude of distinguishing features. As the preceding passage suggests, Stein's typological system emphasizes identities and ignores the particularizing differences of social and historical circumstances. Repetition of a limited set of psychological types, first presented in terms of a specific genealogical and cultural heritage, becomes a universal phenomenon.

Stein's notebooks reveal that her reading of Otto Weininger's *Sex and Character* in 1908 was the catalyst for this new project, which led her to transform a chronicle of an American family into a synchronic study of "kinds." Weininger's "science of character" proposed a new "doctrine of the whole" to challenge the empirical psychology of William James. Leaving behind the "motley world, the changing field of sensations," Weininger sought to identify the "permanent existing something" that underlies the "fleeting changes" of psychic life:

> The character, however, is not something seated behind the thoughts and feelings of the individual, but something revealing itself in every thought and feeling. . . . Just as every cell bears within it the characters of the whole individual, so every psychical manifestation of a man involves not merely a few little characteristic traits, but his whole being, of which at one moment one quality, at another moment another quality, comes into prominence.
>
> Just as no sensation is ever isolated, but is set in a complete field of sensation, the world of the Ego, of which now one part and now the other, stands out more plainly, so the whole man is manifest in every moment of the psychical life, although, now one side, now the other, is

more visible. This existence, manifest in every moment of the psychical
life, is the object of characterology.

Even while Stein was working with William James at Harvard, she was
already more interested in her own intuitive perceptions of character than
in her teacher's empirical research methods. Her essay "Cultivated Motor
Automatism," published in the *Psychological Review* of May 1898, concerns
itself less with the subjects' automatic behavior than with their characters,
which she divided into two basic types. She described one type as "nervous"
and "intensely interested," the other as "phlegmatic." The schematic opposition first sketched in this essay is more fully elaborated in the contrast-
ing, and conflicting, personalities of the lovers portrayed in *Q.E.D.* and
"Melanctha." The last chapter of the 1903 draft of *The Making of Americans*
clumsily introduces another version of it: "[p]assionate women, those in
whom emotion has the intensity of sensation," are opposed to women who
"know not passion" and who "make a resisting compacting mass" to protect
themselves. Julia Dehning, representing the first type, "rushed upon her
sorrow, passionately, fervently heroically." Her sister Bertha is presented
as her opposite, one of the kind that "sits still." The final version of the
novel eliminates this chapter, and this character, but the fundamental
opposition it introduced becomes part of the binary system of classification
Stein began to construct in 1908.

Although Weininger's book stimulated her to systematize her understanding of character, the typology she created in the novel was purely
her own. In her notebooks, she briefly experimented with Weininger's
polarities of male and female, the central categories of his binary system:
"Picasso has a maleness that belongs to genius. Moi ausi." But his misog-
ynistic treatment of sexual differences did not provide a useful model for
Stein's analysis of character. For a time, she also used some of Weininger's
categories (prostitute, mother, servant, saint, masculine woman, and lady),
plus a few of her own invention (mistress and spinster), to analyze her
acquaintances in her notebooks. The categories of servant girl and spinster
appear in the first chapter of the novel, illustrated by long "histories" of
three governesses and three dressmakers who have worked for the Hersland
family. But the two broad categories, "dependent independent" (the "resisting" type) and "independent dependent" (the "attacking" type), clearly
derive from the fundamental opposition that governed Stein's presentation
of character in her earlier narratives. First introduced to label two con-
trasting "ways of loving," these soon became the cornerstones of her elaborate system for classifying the "bottom natures" that inform all human
behavior.

Once she had firmly established the foundations of this system, her desire to illustrate its universal truth came into direct conflict with the exigencies of narrative verisimilitude. "I want sometime to be right about everyone. I want sometime to write a history of everyone, of every kind there is in men and women." Constantly subjecting her writing to the demand of "being right," Stein changed her narrative strategies a number of times, as her pursuit of the "reality" she sought to understand and render in language became increasingly incompatible with the conventions governing fictional *vraisemblance*. By the end of the first chapter, the author is chafing at the limits imposed by the fictional world of her story:

> Sometime there will be written a long book that is a real history of every one who ever were or are or will be living from their beginning to their ending, now there is a history of the Hersland and the Dehning families and every one who ever came to know them.

In the second chapter, in complete defiance of novelistic conventions, the author simply abandons her story of the Herslands and Dehnings to write her own "history of getting completed understanding" of human nature, and the project that began as a fictional narrative of three generations of an American family is transformed into a universal, synchronic "history of every one who ever were or are or will be living."

The Making of Americans systematically violates the reader's expectation that the structure of a novel should roughly correspond to the succession of events in the story it narrates. But, beginning in the first chapter, the text inscribes another history in its temporal dimension, the author's quest for "completed understanding." Midway through the first chapter, the construction of the system becomes the dominant action of the text. The Herslands' three governesses and dressmakers are introduced not because they are necessary to the Hersland story but to contribute to a "kind of diagram for a beginner." Their "histories" occupy nearly as much space in the chapter as those of family members, because "[e]very kind of history about any one is important" to the author's study of "kinds." As storytelling is increasingly subordinated to system building, the linearity of writing (and reading) is activated to trace the gradual unfolding of knowledge: "Slowly there is building up a solid structure of the two different kinds of nature."

From the beginning, the reader is invited to identify with the writer of the text more directly than with its fictional characters: "We need only realise our parents, remember our grandparents and know ourselves and our history is complete." The fictional story of the Herslands and Dehnings is subordinated to this collective history, based on personal experience. "Realising" and "remembering" are presented as two essentially different kinds of knowledge; only the first is "present to our feelings." Repeated throughout the text, the word "realise" explicitly aligns Stein's project with Cézanne's reiterated goal of "realizing" his sensations and emphasizes the primary value of direct present-tense experience in this search for knowledge. Narrative, whether historical or fictional, is almost always governed by the past tense; its story has already concluded before the writing, or the reading, begins. Emile Benveniste has sketched the fundamental opposition between *histoire* (pure narration) and *discours* (discourse) in terms of their different systems of time and pronoun reference. Discourse is governed by the first person and the present tense; its other tenses have meaning in relation to the (always present) time of the speaker at the moment of discourse. Pure narration, on the contrary, excludes the first person and the present tense and, with them, all reference to the instance of discourse. "No one speaks. Events seem to tell themselves," within a past-tense system detached from any reference to the situation of discourse. As Benveniste acknowledges, *histoire* rarely exists in this pure state; to a greater or lesser degree, discursive elements penetrate the narration, momentarily breaking its illusory autonomy. From the beginning, *The Making of Americans* freely combines these two systems, often within a single paragraph:

> Henry Dehning was a grown man and for his day a rich one when his father died away and left them. Truly he had made everything for himself very different; but it is not as a young man making himself rich that we are now to feel him, he is for us an old grown man telling it all over to his children.
>   He is a middle aged man now when he talks about it all to his children, middle aged as perhaps sometimes we ourselves are now to our talking, but he, he is grown old man to our thinking.

As the past tense of the events cedes to the present tense of discourse, the character is moved out of the autonomous time frame of pure narration into the "now" of the discursive moment. This oscillation of tenses recurs throughout the text, as the discourse constantly breaks the illusionistic closure of the fictional past to make itself "present to our feeling."

The temporal dimension of the text traces the author's gradual accumulation of knowledge, which she slowly unfolds for the reader. Direct addresses to the reader soon cease, as she becomes less confident of her audience. She begins the second chapter with the admission, "I am writing for myself and strangers. This is the only way that I can do it." This "I . . . writing" is clearly not a fictional persona. It is the author, stripped of particularizing autobiographical details, seeking knowledge in this process of writing. The truths she discovers, formulated in the present tense, alternate with the past tense of narrative: "Mary *was* not a complete one of such a kind of them. This *is* the kind they are then. Mabel Linker *was* not at all such a kind of one. This *is now* a description of them" (my emphases). As this passage demonstrates in miniature, her discourse constantly engulfs the narrative and its individual characters in the ongoing "now" of her synchronic understanding of "kinds." Understanding becomes simultaneous with writing: "I am writing everything as I am learning anything." The discourse, with its ubiquitous formula "as I was saying," constantly calls attention to itself as an activity unfolding in time. The verbs "know," "understand," and "think" regularly occur in the present progressive aspect:

Always more and more I am understanding.

[A]lways then sometime each one I am ever knowing is a whole one to me.

I am thinking just now certainly thinking just now about some men, about some women.

This unusual usage, which transforms these normally stative verbs into verbs of activity, further emphasizes that knowledge, in this text, is not a static state but a temporal process occurring within the ongoing present of the discourse. This path to wisdom, far from smooth, corresponds neither to the linear, chronological order of narrative nor to the logical order of conventional expository prose. Constant false starts and new beginnings, the "irrelating" and "dulling" effects of textual repetition, are all embedded in the discourse. This enormously long book is the antithesis of what Roland Barthes calls a *texte de plaisir*:

Text of pleasure: which contents, fills, produces euphoria; which comes from culture and does not break with it, is linked to a *comfortable* reading practice. Text of bliss: which imposes a state of loss, which discomforts (perhaps to the point of some boredom), shakes the historical, cultural, psychological assumptions of the reader, the consistency of his tastes, his values, and his memories, brings his relationship to language into crisis.

Resolutely refusing to provide the traditional pleasure of narrative verisimilitude, this text forces its audience to share the author's slow, painful movement toward knowledge in the process of reading.

The second chapter of *The Making of Americans* describes the author's process of understanding, which shapes the entire text:

Sometimes some one for many years is baffling. The repeated hearing, seeing, feeling of repeating in them does not give to me then a history of the complete being in them. Slowly then sometime it comes to be clearer of them, I begin again with listening, I feel new shades in repeating, parts of repeating that I was neglecting hearing, seeing, feeling come to have a louder beating. Slowly it comes to a fuller sounding, sometimes many years pass in such a baffling listening, feeling, seeing all the repeating in some one. Then slowly such a one comes to have real meaning. Many times I begin and then begin again. Always I must not begin a deadened following, always their repeating must be a fresh feeling in my hearing, seeing, feeling. Always I must admit all changing. Always I must have a sensitive and open being, always I must have a loving repeating being. Often listening to them is irritating, often it is dulling, always then there must be in me new beginning, always there must be in me steadily alive inside me my loving repeating being. Then sometime every one is a completed being to me, sometime every one has a completed history to me. Always then it comes out of them their whole repeating, sometime then I can feel and hear and see it all and it has meaning. Sometime then each one I am ever knowing comes to be to me a completed being, and then always they are always repeating always the whole of them.

In this section, numerous paragraphs retrace this same pattern, with only slight variations. Stein's method is circular, constantly returning to her own "loving repeating being" as both origin and final guarantor of the truth she seeks. As one "having loving repeating as a way to wisdom," repetition is both the object of her study and its method: "by repeating I come to know it." The larger structure of the text deliberately models the process sketched in the preceding paragraph:

> [A]lways it has to be told as it has been learned by me very slowly, each one only slowly can know it, each one must wait for little pieces of it, always there will be coming more and more of it, always there will be a telling of every way the two kinds of being are different in everything and always it is hard to say it the differences between them, always more and more I know it, always more and more I know it, always more I come back to begin again the knowing of it, always I will tell it as I learned it, sometime I will have told all of it, always I am telling pieces of it, more and more I will know it, more and more I will tell it, sometime it will be clear to some one and I will be then glad of it.

Stein freely confesses her fears of failure, her increasingly desperate need for an orderly system to unify the disconnected "pieces" of her experience. Her desperate struggle for understanding dominates the entire text. Stein's pursuit of a quixotic dream of total knowledge ends in inevitable failure, but *this* story, which gradually unfolds in the text, makes more compelling reading than the family chronicle it displaces.

Stein's initial premise that character repeatedly reveals itself in individual lives and in family history does not radically differ from the assumptions governing the treatment of character in classic realist narratives. They too present character as a fairly stable entity that manifests itself repeatedly in diverse actions. In family chronicles, character is part of the genealogical heritage that passes from one generation to the next. In traditional novels, however, repetition is subordinated to particularizing differences. Recurrences of personality traits are encoded in a highly particularized linear plot. Family chronicles use inherited similarities of character to highlight the historical circumstances that change the lives of different generations. Patricia Tobin's recent study, *Time and the Novel: The Genealogical Imperative*, focuses on the undermining of "time . . . understood as a linear manifestation of the genealogical destiny of events" in twentieth-century family narratives. Tobin never mentions Stein's *Making of Americans*, but her discussion of the difference between Mann's conventional use of repetition in *Buddenbrooks* and Lawrence's in *The Rainbow* suggests the much greater divergence of Stein's project from traditional family chronicles: "This sameness of experience [in *The Rainbow*] is totally different from Mann's use of the same quality in each generation as the specification of difference, which will allow him to chart decline; rather, sameness here deprives the individual of the unique and singular quality of historical time, and promotes a sense of his or her placement within larger, eternal patterns." The opening pages of Stein's novel use repetition of character traits to trace the rise and decline of her families, but the author quickly became more interested in analyzing, classifying, and describing character as a universal phenomenon than in narrating the particular chain of events or even the larger patterns of action that constitute the experience of a specific family.

Early in the first chapter, the account of Julia Dehning's wedding, adapted from the 1903 draft, uses a conventional device to emphasize the generational recurrence of pesonality traits. Julia "hit the ground as she walked with the same hard jerking with which her mother Mrs. Dehning always rebuked her husband's sinning." Julia's repetition of this characteristic gesture of her mother, described in almost identical words two pages before, illustrates the extent to which the "stamp" of her mother's nature "went deep, far deeper than just for the fair good-looking exterior." As the author examines the relationship between actions and essential "being" more rigorously, she soon discards this traditional method of using a particular gesture to symbolize a personality trait and focuses, instead, on rendering the larger patterns of action that underlie all the specific activities of a character. The elder David Hersland was "always beginning, beginning was living to him." His "ways of eating, his ways of doctoring, his ways of educating" his children, "his way of changing," all manifest the same tendency to begin a project enthusiastically and then become impatient and bored. This pattern, which pervades all his activities, dominates his chronological history as well:

> David Hersland was such a one when he was *in each of his beginnings, soon then* he would be filled up with impatient feeling *and then* there would be in him less of such a big feeling to every one who then looked at him, *later in his life* he was old and weakening and he *then* was shrunk away from the outside of him, he *then* did not have inside him enough to fill him, he was not *then* a big man to every one who saw him.
>
> (my emphases)

This one-sentence paragraph begins with a recurring action and shifts to chronological progression, as the largest pattern of his life duplicates that of his every action. Many similarly constructed paragraphs, moving freely from the "now" of the narrative moment to the future "then," repeat the history of David Hersland's future decline. Others trace the same pattern as a generalized history of his "kind." According to the theory of character that is developing in the text, these patterns do not resolve themselves into a meaningful "whole" until old age:

> In the middle of their living they are always repeating, everybody always is repeating in all of their whole living but in the middle of the living of most men and many women it is hard to be sure about them just what it is they are repeating, they are in their living saying many things then and it is hard to know it about them then what it is in them they are repeating that later in their living will show itself to be the whole of them to any one who wants to watch them.

The repeated synopses of David Hersland's life, which collapse a life span into a sentence, demonstrate how radically this text violates the traditional linearity of narrative to enforce its alternative model of the significant form of human life.

Stein's sentences became longer and longer as she attempted "to put the whole history of the human heart on the head of a pin." The phrase is Faulkner's, who described his own characteristic long sentences as an "attempt to get [a character's] past and possibly his future into the instant in which he does something." Stein was less interested in the specific actions her characters perform than in who they are, but her long sentences present their essential "being" as an ongoing process, not as a static state. They systematically transform past-tense verbs of specific action into the progressive aspect or into participial or gerundival constructions and substantive nouns into gerunds. All of these syntactical procedures create a pervasive sense of continuing activity, unbroken by the finality of simple past-tense verbs of action. As Linda McMiniman has observed, Stein's essential being is " 'permanent action.' It is knowable because of its recurrence, but it defies accurate depiction in the normal noun-laden language of everyday use." In *Three Lives*, Stein used syntactical deformations to render the colloquial speech styles of her characters and to explore their linguistic limitations. In *The Making of Americans*, however, she systematically deviated from syntactical norms in order to embody in language a new vision of truth.

The more intensively she concentrated on pursuing the truth of "being," however, the more widely her perception of this human essence began to diverge from its original grounding in actions. The more centrally she focused on the problem of identifying, and rendering, this "bottom nature" in herself and in others, the more radically she came to question the assumption that actions are reliable manifestations of character. Any plot, any linear sequence of singular events, is contrary to her fundamental intuition that the essential truth of personality is revealed only in the "repeating" that "steadily tells over and over again the history of the complete being" of her characters. In a conventional novel, description works in opposition to narration, because it suspends the temporal movement of the story. By the second chapter of Stein's text, a "complete history" becomes synonymous with a "complete description" of essential "being," and repetition of identities supplants diachronic difference as the form of history in *The Making of Americans*.

In this chapter, the author's analysis of her own history leads her to conclude that her own "bottom nature" did not manifest itself in "ordinary living" for many years:

> There was then always in me as a bottom nature to me an earthy, resisting slow understanding, loving repeating being. As I was saying this has nothing to do with ordinary learning, in a way with ordinary living. . . .
> As I was saying learning, thinking, living in the beginning of being men and women often has in it very little of real being. Real being, the bottom nature, often does not then in the beginning do very loud repeating. Learning, thinking, talking, living, often then is not of the real bottom being. Some are this way all their living. . . .
> There was a time when I was questioning, always asking, when I was talking, wondering, there was a time when I was feeling, thinking, and all the time then I did not know repeating. There was a long time then when there was nothing in me using the bottom loving repeating being that now leads me to knowing.

The first chapter presents larger patterns of action that emerge from the activities of "ordinary living," but as the text progresses, the notion of essential "being" becomes increasingly dissociated from specific actions and these repeated patterns of behavior as well. Already in the first chapter, the author is convinced that children's repeated patterns of action do not reveal their essential natures: "In children as it always is with young living there is much repeating but it is not then so surely themselves they are expressing. . . . [I]n the regular repeating in mostly all children there is less that is really from them more that is just part of the regular living around them." By the time she resumes the narrative of the Hersland family, focusing on the childhood of Martha, she has come to believe so strongly that actions do not reveal character that all narration has become misrepresentation. The anecdote of Martha throwing her umbrella in the mud is narrated twice; both times it is followed by a disclaimer: "it is very hard telling from any incident in any one's living what kind of being they have in them"; "this is a description of an action that many very different kinds of children could have been doing when they were left behind struggling." It "does not now help very much" to understand Martha Hersland's character. Even the narrative fact that "[w]hen she was a very little one sometimes she wanted not to be existing" doesn't help to delineate her individual nature, because "[t]his is a very common thing in mostly every one in the beginning." By this time the author has concluded that none of the traditional resources of narrative will serve to reveal her character's "being":

> [I]t is hard to know the kind of being in any one from just a description of some thoughts, some feelings, some actions in them for it is in their feeling of themselves inside them that the kind of being in them shows in them and that comes out of them slowly in their living, that comes out of them always as repeating, this is very very difficult to make any one understand from a description of them.

In the following chapter, she confesses her inability to imagine connections between actions and "being":

> I have not any dramatic imagination for action in them, I only can know about action in them from knowing action they have been doing any of them . . . I cannot ever construct action for them to be doing, I have certainly constructive imagination for being in them.

Stein's insertion of her 1903 narrative *Fernhurst* into chapter 2, with Martha Hersland in the role of the rejected wife, clearly, if unintentionally, illustrates her point. The clumsy reworking of the story does not conceal th[e] lack of connection between descriptions of Martha's "being" and her [ ] in this conventional narrative. The author freely admits "a little [ ] at resorting to this expedient of "copying an old piece of writing" [ ] "words that sometime had real meaning . . . and have not an[y] in them to the feeling and the thinking and the imagining." By this point in the text, no words have "real meaning" for her except the limited set of adjectives she has invented to label essential "being."

By the third chapter of the novel, which is entitled "Alfred Hersland and Julia Dehning," Stein's search for "completed understanding" had led her far afield from the family narrative she was still committed to writing. Beginning in the second chapter, the author's own "history" breaks the closure of the Herslands' and Dehnings' fictional world and introduces a vast number of characters unconnected to their story to illustrate the truth of her system. Unnamed, these characters are each referred to only as "this one." The only referent the text occasionally provides for the adjective "this" is interior to the discourse ("this one that I am now beginning describing"). Without specific referents, these adjectives function as deictics, situating these characters in direct relation to the writer in the instance of discourse. Concealing their specific identities, the author teasingly reminds the reader of their objective reality in the world of her immediate experience: "I have told this one that I will tell it then. This one will not know then it is this one. That is the very nice thing in this writing. Sometime I will tell everything, everything. Mostly I do tell anything." Occasionally deictic time references situate the anonymous characters in immediate relation to the time of writing: "I saw yesterday afternoon two of them together"; "There were to-night eight of them." For Stein, the proliferation of case histories adds more "reality" to her enterprise:

> Always there are many many millions of every kind of men and women and this makes many stories very much realler, there being so many always of the same kind of them. It makes it realler then when in a story there are twelve women, all alike, and one hundred men, all alike, and a man and a woman completely resembling the one to the other one of them.

By the time she began the task of rendering Alfred Hersland in the third chapter of the novel, Stein's search for understanding had become dizzyingly circular. The text constantly accumulates more "histories" to develop a knowledge of "kinds," but as resemblances become more "real" than differences, each "history" simply repeats the characteristics of the "kind." By the third chapter, these paradigms, which obliterate all traces of individuality, have become the sole means of rendering characters:

> Alfred Hersland then was a kind of them he had a kind of being in him that was in him as more or less engulfing, somewhat passionate, not very bad, certainly not very good, engulfing resisting dependent independent being, needing to own those he would need for loving, very often needing some one poignantly alive to influence him.

> Of the kind of one that Alfred Hersland was in his being they
> range from very good ones through to pretty bad ones, from very tyrannical
> ones to very just ones, from very good ones through to pretty bad ones,
> from very religious ones to completely sceptical ones, from very dominant
> ones to very meek ones, from very passionate ones to completely indif-
> ferent ones and all of these in their living are of the resisting kind of them
> the dependent independent kind of them, those of them should have then
> needing to own those they need for loving.

This passage, one of many similar efforts to "realize" Alfred Hersland,
demonstrates how tautological Stein's process of rendering character has
become.

When she introduced her major categories into the novel, she was
aware that it would be difficult to communicate her understanding of character in these terms:

> It is true then that always every one is of one kind or the other kind of
> them the independent dependent or the dependent independent kind
> of them. It is hard to tell it about them, to describe it how each one is
> of the kind of them that is in that one. *It is hard to tell it about them because
> the same words can describe all of them the one and the other kind of them.*
> . . . It is hard to describe it in them the kind of being each one has in
> them, it is hard to describe it in them it is hard to know it in them, it is
> hard to know it in them, it is only slowly the two kinds of them come
> to be clear to every one who listens to the repeating that comes out of
> them, who sees the repeating that is in them the repeating of the bottom
> nature of them.
>
> (my emphasis)

"Independent dependent" and "dependent independent," each self-can-
celing in terms of ordinary lexical meaning, each the mirror image of the
other, are virtually empty signifiers. Their meaning is more specifically
determined inside the text, partly by their systematic association with other
pairs of words, such as "attacking" and "resisting," and partly by the cu-
mulative effect of specific "histories" which are introduced to illustrate the
two kinds. But in the Alfred Hersland chapter, Stein's means of rendering
individual "histories" are restricted to the same limited set of words that
label essential "being":

> There are only a few words and with these mostly always I am writing
> that have for me completely entirely existing being, in talking I use many
> more of them of words I am not living but talking is another thing, in
> talking one can be saying mostly anything, often then I am using many
> words I never could be using in writing. In writing a word must be for
> me really an existing thing, it has a place for me as living, this is the way
> I feel about me writing.

Moving back and forth from individuals to "kinds," her descriptions end-lessly repeat the few words that "have for [her] completely entirely existing being." This circular process, reenacted within an increasingly self-en-closed, self-referential system, demonstrates the impasse toward which Stein's singleminded pursuit of identities had been leading, with its own inexorable logic.

While Stein was working on the previous chapter of the novel, she was analyzing various painters' relationships to their objects in her note-books. In these analyses she consistently identifies her own work with Cézanne's and Picasso's "direct relationship to the object," their "realisation of the object itself." Throughout *The Making of Americans* her reiterated desire to "realise" her characters explicitly aligns her project with theirs. She repeatedly insists that her knowledge of others is grounded in her immediate experience of them: "They are whole beings then, they are themselves inside them to me. They are then, each one, a whole one inside me. . . . I know it, I am full up with it and I tell it. . . . Sometimes because I am so full of it it keeps pouring out of me all the time when I am first having it." Time and again these metaphors of ingestion and expulsion evoke her intense, even visceral relationship to the objects of her writing.

Stein's perception of Picasso, in her notebooks, as the direct suc-cessor to Cézanne's aesthetic goal of creating a "direct relationship to the object" is fundamentally correct. By 1909, however, Picasso's painting had departed radically from Cézanne's lifelong dedication to "realizing" his im-mediate visual sensations. And the methods of "realizing" her objects that Stein developed as *The Making of Americans* progressed were more closely related to Picasso's recent work than to Cézanne's. . . .

Picasso's diagrammatic, geometrical rendering of his objects parallels Stein's efforts to represent nothing but essential "being" in terms of an all-encompassing system of classification. In her notebooks and in the novel as well, Stein describes both her analysis of individuals and her construction of her system as making "diagrams." John Berger proposes the diagram as the "metaphorical model" of cubism, in terms that are equally applicable to Picasso's project and to Stein's:

> The metaphorical model of Cubism is the *diagram*: the diagram being a visible, symbolic representation of invisible processes, forces, structures. A diagram need not eschew certain aspects of appearances: but these too will be treated symbolically as *signs*, not as imitations or re-creations.
>
> The model of the *diagram* differs from that of the *mirror* in that it suggests a concern with what is not self-evident. . . . It differs from the model of the *personal account* in that it aims at a general truth.

But C. S. Peirce's more rigorous consideration of the geometrical diagram clarifies the crucial difference between Picasso's diagrammatic reduction of his objects and Stein's. As Peirce emphasizes, the geometrical diagram is an iconic design, a "representamen of what it represents . . . by virtue of its being an immediate image." The pyramidal diagram that Picasso proposes as a "real" nose, however reductive, still has a degree of relational similarity to the object it signifies. Stein's medium is language. She insists that the few words she uses have "completely weight and form and really existing being" for her, but these adjectival labels are still arbitrary signs, which cannot create the "direct relationship to the object" that a geometrical diagram can.

Years later, Stein came close to admitting that her system of classification failed to provide her with adequate means of "realizing" her objects. In "The Gradual Making of *The Making of Americans*," she acknowledged that her knowledge of "types of people" still left her with the difficulty of "put[ting] into words . . . a whole human being felt at one and the same time." To demonstrate that she "became very consciously obsessed by this very definite problem," she went on to quote an anecdote from the Alfred Hersland chapter that concerns a little boy "killing things to make collections" of butterflies and beetles. In its original context, it is not presented as an explicit comment on the author's own project, but, as the later essay suggests, it is an apt comment on the perils of classification. Throughout the novel, Stein insists that she is "full" of her characters' essential "being." She declares that the understanding she achieves through her love of repetition is an "earth feeling," identical to the "earthy . . . sense of the significance of objects" that she attributes to Picasso in her notebooks. She repeatedly assures the reader that her knowledge of "being" comes from "many years of listening, seeing, living, feeling, loving the repeating" that gradually clarifies individuals' "living, loving, eating, pleasing, smoking, thinking, scolding, drinking, working, dancing, walking, talking, laughing, sleeping" into "completed understanding." But her discourse endlessly repeats only the few words that label the conclusions of these observations as she goes on incorporating more and more cases into her paradigms.

The structure of Stein's prose, with its endless repetitions and reformulations, effectively enacts the movements of her own mind, endlessly revolving inside the increasingly restrictive boundaries of her self-created system, but it does not render the process by which she gradually achieved her knowledge of individuals. While her prose repeatedly proclaims her ecstatic union with her objects, the reader, who has no means of sharing in the process, is likely to become bored with these reiterated reports of her conclusions. In *Le Plaisir du texte*, Barthes has observed, "Boredom is not far from bliss [*jouissance*]: it is bliss seen from the shores of pleasure." Later in this text, Barthes acknowledges that repetition can create this state of bliss: "There are abundant ethnographic examples: obsessive rhythms, incantatory music, litanies, rites, and Buddhist nembutsu, etc.: to repeat excessively is to enter into loss, into the zero of the signified. However: for repetition to be erotic, it must be formal, literal, and in our culture, this flamboyant (excessive) repetition reverts to the eccentric." Many readers have experienced Stein's endless repetitions as this kind of liberation from meaning, although not all have found the experience equally blissful. But Stein never intended this effect; she wanted repetition to render the "last touch of being" of her objects.

According to Kierkegaard, "When the Greeks said that all knowledge is recollection they affirmed that all that is has been; when one says that life is a repetition one affirms that existence which has been now becomes." Stein describes her experience of repetition in individuals similarly, as a perception that is constantly renewed in the present. But her system of classification works against her desire to "realize" this experience for the reader. As she frequently acknowledges, the search for resemblances is grounded in recollection; classification of "being" presupposed "*completed* understanding." Gilles Deleuze begins his study *Différence et répétition* by emphasizing, "Repetition is not generalization. . . . To repeat is to conduct oneself with regard to something unique or singular, which has no likeness or equivalent." In opposition to this vital singularity, he argues, "Generalization is of the order of laws. But the law determines only the resemblance of subjects who are subjugated to it, and their equivalence to the terms that it designates." In these terms, Stein's two goals were fundamentally incompatible from the beginning; the "law" of her totalizing system inevitably obliterated the essential singularity of her perception of repetition in individual lives. Once this system begins to dominate the text, the figure of repetition itself is the only trace that remains of the experience she intended to "realise."

Many of the most compelling passages in *The Making of Americans* reveal the intensity of Stein's need to perceive individuals as "whole" and to create an ordered system of resemblances that would reduce the plethora of individual differences to a unified field of knowledge. Early in the novel, she expresses her faith that repetition "gives to every one who feels it in them a more certain feeling about them, a more secure feeling in living. . . . Always more and more then there is contentment in the secure feeling repeating in every one gives to every one." She soon needs more than this perception of repetition to satisfy her desire for order: "The important thing then [in] hearing, feeling, seeing all the repeating coming out from such a one is to realise the *meaning* of the being, it is not enough to realise all the repeating in such a one" (my emphasis). Her goal is to achieve the "completed friendly feeling of the whole being," but in the second chapter the author begins to acknowledge that sometimes she perceives nothing but "pieces." As the text progresses, this sense of fragmentation increasingly threatens to destroy the validity of the system. Without the certainty that each individual is a "whole one, a complete one so that there can then be a solid basis of comparison, . . . there are so many ways of seeing, feeling resemblances in some one, some one resembles so many men and women that it is confusing, baffling, then the one learning kinds in men and women is despairing, nothing then to that one has any meaning, it is then to that one all of it only an arbitrary choosing."

This idea of character as a collection of disconnected pieces was already present in Stein's earlier texts. Adele in *Q.E.D.* and Jeff in "Melanctha" both struggle to comprehend the multiplicity of their lovers' personalities. Significantly, Jeff experiences a sense of unity only after he abandons the conceptual grid of his moral categories and gives in to his feelings: "I got a new feeling now . . . and I see perhaps what really loving is like, like really having everything together, new things, *little pieces all different*, like I always before been thinking was bad to be having, all go together like, to make one good big feeling" (my emphasis). After Stein brilliantly demonstrated the inadequacy of Jeff's attempts to categorize the complexity of Melanctha's personality in the language he has at his disposal, in *The Making of Americans* she tried to forge a language of classification, with an even more limited lexicon than Jeff's, that would master the rich diversity of personality. The author's own language eventually proved to be no more powerful than that of the character she created in "Melanctha." By the Alfred Hersland chapter, if not before, Stein's repetitions seem to demonstrate as much helplessness and futility as Jeff's. The complexity of her own experiences exceeds the restrictions imposed by her conceptual system: "[E]very one is to me just now as pieces to me." In this chapter, her persistent inability to "realise" Alfred Hersland makes her doubt her ability to perceive or create the wholeness she so fervently desires. Her increasing sense of fragmentation, which undermines her faith in her totalizing system, produces an outburst of metaphysical despair:

> Why should anything any one keep on going if not ever at any time anything any one will be a whole one . . . now mostly every one is a

piece of a one, not all the being as a complete one and yet every one has their own being in them and putting all of each kind of them together to make a whole one can not be to me a satisfaction, cannot give to me any real satisfaction can not be a satisfactory way in my feeling of having completion of having anything or any one a whole one cannot give to me any reason why the world should keep on being, there is not any reason if in repeating nothing is giving to me a sensation of a completed one.

Within two years, she would embrace this sense of fragmentation as the only "reality" and create a new mode of writing to celebrate it. In 1938 she proclaimed it the "splendor" of the twentieth century:

The twentieth century is more splendid than the nineteenth century, certainly it is much more splendid. The twentieth century has much less reasonableness in its existence than the nineteenth century but reasonableness does not make for splendor. . . . So the twentieth century is that, it is a time when everything cracks, where everything is destroyed, everything isolates itself, it is a more splendid thing than a period where everything follows itself. So then the twentieth century is a splendid period, not a reasonable one in the scientific sense, but splendid.

None of her later writings acknowledges either the agonizing personal struggle that preceded this affirmation of the radical epistemological break between *The Making of Americans* and her later writings. Her totalizing system of classification, however eccentric, was meant to be "reasonable . . . in the scientific sense," resembling the classical taxonomies of natural history. Like Linnaeus's system, Stein's selects one element as a basis for studying identities and differences, ignoring all the rest, and uses it as the determinant of character. Basing her taxonomy on the Jamesian method of introspection supplemented by observation of others' behavior, she analyzed herself and a large number of acquaintances. She was pursuing the ideal order of classical science, a conceptual grid that would impose coherence on the vast field of human behavior.

In the Alfred Hersland chapter, the author's persistent failure to "realise" the central character as a coherent whole creates an increasingly urgent need for total knowledge and increasingly impossible criteria for achieving it. No longer content with paradigms based on identities, she begins to require a different form of comprehensiveness as well. However closely she studies a person, she feels that her observations are always incomplete, because they cannot include "what they are saying to other ones, what they are feeling." Eventually her desire for comprehensive factual data becomes so urgent that nothing will satisfy her but a "complete record of each one, what each one did, what each one had as being in her in him, what each one could be doing, thinking, feeling, knowing." Although she has little hope of achieving this knowledge, still she pursues her impossible dream. Exhaustive enumeration becomes her new criterion for mastering the truth: "It would be a very complete thing in my feeling to be having complete lists of every body ever living and to be realising each one and to be making diagrams of them and lists of them and explaining the being in each one and the relation of that being to other beings in other men and other women and to go on then explaining and realising and knowing the complete being in each one and all the kinds there are in men and women." In the first chapter of the novel, case histories serve to develop her paradigms, to "make a kind of diagram" of essential being. By this point in the text, the paradigm, no longer satisfying in itself, must be supplemented by a complete inventory of every individual. In addition to spawning the innumerable case histories that fill the second and third chapters of the novel, this impulse to produce a comprehensive inventory overflowed into A Long Gay Book and Many Many Women, both of which began as collections of short descriptions of anonymous individuals. In the Alfred Hersland chapter of the novel, new categories and lists proliferate, as the author frantically pursues her two conflicting ideas of comprehensive knowledge, the totalizing paradigm and the exhaustive inventory.

The more strongly her continuing empirical observations threaten the unifying coherence of her system, the more clearly her struggles reveal the metaphysical assumptions that impel her quest for totalizing knowledge:

> Sometime I want to be completely certain. I am one that in this way am wanting to be completely certain, am wanting to be right in being completely certain and in this way only in me can it come to be in me that to be dead is not to be a dead one. Really to be just dead is to be to me a really dead one. To be completely right, completely certain is to be in me universal in my feeling, to be like the earth complete and fructifying.

Only a mastery of truth will overcome her terror of meaningless mortality. For Stein, infancy is the mirror image of death, a discontinuity of consciousness at the time of origin that equally threatens the "universal" feeling:

> There are some when they feel it inside them that it has been with them that there was once so very little of them, that they were a baby, helpless and no conscious feeling in them, that they knew nothing then when they were kissed and dandled and fixed by others who knew them when they could know nothing inside them or around them, some get from all this that once surely happened to them to that which was then every bit that was then them, there are some when they feel it later inside them

that they were such once and that was all that there was then of them, there are some who have from such a knowing an uncertain curious kind of feeling in them that their having been so little once and knowing nothing makes it all a broken world for them that they have inside them, kills for them the everlasting feeling; and they spend their life in many ways, and always they are trying to make for themselves a new everlasting feeling.

Stein's celebration of repetition is an attempt to repair this breach, but time and again her text obsessively returns to the fact of death, repeating its haunting refrain, "Dead is dead." Repetition alone did not suffice to overcome her fear of mortality. Only the certainty of complete knowledge could give her the "everlasting feeling" she craved:

> I know then there can be a history of each one and of all kinds all the kinds in men and women. This is a pleasant feeling, this is comforting to me just now when I am thinking of every one always growing older and then dying. . . . [A]s I am saying I am having a pleasant completely completed feeling and always then it is a comfortable and calming thing this being certain that each one is one of a kind of them in men and women and that there are always very many of each kind existing, that each one has their own being in them is then completely interesting, that each one sometime is to be a dead one is then not discouraging, and so then I am having a completely pleasant and completed feeling, I who am completely certain that each one is of a kind in men and women, I who am always almost always knowing several of each kind of them I come to know in living, I who am expecting sometime perhaps to be knowing all there ever can be, were or are or will be of kinds in men and women. I have then even with sombre certain feeling that each one is always an older one and sometime a dead one I have then knowing each one is of one kind in men and women I have then a pleasant feeling, a contented a completed feeling as I have been saying. I have a quiet sombre feeling I have not so much an afraid feeling in being living now when I am certain, and I am knowing them, that there are a number of kinds in men and women, no such a great number of them, quite a number of them.

The author's sense of having achieved this synchronic understanding that obliterates history, by "knowing all there ever can be, were or are or will be of kinds in men and women," is intermittent at best, and it does not help her to resolve the problem of rendering the individual character of Alfred Hersland. In 1910, during this period of struggle recorded in the Alfred Hersland chapter of the novel, she began writing portraits of her friends. Leaving behind the apparatus of her descriptive system, she created a new method of rendering individual personalities in terms of their characterizing actions. At the same time she was mastering this new technique, she was still pursuing the lure of "completed understanding" in the novel. But at the end of the Alfred Hersland chapter, the author announces, "This is the ending of just this way of going on telling about being being in some men and in some women." This proclamation marks the end of Stein's quest for a totalizing system, which had seemed to her the only way of overmastering discontinuity and death. The final chapter of the novel is a powerful rendition of the life and death of David Hersland, written in the style of the early portraits. At the beginning of it, admitting that her quest for complete knowledge is doomed, the author still associates this failure with death:

> I am now again and again certain that I will not ever be realising experiencing in each one of very many men and very many women, I can realise something of experiencing in some of them, in them as kinds of them but I am needing to have it in me as a complete thing of each one ever living and I I know I will not, and I am one knowing being a dead one and not being a living one, I who am not believing that I will be realising each one's experiencing.

David Hersland dies young; his death pervades her somber presentation of his life. After finishing this paean to death, Stein went on to liberate herself and her writing from the certainties of all totalizing systems of knowledge and to celebrate the difference and discontinuity that had seemed so threatening as the "reality" of the twentieth century.

Chronology

1874   Gertrude Stein born in Allegheny, Pennsylvania, on February 3 to Daniel Stein and Amelia (Keyser) Stein.

1878   Stein family lives briefly in Passy, France.

1880   Family moves to Oakland.

1888   Amelia Stein dies of cancer.

1891   Daniel Stein dies. Family, now in the care of eldest brother Michael, moves to San Francisco.

1892   Family separates. Stein and sister Bertha live with maternal aunt in Baltimore. Brother Leo leaves the University of California at Berkeley, transfers to Harvard.

1893   Stein enters the Harvard Annex (renamed Radcliffe College in 1894).

1894   Studies under Munsterberg in the Harvard Psychological Laboratory.

1896   "Normal Motor Automatism" published in *Psychological Review*. Stein travels abroad.

1897   Fails Radcliffe's Latin entrance examination, and is refused her B.A. Joins Leo Stein, who is studying biology, in Baltimore. Enters Johns Hopkins School of Medicine.

1898   Awarded her Radcliffe B.A.

1901   Fails four courses in last term of medical school. Conducts research on the brain.

1902   Gertrude and Leo Stein settle in London. Stein reads extensively in the British Museum. Leo Stein leaves for Paris.

1903   Returning to New York, Stein begins early drafts of *The Making of Americans* and *Things as They Are*. Gertrude and Leo Stein move to 27 rue de Fleurus, in Paris.

1904   After seeing Charles Loeser's collection of Cézannes in Florence, the Steins begin collecting paintings.

1905   Begins *Three Lives*. Meets Picasso through the art dealer Clovis Sagot.

1906   *Three Lives* completed. Stein sits for Picasso portrait.

1907   Meets Alice Toklas in Paris.

1908	Toklas begins transcribing *The Making of Americans.*
1909	*Three Lives* published, her first book in print. Alice Toklas joins the Steins at the rue de Fleurus.
1911	Completes *The Making of Americans.*
1912	Stieglitz publishes "Picasso" and "Matisse" in *Camera Work.*
1913	Travels to England to arouse interest of publishers. Definitive separation from Leo Stein.
1914	*Tender Buttons* published. War begins.
1915	Stein and Toklas flee to Spain after zeppelin raids.
1916	Return to Paris after the Battle of Verdun.
1917	Stein drives her own car as supply truck for American Fund for French Wounded. Opens distribution depot in Perpignan, then stationed in Nîmes.
1918	Provides civilian relief in Alsace.
1919	Returns to Paris.
1921	Meets Sherwood Anderson. Lipchitz sculpts bronze of her head.
1922	*Geography and Plays* published. Meets Ernest Hemingway. Awarded the Medaille de la Reconnaissance Française for wartime activities.
1924	*The Making of Americans* serialized in *Transatlantic Review.*
1925	Contact Editions publishes *The Making of Americans.*
1926	Delivers "Composition as Explanation" at Cambridge and Oxford Universities. Meets Virgil Thomson, Bernard Fay.
1931	Plain Edition publishes *Lady Church Amiably.*
1932	Writes *The Autobiography of Alice B. Toklas* (1933).
1934–35	First performance of *Four Saints in Three Acts.* Arrives in New York City; lecture tour of United States.
1936	Lectures again at Cambridge and Oxford.
1937	Stein attends opening of *A Wedding Bouquet* in London. Meets Thornton Wilder. Evicted from 27 rue de Fleurus.
1938	Stein and Alice Toklas move to 5 rue Christine.
1940	Paris occupied.
1943	Stein and Toklas move to "Le Colombier" in Culo, where German and Italian soldiers are billeted at various times.
1944	Stein and Toklas return to Paris.
1945	Tours American army bases in occupied Germany. Lectures in Brussels.
1946	*Yes Is For a Very Young Man* performed for the first time at Pasadena Playhouse. Dies on July 27, following operation for cancer.

Contributors

HAROLD BLOOM, Sterling Professor of the Humanities at Yale University, is the author of *The Anxiety of Influence*, *Poetry and Repression* and many other volumes of literary criticism. His forthcoming study, *Freud: Transference and Authority*, attempts a full-scale reading of all of Freud's major writings. A MacArthur Prize fellow, he is the general editor of *The Chelsea House Library of Literary Criticism*.

SHERWOOD ANDERSON is the author of *Poor White* and *Winesburg, Ohio*. He was one of the first American writers to become interested in the work of Gertrude Stein.

KATHERINE ANNE PORTER wrote *Ship of Fools* and *Pale Horse, Pale Rider*. Her collection of essays, *The Days Before*, contains several pieces on Gertrude Stein.

EDMUND WILSON, critic and writer, monitored the careers of writers throughout the 1920s, 30s and 40s (see *Axel's Castle*, *The Shores of Light*).

WILLIAM CARLOS WILLIAMS, a physician, poet and writer, wrote *Paterson, New Jersey*, *In the American Grain* and *A Voyage to Pagany*.

THORNTON WILDER, novelist and playwright, is the author of *Our Town*, *The Skin of Our Teeth* and *The Matchmaker* (later *Hello, Dolly!*).

DONALD SUTHERLAND, educator and writer, is the author of *Gertrude Stein: A Biography of Her Work*.

ALLEGRA STEWART is Professor Emeritus at Butler University. She is the author of *Gertrude Stein and the Present*.

B. L. REID, educator and writer, is the author of *Art By Subtraction: A Dissenting Opinion of Gertrude Stein*.

RICHARD BRIDGMAN, a writer and Gertrude Stein scholar, is the author of *Gertrude Stein in Pieces* and many articles on her work.

NORMAN WEINSTEIN is the author of *Gertrude Stein and the Literature of the Modern Consciousness*.

JUDITH P. SAUNDERS is Assistant Academic Dean at Marymount College.

CATHARINE R. STIMPSON teaches English at Rutgers University. She is the author (with Ethel S. Person) of *Women, Sex and Sexuality* and editor of *Women and the American City*.

WILLIAM H. GASS, educator and writer, is the author of *The Habitations of the Word* and *The World Within the Word*.

MARIANNE DeKOVEN, educator and writer, is the author of *A Different Language: Gertrude Stein's Experimental Writing*.

JAYNE L. WALKER is the author of *The Making of a Modernist: Gertrude Stein from Three Lives to Tender Buttons*.

Bibliography

Aldington, Richard. "The Disciples of Gertrude Stein." *Poetry* 17 (Oct. 1920): 35–40.

Bridgman, Richard. *The Colloquial Style in America.* New York: Oxford University Press, 1966.

———. *Gertrude Stein in Pieces.* New York: Oxford University Press, 1970.

Brinnin, John Malcolm. *The Third Rose: Gertrude Stein and Her World.* Boston: Little, Brown, 1959.

Cargill, Oscar. *Intellectual America, Ideas on the March.* New York: Macmillan Publishing Co., Inc. 1941.

Cooper, David D. "Gertrude Stein's 'Magnificent Asparagus': Horizontal Vision and Unmeaning in *Tender Buttons.*" *Modern Fiction Studies* 20 (Autumn 1974): 337–49.

Corke, Hilary. "Reflections on a Great Stone Face." *The Kenyon Review* 23 (Summer 1961): 367–89.

DeKoven, Marianne. *A Different Language: Gertrude Stein's Experimental Writing.* Madison: University of Wisconsin Press, 1983.

Eagleson, Harvey. "Gertrude Stein: Method in Madness." *Sewanee Review* 44 (April–June 1936): 164–77.

Evans, Oliver. "Gertrude Stein as Humorist." *Prairie Schooner* 21 (Spring 1947): 97–102.

Gallup, Donald. "A Book is a Book." *New Colophon* 1 (Jan. 1948): 67–80.

———. "The Making of *The Making of Americans.*" *New Colophon* 3 (1950): 54–74.

Gass, William H. *The World Within the Word.* Boston: Nonpareil Books, 1979.

———. "Gertrude Stein: Her Escape from Protective Language." *Accent* 18 (Autumn 1958): 233–44.

Hass, Robert Bartlett, ed. *A Primer for the Gradual Understanding of Gertrude Stein.* Los Angeles: Black Sparrow Press, 1971.

Haas, Robert Bartlett, and Gallup, Donald. *A Catalogue of the Published and Unpublished Writings of Gertrude Stein.* New Haven: Yale University Press, 1941.

Hoffman, Michael J. *The Development of Abstractionism in the Writing of Gertrude Stein.* Philadelphia: University of Pennsylvania Press, 1965.

Kazin, Alfred. *Contemporaries.* Boston: Little, Brown, 1962.

Levinson, Ronald. "Gertrude Stein, William James, and Grammar." *American Journal of Psychology* 54 (Jan. 1941): 124–28.

Malone, Kemp. "Observations on *Paris France.*" *Papers on Language and Literature* 3 (Spring 1967): 159–78.

Miller, Rosalind. *Gertrude Stein: Form and Intelligibility.* New York: Exposition Press, 1949.

Moore, Marianne. "The Spare American Emotion." *Dial* 80 (Feb. 1926): 153–56.

Porter, Katherine Anne. *The Days Before.* New York: Harcourt, Brace, 1952.

Reid, Ben. *Art by Subtraction: A Dissenting Opinion of Gertrude Stein.* Norman, Okla.: University of Oklahoma Press, 1958.

Rogers, W. G. *When This You See Remember Me: Gertrude Stein in Person.* New York: Rinehart, 1948.

Simon, Linda, ed. *Gertrude Stein: A Composite Portrait.* New York: Avon Books, 1974.

Skinner, B. F. "Has Gertrude Stein a Secret?" *Atlantic Monthly* 153 (Jan. 1934): 50–57.

Sprigge, Elizabeth. *Gertrude Stein: Her Life and Work.* New York: Harper, 1957.

Stein, Leo. *Journey Into the Self.* Edited by Edmund Fuller. New York: Crown Publishers, 1950.

Sutherland, Donald. *Gertrude Stein: A Biography of Her Work.* New Haven: Yale University Press, 1951.

Toklas, Alice B. *What Is Remembered.* New York: Holt, Rinehart, and Winston, 1963.

Walker, Jayne L. *The Making of a Modernist: Gertrude Stein from Three Lives to Tender Buttons.* Amherst: University of Massachusetts Press, 1984.

Weinstein, Norman. *Gertrude Stein and the Literature of the Modern Consciousness.* New York: Frederick Ungar Publishing, 1970.

Wilcox, Wendell. "A Note on Stein and Abstraction." *Poetry* 55 (Feb. 1940): 254–57.

Wilder, Thornton. Introduction to *Four in America,* by Gertrude Stein. New Haven: Yale University Press, 1947.

———. "Gertrude Stein Makes Sense." *47: The Magazine of the Year* 1 (Oct. 1947): 10–15.

Williams, William Carlos. *Selected Essays of William Carlos Williams.* New York: Random House, 1954.

Wilson, Edmund. *Axel's Castle.* New York: Scribner's, 1931.

———. *The Shores of Light: A Literary Chronicle of the Twenties and Thirties.* New York: Farrar, Straus, and Cudahy, 1952.

Yalden-Thomson, D. C. "Obscurity, Exhibitionism, and Gertrude Stein." *Virginia Quarterly Review* 34 (Winter 1958): 133–37.

Acknowledgments

"An American Impression" by Sherwood Anderson from *The Portable Sherwood Anderson* edited by Horace Gregory, copyright © 1977 by Horace Gregory. Reprinted by permission.

" 'Everybody is a Real One' " by Katherine Anne Porter from *The Days Before* by Katherine Anne Porter, copyright © 1952 by Katherine Anne Porter. Reprinted by permission.

"Gertrude Stein" by Edmund Wilson from *Axel's Castle* by Edmund Wilson, copyright © 1959 by Edmund Wilson. Reprinted by permission.

"The Work of Gertrude Stein" by William Carlos Williams from *Selected Essays of William Carlos Williams* by William Carlos Williams, copyright © 1954 by William Carlos Williams. Reprinted by permission.

"Four in America" by Thornton Wilder from the Introduction to *Four in America* by Gertrude Stein, copyright © 1947 by Yale University Press. Reprinted by permission.

"Three Lives" by Donald Sutherland from *Gertrude Stein: A Biography of Her Work* by Donald Sutherland, copyright © 1951 by Yale University Press. Reprinted by permission.

"The Quality of Gertrude Stein's Creativity" by Allegra Stewart from *American Literature* 28 (January 1957), copyright © 1957 by Duke University Press. Reprinted by permission.

"An Evaluation: 'Think of Shakespeare and Think of Me' " by B. L. Reid, from *Art by Subtraction: A Dissenting Opinion of Gertrude Stein* by B. L. Reid, copyright © 1958 by University of Oklahoma Press. Reprinted by permission.

"Things As They Are and *Three Lives"* by Richard Bridgman from *The Colloquial Style in America* by Richard Bridgman, copyright © 1966 by Richard Bridgman. Reprinted by permission.

"*Four Saints in Three Acts:* Play as Landscape" by Norman Weinstein from *Gertrude Stein and the Literature of the Modern Consciousness* by Norman Weinstein, copyright © 1970 by Frederick Ungar Publishing Co., Inc. Reprinted by permission.

"Gertrude Stein's *Paris France* and American Literary Tradition" by Judith P. Saunders from *South Dakota Review* 1, vol. 15 (Spring), copyright © 1977 by *South Dakota Review.* Reprinted by permission.

"The Mind, the Body, and Gertrude Stein" by Catharine R. Stimpson from *Critical Inquiry* 3, vol. 3 (1977), copyright © 1977 by *Critical Inquiry.* Reprinted by permission.

"Gertrude Stein and the Geography of the Sentence: *Tender Buttons*" by William H. Gass from *The World Within the Word* by William H. Gass, copyright © 1976 by William H. Gass. Reprinted by permission.

"Melody" by Marianne DeKoven from *A Different Language: Gertrude Stein's Experimental Writing* by Marianne DeKoven, copyright © 1983 by The Board of Regents of the University of Wisconsin. Reprinted by permission.

"History as Repetition: *The Making of Americans*" by Jayne L. Walker from *The Making of a Modernist: Gertrude Stein from Three Lives to Tender Buttons* by Jayne L. Walker, copyright © 1984 by Jayne L. Walker. Reprinted by permission.

Index